More Advance Praise for

"As the champion of the American Heart Association, Cass Wheeler has helped improve the lives of millions of Americans who suffer from heart disease and stroke. If, like Cass (and me), you believe the status quo is not good enough, this book will inspire you to take bold, innovative action . . . a must read for all nonprofit staff and volunteers."
William D. Novelli, Chief Executive Officer,
American Association of Retired Persons (AARP)

"Great coaching for leaders of nonprofit organizations at any level! A wonderful way to learn from a leader who has 'been there'!"
Marshall Goldsmith, the *New York Times* and *Wall Street Journal* #1 best-selling author of *What Got You Here Won't Get You There*

"In *You've Gotta Have Heart*, Cass Wheeler has given a marvelous gift to all of us who are committed to leadership in the nonprofit field, just as he has done through his remarkable leadership of the American Heart Association. He shares his years of leadership experience in clear, concise ideas that will enable all nonprofit leaders to become more effective in reaching their goals."
Bill George, author of *True North* and former Chairman and CEO of Medtronic

"*You've Gotta Have Heart* is a magisterial and inspiring book. At one and the same time an essay and a memoir. Brilliantly recaptures the secrets to AHA's success and the specific challenges that nonprofits face if they want to survive into the future. Remarkable ideas remarkably set forth."
Valentin Fuster, MD, PhD; Director, Mount Sinai Heart;
past President, American Heart Association

"*You've Gotta Have Heart* is a timely guide to managing change in the rapidly evolving world of nonprofit organizations. Throughout the book Cass Wheeler shares motivational stories, wisdom, and immensely practical advice from his remarkable journey at the helm of the American Heart Association. He writes to inspire the leader within all who work to serve the greater good in their professional and personal lives. I loved it and you will too."
Carol Cone, Chairman and Founder, Cone, Inc.

"Cass Wheeler has written a 'must read' book for anyone involved in advancing the essential work of nonprofit organizations' service to communities and our nation. At this critical time, as stakeholders demand more from these significant organizations, this book provides a comprehensive and practical guide for managers, employees, boards of directors, volunteers, donors, and others."

Reed V. Tuckson, MD, FACP; Executive Vice President and Chief of Medical Affairs, UnitedHealth Group

"The American Heart Association is one of the most successful not-for-profit organizations in America, due in no small measure to the leadership of Cass Wheeler and his embrace of for-profit principles to drive results in this not-for-profit world. Volunteers and staff at any level can learn and apply the concepts from You've Gotta Have Heart."

James J. Postl, retired President and Chief Executive Officer, Pennzoil–Quaker State Co.

"In *You've Gotta Have Heart*, Cass Wheeler understands that the soul of a company is embedded in the ways it reaches beyond business needs to better communities, customers, and employees. A 'heartfelt mission' built into the very DNA of an organization is a recipe for success."

Shawn Dennis, Senior Vice President and Chief Marketing Officer, American Girl Company

"*You've Gotta Have Heart* is a definite 'must have' for any leader's bookcase covering a broad scope of topics. Cass Wheeler has brought together an impressive array of tools, techniques, and guidelines for organizational success, gleaned from his exceptional career as the head of one of the world's most successful nonprofits."

Robert Barner, Director of Talent Management & Learning, Accredo Health, and author of *Bench Strength: How to Improve the Depth and Versatility of Your Leadership Team*

YOU'VE GOTTA HAVE
HEART

Achieving Purpose
Beyond Profit
in the Social Sector

CASS WHEELER

HarperCollins
Leadership

An Imprint of HarperCollins

You've Gotta Have Heart

© 2022 Cass Wheeler

All rights reserved. No portion of this book may be reproduced, stored in a retrieval system, or transmitted in any form or by any means—electronic, mechanical, photocopy, recording, scanning, or other—except for brief quotations in critical reviews or articles, without the prior written permission of the publisher.

Published by HarperCollins Leadership,
an imprint of HarperCollins Focus LLC.

Any internet addresses, phone numbers, or company or product information printed in this book are offered as a resource and are not intended in any way to be or to imply an endorsement by HarperCollins Leadership, nor does HarperCollins Leadership vouch for the existence, content, or services of these sites, phone numbers, companies, or products beyond the life of this book.

Bulk discounts available. For details visit:
www.harpercollinsleadership.com/bulkquotes
Email: customercare@harpercollins.com

ISBN 978-1-4002-3252-9 (TP)

CONTENTS

Acknowledgments	*vii*
Introduction: Leading with Heart: A Purpose Beyond Profit	1
1: A Mission Statement Is Not the Same as a Sense of Mission	18
2: When Everyone Points North: Developing a Clear Decision-Making Framework and Business Model	37
3: The Power of a Breakthrough Goal	61
4: Break Out the Big Brass *Brand*	74
5: Bold Moves and Best Practices	102
6: Building the Best Staff	120
7: Inspiring the Best Work: Managing Nonprofit Employees	143
8: Recruiting and Guiding Volunteers and the Board of Directors	156
9: Influencing Public Policy: Nonprofit Advocacy and Lobbying	180
10: Heart-to-Heart Alliances: Becoming a Partner of Choice	198
Conclusion	219
Notes	221
Index	223

ACKNOWLEDGMENTS

This book is dedicated to the volunteers and staff, both past and present, of the American Heart Association. If not for their hard work and dedication, I would not have had these successes to write about. In all that we do and accomplish, we do so because we stand on the shoulders of giants. I have been blessed over the years to be surrounded by giants.

You will note that I refer to very few individuals in the book by name, and this is intentional. One reason is that this is not a history of the American Heart Association, and secondly, it would be impossible to list literally thousands of volunteers and staff who are responsible for the success of the organization. I would like to single out a few people who formed a community with me to help make this book a reality. Without them, it would never have been written.

First, my family, who saw me even less than usual over a period of months: my wife, DeLisa, and my children, Kevin, Kristen, Austin, and Chloe; my daughter-in-law, Marchelle; and my grandchildren, Trinity and Cash.

Thank you to Jacquie Flynn and the team at AMACOM books, including Jenny Wesselmann, Kama Timbrell, Penny Anna Makras, Cathleen Ouderkirk, Jennifer Holder, and Jim Bessent, and at North Market Street Graphics, Lainey Harding, Mike Dunnick, Rhonda Stough, and Ginny Carroll.

A special thanks goes to Deborah Driskill, who saw a book in me long before I did and was determined to make it a reality by leading me to John Walvoord and, ultimately, to my agent, Jan Miller, of Dupree/Miller and her associate, Nena Madonia. Many thanks to Jan and Nena for all of their efforts on my behalf. Thank you as well to Wes Smith, for shaping the book in its earlier days.

Another special thanks goes to Lindsey Pollak, my reverse mentor and the person who put muscle on the skeleton of the book. And then a community who reviewed the manuscript and significantly enhanced its quality: Natalie Alfrey, Roger Brown, Diana Foster, Mary Beth

Fiske, Evan Gotlib, Robin Johnson, Pat Read, Melissa Scholl, and Kristen Wheeler.

I also want to acknowledge my dear friend, mentor, and predecessor, Dudley Hafner, who saw my potential and always gave me the benefit of the doubt. I would never have become CEO without his guidance. I continue to stand on his shoulders. During my tenure as CEO, Robin Johnson, of Vidalia and Associates, periodically served as my executive coach and improved my performance by providing a set of outside eyes.

I also want to acknowledge the support of my best friends, Jeff Blansit and Sheilah Blansit.

Last, this book is in memory of my parents, Honey and Skip, who always believed in me and stood by me. I only wish they could read it and be proud.

INTRODUCTION

LEADING WITH HEART

A Purpose Beyond Profit

When Jeannie was born in February 1986, she was to be immediately given up for adoption. But because she had a serious heart defect and other medical issues, her adoptive parents-to-be backed out.

A second family, the Bornemanns, claimed Jeannie as their daughter. They saw her for the first time when she was just three days old. She had IVs in her head, chest, and both hands and feet, and she had tubes in her nose.

Their first words were "Hi, teeny Jeannie! Mommy and Daddy are here!"

Jeannie had an extremely rare set of conditions—transposition of the great vessels, pulmonary stenosis, and a ventricular septal defect. Her heart's chambers and arteries were reversed. Not much was known about this condition then—more research was desperately needed.

Jeannie's doctors inserted a flexible tube called a shunt to increase blood flow. It was all they could do. They hoped that she would get bigger and stronger and that research would provide new knowledge and tools to help them help her.

Jeannie didn't grow normally. When she was 5, she weighed just 22 pounds and was 29 inches tall. But she was finally strong enough for the corrective surgery that doctors had been waiting to do.

Jeannie's quality of life improved a lot after her surgery. She went to school, played T-ball and soccer, and followed her medical instructions without complaint. Despite a severe hearing impairment, she became a fanatic music lover, especially the music of Elvis. She loved people and life and looked like any other normal, healthy kid—except she was hearing impaired, legally blind, and undersized and had a heart defect.

In 1999, at age 13, Jeannie was looking forward to spending a week at a special camp. It was a place where kids with heart disease could make friends, share experiences, and enjoy hiking, fishing, horseback riding, making crafts, and singing around the campfire—while being supervised by doctors, nurses, and other volunteer camp counselors. Swimming was a favorite activity, because, since all the kids have surgical scars, no one is embarrassed—they even compare scars!

The day before camp started, Jeannie fell from a tree, breaking her collarbone. She was undaunted and still went to camp.

By the next year, Jeannie's health had begun to decline. Research advances offered new hope, and Jeannie's cardiologist proposed a heart transplant. Her parents were afraid—but not Jeannie.

On the night before she was set to go back to camp, the call came. A heart was available. Jeannie missed camp that year but got her new heart.

Jeannie had severe complications after her transplant. She spent thirteen of the next thirty-six months in the hospital. Between hospital stays, she lived the fullest life she could, singing on stage in high school, acting with a performing arts group, going to two homecoming dances, and traveling.

When she was 17, Jeannie got very sick and again went to the hospital. While she was there, she wrote a short note about the fun she'd had at camp: making friends, doing crafts, hearing silly jokes, and singing a song that ended like this:

> When the bugs bite, when the bees sting, when I'm feeling sad, I simply remember my Boggy Creek things, and then I don't feel so bad.

Jeannie Bornemann died in 2004. American Heart Association research and programs had helped keep her alive for eighteen years, but the knowledge we needed—that she needed—ran out.

Lots of people are alive today because of American Heart Association research and programs. Our work brings hope, health, and life to millions of people, throughout America and around the world.

The Bournemanns commented that if she were alive today, Jeannie would say, "Thank you from the bottom of my new heart." We're grateful for that, but sadness remains. We're proud of our successes, but our limitations—like our inability to maintain the miracle of Jeannie Bournemann's life—are what drive us to work harder and do more every day.

There are lots of Jeannies and other people living longer today because of the American Heart Association's research and programs. I believe our work gives meaning to Jeannie's life and provides hope for millions of people throughout America and across the world. Personal stories like these drive each of us to do our best work every day. And yet I have to say that deaths like Jeannie's frustrate me that we haven't done more. We still have so much work to do.

Deaths like that of Jeannie Bornemann make me sad and angry, and that is a good thing. I believe dissatisfaction with the status quo should be part of our organizational culture at the American Heart Association. The hopes and lives of many people we will never meet rest on our shoulders, and we must continually challenge ourselves to do more. We need to keep reassessing our program offerings, the research we fund, our structure, our volunteer and staff talents, our fund-raising goals and procedures, and our impact. People are suffering and dying every day from heart disease and stroke, and we must do all we can to save them.

I know that you have the same passion for the issues your organization works to support or affect. This is why the status quo is not good enough. Taking bold, innovative action is an absolute mandate, whether the work of your organization is focused on health, the arts, poverty, homelessness, domestic abuse, children, religion, the environment, a particular local issue, or any other concern.

THE 5 PERCENT CHALLENGE

As someone who has spent forty-plus years in the nonprofit community, I have learned a lot, read a lot, tried a lot, succeeded a lot, and failed more than a few times, too. In this book, I am sharing it all. I explain the theories and strategies I have adopted, how I have executed them, and the results we have achieved. This book is about being bold, working hard, and making a difference in the world today and into the future. Although we are all competing for a limited number of donor dollars, I believe that the better each nonprofit does, the stronger and more successful the entire country becomes. Imagine an America without a vibrant charitable community. The work of these organizations and their millions of volunteers and staff keeps us in touch with our humanness and ensures that the diverse needs of our communities are met.

What kinds of organizations constitute our community? The Panel on the Nonprofit Sector describes eight categories of charitable organizations:

1. **Arts, culture, and humanities:** This includes organizations such as museums, symphonies, orchestras, and community theaters.
2. **Education and research:** This includes organizations such as private colleges and universities, independent elementary and secondary schools, and noncommercial research institutions.
3. **Environment and animals:** This includes organizations such as zoos, bird sanctuaries, wildlife organizations, and land protection groups.
4. **Health services:** This includes organizations such as hospitals, public clinics, and nursing facilities.
5. **Human services:** This includes organizations such as housing and shelter providers, organizers of sports and recreation programs, and youth programs.
6. **International and foreign affairs:** This includes organizations that provide overseas relief and development assistance.
7. **Public and societal benefit:** This includes organizations such as private and community foundations and civic, social, and fraternal organizations.
8. **Religion:** This includes organizations such as houses of worship and their related auxiliary services.

Imagine all of these organizations disappearing in the blink of an eye. How different would our world be? One thing is certain: We would be a weaker America. And if we can strengthen these organizations, we can build a stronger America.

The advice that I share in this book comes with a challenge to you. You might know principles and concepts, but how good are you at executing? It is one thing to adopt a theory or strategy, but it is quite another to make that theory a reality for your organization. This book is about implementation. It is about creating measurable results. It is about bringing common sense into common behavior. Because I am such a stickler for clear objectives and outcomes, I have one for this book:

My goal for this book is for you to increase your organization's or your operation's effectiveness by 5 percent (or better) over your current projections.

It is up to you to determine the specific metrics for achieving this goal. Depending on your unique situation, this may mean 5 percent higher revenue from fund-raising, 5 percent better retention of staff and volunteers, or 5 percent more people served by your programs—in short, the goal is to become 5 percent more effective in a way that is most meaningful for you. No matter what target you select, it is about making a commitment to apply these strategies in a measurable, meaningful way.

> **Lesson Learned**
>
> No matter how successful your organization is today, you can—and should—always aim for bigger and better results. As well-known business author and consultant Jim Collins has said, "Good is the enemy of great."

To help you do this, I invite you to take an inside look at my leadership as CEO of the American Heart Association over the past eleven years, as well as my work in various levels of the organization prior to becoming CEO. I share some stories from other organizations, but for the most part this book sticks closely to my personal experience, about which I can provide the greatest detail and insight. Along the way I highlight lessons you can apply to your organization and helpful how-to lists, dos and don'ts, and other takeaways to make my experiences applicable to organizations of various sizes and missions.

This book is not just for large nonprofit organizations. The principles and concepts can be applied to all organizations and to you professionally. This includes readers who serve on nonprofit boards, committees, or task forces. It likewise includes paid staff and volunteers at all levels.

Among many other lessons and topics, five overarching themes appear throughout this book. They are the key philosophies that I have adopted over the course of my career, and I briefly outline each one in this introduction.

The first theme is the most fundamental: Our organizations exist for a purpose beyond profit. Sometimes we become preoccupied with the politics, fund-raising, and programmatic activities on our daily to-do lists. Although this might happen, we must never lose sight of our core mission of public service.

> **Theme #1: Nonprofits Exist for a Purpose Beyond Profit**
>
> Our sense of mission and dedication to our particular cause must be top of mind in all that we do. We all must work and lead with our hearts by staying focused on serving our constituents and bettering our world.

THE STATE OF THE NONPROFIT SECTOR

There are currently more than 1.5 million registered nonprofits in the United States alone. They generate annual revenues of $260 billion. In total, nonprofit organizations in the United States employ more than 14 million people. In 2005, there were 63.4 million volunteers working for nonprofit organizations in this country, up from 59.5 million in 2002, according to the U.S. Bureau of Labor Statistics.

All nonprofits are under growing pressure to make the most of what they've got while also facing increased and intense competition for financial and volunteer resources. Recruiting and keeping talented employees, grassroots organizers, volunteers, and fund-raisers has also become a major challenge for nonprofits. Chapter 1 discusses in greater detail many of the challenges facing nonprofits.

A major question in our community today is whether nonprofit organizations should embrace strategies more commonly used by the for-profit business sector. I believe the answer is yes. We really have no other choice. However, we must be careful in choosing which for-profit tactics we select and how we adapt them to our realities. The following chapters discuss how we approached those decisions at the American Heart Association—for example, buying paid advertising, developing partnerships with for-profit corporations, and implementing aspects of the Sarbanes-Oxley law even though nonprofits are generally not required to do so—and how we stayed true to our mission in the process.

> **Theme #2: Nonprofits Must Embrace Some Strategies from the For-Profit World**
>
> The lines are blurring between nonprofits and for-profits thanks to cause-related marketing, the Internet, and other modern business realities. To be sure, we must stay true to our missions and purpose and not compromise our organizations simply to make more money or serve more people. But we must embrace some of the tactics and practices of for-profit corporations to stay competitive and achieve our goals.

IF YOU ARE READING THIS BOOK, YOU ARE A LEADER

Do you have to be a CEO or executive director to benefit from this book? Absolutely not. I believe that anyone—whether volunteer or paid staff—can make a conscious choice to be a leader, and by picking up this book you have already made this choice. Leaders exist formally and informally at all levels and in all departments of an organization. The first three chapters of this book—which discuss mission, disciplined decision making, and breakthrough goals—are not just for CEOs. Every project, effort, or organization should have a mission statement and everyone can benefit from disciplined decision making and breakthrough goals. You can make a 5 percent difference in your entire organization or in your discrete area of influence.

In fact, if you are a volunteer or staff at any level, you have two jobs: (1) to accomplish your objectives and make your individual operation a success and (2) to help make your organization a success. Some people see only their first role, but if you really want to make a difference, add in the second responsibility. My intention is for this book to have relevance for anyone who works for, volunteers with, donates to, or cares about the nonprofit community.

ABOUT ME

My own career had humble beginnings, both literally and figuratively. I started out in the oil business, at Lyle's Humble Oil Service Station, in Fort Worth, Texas, where I worked throughout my high school years. In those days, I had more partying skills than organizational skills. At one point, I was suspended from high school for three days for utter nonsense, and I even received a few F's in citizenship. Most of my classmates probably would have voted me *least* likely to succeed. Becoming CEO of a nonprofit organization was far from my obvious destiny.

During my college years as an advertising major at the University of Texas at Austin, I moved from gas pump jockey and grease monkey to the ground level in nonprofit work. My first nonprofit job was for the American Cancer Society. It was part-time and low-tech. I ran an Address-O-Graph machine with databases for volunteers throughout Texas. My office was a warehouse shared with a couple other college students and administrative assistants.

It was good training, because I learned from the bottom up how nonprofits worked. More important, I was infused with a sense of mission. I liked the people I worked with; we had fun together, and we were bonded by the feeling that we were part of something larger than ourselves. Even in that lonely warehouse out in the middle of nowhere we felt that our work helped save lives. We believed that we were doing good things.

That sense of mission was important to me, perhaps in ways that I didn't realize for many years. I had lost two little sisters early in my life, and even though I was very young and not all that aware, it could be that their deaths instilled in me a deep desire to help others. I am not saying that I have carried that conscious thought with me every day, but throughout my life I have always been drawn to activities that contributed to the public welfare, and I wanted to make life a little better for everyone I touched. Since you are reading this book, I have a feeling something similar might drive you as well.

Perhaps I inherited my sense of volunteerism from my parents. Neither one had a college education or much money, but they made it a priority to give to those less fortunate. My father was 6 and had three younger siblings when their father died. He became the breadwinner as a young teenager and helped raise his brothers in a state of near poverty. No matter how difficult his childhood and young adulthood had been, he always told me, "When you are really feeling down and think things are awful, just drive out to some nearby community and you can always find people a heck of a lot worse off than you are."

When I was 8 years old, there was a huge flood in Fort Worth, and many services were shut down for days. Not too far away from us, maybe three or four miles, was a low-income community that did not have drinking water until the floodwaters receded. I remember spending a weekend filling water containers, then getting in the car with my father and delivering water to the people in that community. We did that for two days straight, driving back and forth.

Like most dedicated volunteers, my parents never stopped giving to others, even as they aged. Almost every time I visited them as an adult my mother was in the kitchen cooking, not just for our family but for a neighbor or friend or church member who needed help. When I arrived on their doorstep every Christmas, I never knew who else would be at our table. There might also be a college student who could not make it home, a young couple with no friends in town, or a recent widow who needed a comforting place to go. Perhaps it isn't such a surprise that I ended up in nonprofit leadership after all.

THERE IS NO RIGHT WAY TO DO THE WRONG THING

The billions of dollars pouring into charities and nonprofit organizations today has created enormous opportunities, but it also has resulted in intense media and government scrutiny—and in a growing number of calls for nonprofits to become more disciplined, more efficient, and more effective. Unfortunately, high-profile scandals among charitable organizations in recent years have taken a toll on the public's perception of this sector. It is distressing that only 58 percent of respondents in a recent survey agreed that most charitable organizations are honest and ethical in their use of donated funds. Exemption from taxation is a privilege, and we must earn it every day. We owe it to our donors to be effective and honest, not just well intentioned.

In terms of transparency and accountability, the American Heart Association goes above and beyond what most for-profits and nonprofits do, to the extent of posting all of our financial and other pertinent information on our website. The Wise Giving Alliance (WGA) of the

Better Business Bureau has a comprehensive set of twenty criteria that must be met by nonprofits—it is the gold standard. The American Heart Association was the first organization to receive the WGA Seal of Approval. In several upcoming chapters, I will explain what the American Heart Association does to meet the highest expectations of those who volunteer and donate to the organization.

> **Theme #3: Credibility Is Everything**
>
> When it comes to ethics, nonprofit organizations are held to a higher standard. And, like it or not, perception is reality. Even the faint whiff of impropriety or conflict of interest can be fatal. Nonprofits—and nonprofit leaders—must have the highest ethical standards and make sure they are visible to our staff, volunteers, donors, and the general public.

LEADING THE AMERICAN HEART ASSOCIATION

To fill in the rest of my background: After graduating from college, I spent several years at the American Cancer Society, as well as a stint in the for-profit sector as a stockbroker. In 1973 I joined the American Heart Association, Texas Affiliate, in Austin, as vice president for field operations and, later, executive vice president. In 1982, I joined the National Center in Dallas as chief operating officer. In 1996, I became senior vice president for field operations, and in 1997 I became CEO.

During my tenure as CEO, the American Heart Association has made major changes to structures and processes, which have dramatically increased the organization's success in many areas. As you will read about in Chapter 2, we merged the American Heart Association's fifty-six state and metropolitan affiliates into fifteen regional affiliates (now reduced to eight) and adopted a single corporate type of structure. During my tenure as CEO, the organization also approved a far-reaching health breakthrough goal that called for the reduction of coronary heart disease, stroke, and their concomitant risks by 25 percent by 2010 (more about this in Chapter 3). This first-ever strategic plan with a measurable outcome goal brought a new focus to the association, as all of our endeavors are now evaluated based on their contribution to achieving this goal.

> **Structure of the American Heart Association**
>
> Throughout, this book refers to the American Heart Association's National Center and its regional affiliates. Here are quick definitions of these terms:
> *National Center:* This is the headquarters in Dallas, Texas.
> *Regional affiliates:* These currently consist of eight multistate territories across the United States that serve and coordinate local and metro operations in most communities.

In another bold move for the nonprofit community, we brought in a professional advertising agency and consultants to build the brand and strengthen the political clout of the American Heart Association. Thanks in part to these intensified marketing efforts, which Chapter 4 explores, the American Heart Association has become one of America's greatest brands, according to the American Brand Council. The American Heart Association was one of very few nonprofits to be ranked with major businesses such as Disney, State Farm, and Barnes & Noble.

During my tenure, the American Heart Association has also experienced its greatest period of financial growth, with annual revenues increasing from $400 million to $650 million over the last eleven years. Here are some of the highlights of the past decade:

- Creating the American Stroke Association as a division of the American Heart Association.
- Launching Go Red For Women, an award-winning national campaign to raise women's awareness of heart disease, their number one killer.
- Joining with the William J. Clinton Foundation and Governor Mike Huckabee of Arkansas to create the Alliance for a Healthier Generation, to fight the alarming epidemic of childhood obesity.

About the American Heart Association

The American Heart Association is the nation's oldest and largest voluntary health organization dedicated to building healthier lives, free of cardiovascular diseases and stroke.

Founded: 1924
National headquarters: Dallas, Texas
Website: www.americanheart.org
Annual revenue: $650 million
Employees: 3,500
Volunteers and donors: 22.5 million

Here are just some of the highlights of the American Heart Association's accomplishments:

- Research expenditures over the last ten years total $1.4 billion.
- The American Heart Association Contact Center receives an average of 1,200 calls a day.
- The average number of monthly visits to the www.AmericanHeart.org website is 3 million. The average number of website visits per day is 44,000.
- More than 750,000 walkers participate in over 515 American Heart Walk events each year, raising over $100 million.
- Nearly 11 million people have been trained in cardiopulmonary resuscitation (CPR).
- The Professional Membership Program consists of 25,000 scientists around the world who serve on sixteen Scientific Councils.
- More than 12,000 abstracts are submitted for Scientific Sessions each year, from fifty different countries. Nearly 3,100 speakers are invited to present.
- Total attendance at Scientific Sessions is around 26,000—half from outside the United States.
- More than 100 companies with over 800 products participate in the Food Certification Program.

- Strategic alliances have been formed with more than ninety organizations at the national level, including the Clinton Foundation, the National Football League (NFL), and those that have major influence over the health-care system, such as the Centers for Medicare and Medicaid and the Centers for Disease Control and Prevention.
- Partnerships have been formed with groups that provide health-care coverage to over 100 million Americans.

- Introducing Get With The Guidelines to help hospitals improve care and survival rates for heart and stroke patients. It is estimated that these guidelines could eliminate 80,000 heart attack deaths every year. In December 2004, it was the first hospital program to receive the Innovation in Prevention award from the U.S. Department of Health and Human Services.
- Collaborating with the Joint Commission of Healthcare Organizations to develop a Primary Stroke Center Certification program and with the National Committee for Quality Assurance to develop a recognition program for doctors and hospitals.
- Increasing online activities, resulting in *Forbes* magazine recognizing the American Heart Association with a Best of the Web award for health information.

Although not every nonprofit has the resources and size of the American Heart Association, any organization can apply the principles and strategies we have used to achieve all of the goals discussed here. Every nonprofit can be more forward-thinking, creative, disciplined, visionary, and successful. Reading this book will equip you with the tools and strategies to help your organization become as successful as you can imagine.

LEADERSHIP IS A TEAM SPORT

Although some people possess innate talent for leading, the practice of leadership is very much a learned skill. A big part of that learning is to acknowledge how much leaders need other people. I am always willing to put my ego aside because I know that I can learn from anybody—inside, outside, or at any level of the organization. A lot of leaders, particularly CEOs, think they need to be omnipotent or omniscient. They believe it is a sign of weakness to admit they don't know something or to ask for help. They could not be more wrong. Leadership is very much a team sport.

This means, of course, that it is incredibly important who is on your team. This book shares many ideas and tactics for making sure that you partner with the right people, and it helps you develop the people you already have on board. This includes staff members, volunteers, board members, and strategic partners. Once you have acquired the best people, how to do you keep them on board and drive them to perform at their best? The short answer is to make everyone feel valued, engaged, and included. Chapters 6, 7, 9, and 10 discuss this topic in thorough detail.

> **Theme #4: Surround Yourself with the Best People**
>
> Surround yourself with people you think are smarter and more talented than you—and listen to them. Know where you are going and how you are going to get there, but engage and support the team in setting the vision and achieving the goals. Create a positive environment by setting the tone and leading by example. No matter what other purposes are important, people always make the difference.

THE ROLE OF THE NONPROFIT LEADER

Many outside people think that the nonprofit sector has lower standards and a slower pace than the for-profit sector. Some others may perceive that the nonprofit CEO or executive director has all the answers. Let's dispel those myths right off the bat. These days, a nonprofit leader cannot create results through mandate. He or she must build commitment, create consensus, and be active on the front line. Constantly driving change in the organization is a given for this kind of proactive leadership.

You must have in-depth understanding of your organization's area of focus (health, education, the environment, etc.). You must be informed and strategic, yet hands-on. The environment in which nonprofits function today calls for far more accountability and transparency with the general public, regulatory bodies, and the organization's volunteers, staff, and constituencies.

You can keep your edge by reading the latest business books, perusing business journals such as the *Harvard Business Review* and the electronic BoardSource, and interacting with peers regularly. CEOs and staff often belong to organizations such as the Independent Sector, the American Society of Association Executives, the National Human Services Assembly, and the National Health Council to keep up with best practices. In addition, they and their senior staff attend outside conferences conducted by local colleges, universities, or chambers of commerce, which can provide new insights. Good ideas and benchmarks come not only from other nonprofits but also from for-profit organizations.

As you will see, I am a heavy reader of business books, subscriber to expert blogs, and listener at conferences and speeches. I also spend as much time as possible interacting with the people the AHA serves in local communities. I encourage you to do the same. You will see that many leaders do these sorts of things, too, but they are not all equally good at taking the best ideas and executing them extremely well. This is your challenge. Theories are great, but they mean nothing without strong execution.

THE SOFT STUFF

Joseph Nye, dean of Harvard's Kennedy School of Government, coined the term *soft power*, defined as the ability to get what you want by attraction rather than coercion. Nonprofit leaders actually excel in this area. Nonprofit leaders may be more effective than for-profit leaders. In a 2008 study by the Community Resource Exchange, over 2,500 management leaders in the nonprofit and for-profit sectors were studied on seventeen dimensions. For-profit leaders scored higher in only three dimensions. Of the other fourteen, the most dramatic differences appeared in the six dimensions characterized by sensitivity to people and the use of personal versus hierarchical power. For complete results go to www.nonprofitquarterly.com.

Leaders create vision and bold goals, they drive change, and they take prudent risks. We build, challenge, and empower outstanding teams. We execute and hold ourselves accountable for measurable outcomes. But, equally as important, we also set the tone for our colleagues, volunteers, and the people we serve. Therefore, we must attend to the softer, intangible side of leadership. Leadership is about being excellent in your work *and* being a good role model. Often, when the intangible, softer elements (such as transparency, strong relationships, trust, and open communication) are in place, these elements move the hard resources (such as dollars and people). The following leadership practices are explored in greater detail in Chapter 7, and many other practices are defined throughout the book:

- **Be authentic.** People want to make sure that you walk the walk as well as talk the talk. Be an example to everyone around you.
- **Admit your mistakes.** Be willing to show your vulnerability and say, "I made a mistake," or "I do not have all the answers." People want to know they work with someone who is a real person, who will be honest and straight with them.
- **Be confident.** Vulnerability is important, but it must be coupled with a confident demeanor. If your operation or team is in crisis, the worst thing you can say is, "I do not know how we are going to get through this!" People need to have confidence in their leaders.
- **Be consistent and transparent.** Consistency and predictability breed confidence and trust. When you make important decisions that will affect other people, be sure to explain your process. Decisions should have a context, so they do not seem to come out of nowhere.
- **Overcommunicate.** You must communicate, communicate, communicate and listen, listen, listen. Address issues proactively and aggressively communicate what is going on so that everyone feels "in the know."

I hope that you will take the practices in this book that most apply to you and then go forth and execute them to the best of your ability.

> **Theme #5: Soft Resources Can Move Hard Resources**
>
> You have to tend to the soft resources (trust, relationships, communication, etc.) in addition to the hard resources (finances, people, etc.). Oftentimes, if the soft resources are healthy, they will realign the hard resources and speed up execution.

Ultimately, these five themes add up to a prescription for a healthy, happy, long-living nonprofit organization. I hope that you will not only apply many of the strategies in this book but also share them with other volunteers and staff. After all, strong nonprofit leadership is about not just creating a better future for ourselves and organizations, but creating a better future for our world. That mission infused my work with the American Heart Association and is the reason I have written this book. I have always loved this Greek proverb and encourage you to keep it in mind while reading:

> *A society grows great when old men plant trees whose shade they know they shall never sit in.*

I am proud of my accomplishments, but I hope that my greatest legacy is helping to build the next generation of successful nonprofit volunteer and staff leaders and effective nonprofit organizations. Now let's get down to the business of planting!

CHAPTER 1

A MISSION STATEMENT IS NOT THE SAME AS A SENSE OF MISSION

It has been trendy in recent decades for businesses and organizations of all kinds to develop mission statements and post them in prominent places. That is a good thing, a healthy thing, and a practice to be encouraged. But a mission statement is not the same as a true sense of mission. One is a reminder, and the other is a deeply felt passion.

Nonprofit organizations, whether large like Goodwill Industries and the American Heart Association or small like a local PTA or church group, would not and could not exist without a pervasive sense of mission. Without a cause that resonates with volunteers and donors, momentum falters and, over time, initiatives die. For-profits can have a powerful sense of social mission about their products and services, but they also exist to make a profit. This is not a bad thing, of course. But nonprofits are different. Mission is our sole driver.

When I wake up in the morning, my mind is on the lives the American Heart Association is saving. Wherever I travel, I talk about heart health. When I scan the e-mail messages that come in overnight on my BlackBerry, I am often greeted by the story of someone who called 9-1-1 because he learned about the warning signs of a heart attack on the AmericanHeart.org website. Or I receive a note from a mother who is feeding her children healthier foods because her son came home from school talking about the fun of participating in the Let's Just Play Go Healthy Challenge, a campaign the American Heart Association launched with the William J. Clinton Foundation and Nickelodeon in 2006. I am grateful every day for the staff, volunteers, and donors of the AHA who make these successes possible, and I consider it part of my job description to be the organization's strongest advocate (yes, that includes avoiding high-cholesterol foods and exercising regularly!).

Fortunately for those of us who care deeply about nonprofit organizations, a sense of mission is abundant in the United States. The spirit of volunteerism and nonprofit work is a vital part of the heritage of our country. In the early 1800s, Alexis de Tocqueville noted that in U.S. communities we form organizations to address common problems that in Europe are served by the government or the church. Regardless of how you define the role of government, most would agree that our country is enhanced by volunteerism; we are a nation with enormous needs, and certainly the government cannot do it all. We are enhanced by volunteerism because it creates a stronger sense of community and connectedness in a large country, not just because there is a need.

A sense of mission is absolutely vital to nonprofit organizations. Although those of us in the nonprofit sector possess a dedication to the causes and people we serve, we know that we cannot fulfill our goals through heart and soul alone. We also need good leadership and good management. That is what this first chapter is all about: combining a sense of mission with a sense of business. Nonprofit organizations need a deep commitment to both in order to survive and thrive.

Lesson Learned

Nonprofit organizations need to combine a sense of mission with a sense of business. Both must be embraced for these organizations to survive and thrive into the future.

CHALLENGES FACING THE NONPROFIT COMMUNITY

How well are nonprofits serving their missions today? More important, could they do better? It is imperative to always think about doing better and improving. All organizations today—for-profit and nonprofit—are in a constant race to do better. As everyone applies better and smarter ways of working, all of us can do more good in the world. This is a powerful proposition in the nonprofit sector. If each nonprofit could achieve its mission a bit more effectively and efficiently, imagine the exponential good they could do—less poverty, better health care, safer neighborhoods, better schools, cleaner air, more opportunity, decreased suffering. Your organization or initiative may not need a massive overhaul, but even small tweaks can make a huge difference. Regardless of how good any of us are, we can always get better.

This book is for everyone interested in the success of the nonprofit sector—leaders, staff, board members, donors, volunteers, and customers of both nonprofits and for-profits. We would all like to serve more people and, when it comes to our missions, knock the ball out of the park. But several significant challenges exist:

1. **More competition in the nonprofit sector.** While donations continue to rise, so do the number of nonprofit organizations in existence. Nonprofits are under increasing pressure to make the most of donated dollars and differentiate themselves from other organizations in the face of this intense competition. Not only do nonprofits compete for donations, but they also compete for top talent—both staff and volunteers. It is increasingly difficult to recruit and keep talented executives, grassroots organizers, volunteers, and fund-raisers.

2. **Blurring lines between nonprofit and for-profit organizations.** More for-profit organizations are becoming involved in cause-related marketing, foundation work, and other ventures that were previously in the domain of nonprofits. Think of museum and hospital gift shops, nonprofit credit counseling agencies, the Avon Walk for Breast Cancer, and other instances of fuzziness along the for-profit/nonprofit divide. This means that consumers are faced with many more options for where to give their money, time, and attention to the causes they want to support. The *New York Times* recently reported a trend toward a convergence of interest between nonprofits and for-profits and suggested that, increasingly, the two sectors should work on aligning around strategic objectives.

3. **Inadequate definitions of what constitutes success.** In the for-profit sector, shareholders measure a company's success primarily by profit. In the nonprofit sector, there is no clear measure. The sector as a whole has done a very poor job over the years of defining suc-

cess. It has been soft; it has been process oriented. It has not been as focused on end results as it should or could have been. In an effort to assess the effectiveness of various charities, some watchdogs groups (type the term *charity watchdog* into an Internet search engine and you will find several examples), recently established a somewhat oversimplified mathematical formula to measure the success of nonprofits of all sizes and missions. This formula states that the cost of fund-raising and general management should not exceed 25 percent of expenditures. The problem is that this measure does not consider whether an organization is actually accomplishing anything! It is a well-intentioned idea but not particularly helpful for donors.

Each of these factors has led to a growing debate in the nonprofit field during the past several years over which for-profit business strategies nonprofit agencies should embrace without undermining the heart and soul of the organizations' missions. The answers may vary depending on each individual organization, but there is no doubt that all nonprofits must apply some businesslike, bottom-line mentalities and high-level accountability to maintain credibility and stay viable. Good intentions are no longer enough. There is no other option if nonprofits are to survive and thrive in the twenty-first century.

Why am I so steadfast in my belief that implementing for-profit practices is the right thing to do? Let's look more closely at the challenges facing nonprofits.

Growth in the Number of Nonprofits

As of 2006, there were 1,478,194 nonprofit organizations registered with the Internal Revenue Service (IRS), including public charities, private foundations, and other 501(c)(3) nonprofit organizations (such as civic leagues, social and recreational clubs, social welfare organizations, and chambers of commerce). This represents a 36.2 percent growth from ten years earlier, when there were 1,084,939 nonprofits registered.[2] Today, charitable nonprofits and religious organizations employ more than 14 million people in the United States—that is 11 percent of the national workforce. In 2005, there were 63.4 million volunteers working for nonprofit organizations in this country, up from 59.5 million in 2002, according to the U.S. Bureau of Labor Statistics.

Nonprofits are a major force in the American economy, and the sector is growing larger every year. In California alone, 400 new nonprofits are formed each month.

Much of the growth is due to a remarkable boom in American philanthropy. Massive wealth has ignited an unprecedented level of philanthropy by the world's wealthiest and most powerful individuals. Traditional philanthropic organizations launched by Carnegies and Rockefellers have been joined by those of the billionaires who created Google, eBay, and Microsoft, and others formed by mere multimillionaires, celebrities, rock stars, athletes, and former presidents.

The Internet has also fueled the growth in the number of charities because it is easier for newer organizations to reach out to donors and easier for the donors to give. Websites such as JustGive.org enable anyone with an Internet connection to donate funds. According to the Center on Philanthropy at Indiana University, approximately 67 percent of all American households donate to charity.[3]

The billions of dollars pouring into charities and nonprofit organizations have created enormous opportunities but have also resulted in intense media, government, and consumer scrutiny—and in growing calls for nonprofits to become more disciplined, more efficient, and more effective. If you want people to give their dollars to your organization, you must show exactly where those dollars are going and what good they are doing. To use business terminology, you must be able to document for donors a return on investment (ROI).

Megabillionaire Pierre Omidyar, founder and chairman of eBay, threw down the gauntlet when he challenged his own philanthropic organization, Omidyar Network, to invest more effectively in its goal to build community in the physical world just as his business has done in the virtual world. I believe we will see more of this as for-profit leaders, such as Omidyar, Bill Gates, and Oprah Winfrey, apply their business acumen to the running of their philanthropic organizations. Donors will notice, too, and demand that other nonprofits apply business discipline to their operations.

Blurring Lines

Thirty thousand websites exist to help Americans with health issues. Do consumers notice—or care—which ones are nonprofit and which

> **Lesson Learned**
>
> To be successful, nonprofits of all sizes must operate with great discipline and measurable effectiveness while also maintaining their philanthropic sense of mission. Otherwise, philanthropic dollars will go elsewhere.

are for-profit? Avon, a for-profit company, hosts a walk for breast cancer to benefit its nonprofit charitable foundation. Microsoft, another for-profit sponsors a campaign in which every time you start a conversation using its Instant Messenger software the company shares a portion of the program's advertising revenue with nonprofit organizations dedicated to social causes. Couples who create wedding registries on WeddingChannel.com are invited to donate a portion of their gift givers' purchases to the charity of their choice. Frequent flyer and credit card loyalty programs also include the option to donate miles and points to nonprofit organizations.

MTV's Think MTV (www.mtv.com/thinkmtv) program uses the combined power of celebrity and technology to engage young people in volunteerism. The site gives young people information about how to get involved and mobilize other people with similar interests. Those registering on the site can get involved in causes ranging from stopping the genocide in Darfur to issues in their local communities. Kids who use the site to do good can win rewards that include prizes such as hanging out with celebrities like Bono, Jay-Z, Brad Pitt, Chris Rock, and Rosario Dawson. In addition, they get access to exclusive MTV events and exposure on MTV and other national media outlets, plus the chance to win grants, scholarships, and more. The site also carries advertising from for-profit corporations with cause-related marketing messages.

If you are having trouble telling the difference between for-profits and nonprofits these days, you are certainly not alone. There is nothing less than a competition for mindshare going on between for-profits and nonprofits. This is why nonprofits must always stay true to the fact that they exist for a purpose beyond profit. Our missions—our deep, passionate commitments to our causes—are our beacons in the storm. The more the world changes and the more the lines blur between nonprofits and for-profits, the more crucial it is for us to stay true to our missions.

> **Lesson Learned**
>
> Today, nonprofits and for-profits often compete with each other, particularly for mindshare of the public. If nonprofits do not perform well and differentiate themselves, they will be left behind. Nonprofits can compete by adopting some of the strategies of for-profit corporations, and they can differentiate themselves by emphasizing a dedicated sense of mission—having a purpose beyond profit.

Another reason for blurring lines is that more for-profits and nonprofits are joining together in alliances, marketing campaigns, product development, and other ventures. The American Heart Association has embraced this trend with gusto. Over the years, I have had the opportunity to work with for-profit executives and corporations that have a passion about their mission that is equal to ours. As Chapter 10 describes in more detail, the AHA has partnered with such organizations as Macy's, Pfizer, and Microsoft.

The American Heart Association has an entire department devoted to building corporate relationships. Corporate relationships have made a significant difference in advancing the organization's mission—quite simply, allowing the organization to do more. Of course, nonprofits must also keep in mind that, when establishing partnerships (particularly when there is a significant financial transaction), the public can perceive a conflict of interest. Many years ago, the American Heart Association established corporate relations policies to try to guard against that perception—a perception that would benefit neither the organization nor the corporation.

Nonprofits also must be in touch with the reality that most of these contributions or sponsorships come from a corporation's advertising and/or promotional budgets. Corporations want to do good and they want to help us advance our missions, but their primary goal is to make money. They are in business to sell their products or services and make a profit for their shareholders. Be aware that a corporation's need to make a profit may occasionally come into conflict with the mission of your nonprofit organization.

Evolving Definitions of Success

The nonprofit community is recognizing the desire for accountability and oversight with some ambivalence but no shortage of suggestions. We certainly want to do the right thing, but we also do not want a lot of government intervention, rules, or regulations. The Senate Finance Committee has rightly pointed out instances of lavish or inappropriate spending by nonprofit organizations. In 2004, they asked Independent Sector (a leadership forum for charities, foundations, and corporate giving programs) to form the Panel on the Nonprofit Sector to make recommendations for how nonprofits could better measure their success.

The panel—of which I was co-convener with Lorie Slutsky, president of the New York Community Trust, and Paul Brest, president of the Hewlett Foundation—was an independent effort by charities and foundations to ensure that the nonprofit community would remain a vibrant and healthy part of American society. It consisted of twenty-four nonprofit and philanthropic leaders, whose organizations are diverse in their location, mission, perspective, and scope of work. The panel took a number of steps to receive input from organizations across the country and conducted a series of field hearings to explain and obtain feedback on its work.

Ultimately, in June 2005, the panel issued a report to Congress and the nonprofit sector, *Strengthening Transparency, Governance, and Accountability of Charitable Organizations* and followed up with a supplemental report by the same name in April 2006. In a nutshell, the report presented three clusters of recommendations: (1) things that Congress should do, (2) things that regulatory bodies should do, and (3) things that the nonprofit sector should do itself.

To help nonprofits take action on the panel's recommendations to Congress, the panel released *Principles for Good Governance and Ethical Practice: A Guide for Charities and Foundations* in October 2007. This guide represents the first time that members of the American nonprofit community have come together to develop principles of ethical conduct, accountability, and transparency. The guide outlines thirty-three practices designed to support board members and staff leaders of every nonprofit organization as they work to improve their own operations. This is an excellent first step for nonprofits toward defining their own parameters for accountability and success. The thirty-three recommendations are divided into four categories. As you can see from the category titles, the recommendations represent an effort to steer nonprofits toward business strategies:

1. Legal compliance and public disclosure
2. Effective governance
3. Strong financial oversight
4. Responsible fund-raising

If you choose to read the panel's report and implement its recommendations, I would add one important reminder: Even if your organization follows the report's recommendations, you still need to focus on the end result—the bottom line for your organization. The goal of implementing more businesslike practices is not just to run a more effective organization; it is to improve the results your organization achieves.

Recommended Resources

Independent Sector (www.independentsector.org) provides databases on a variety of topics as well as offering helpful tool kits related to nonprofit governance, lobbying, giving, volunteering, regulations, ethics, accountability, and more.

The **National Council of Nonprofit Associations** (www.ncna.org) is a network of state and regional nonprofit associations that helps small and midsize nonprofits manage and lead more effectively, collaborate and exchange solutions, and achieve greater impact in their communities.

In the summer of 2007, Congress passed legislation that included the most far-reaching reforms to charitable regulation since 1969—and those of us at nonprofit organizations were gratified that about 95 percent of the provisions Congress included reflected the panel's recommendations. The fact is clear that nonprofits are being held more accountable for such things as transparency, better governance, and proper review of compensation practices.

In addition to government oversight, there are several charity watchdog agencies that report on nonprofit activities. Thanks to the Internet, their findings are available to donors, volunteers, and the general public at the click of a mouse. Although I have some problems with the arbitrary measures of success of many online watchdog groups, some are helpful in their assessments. The gold standard is the Wise Giving Alliance, a division of the Better Business Bureau. The Wise Giving Alliance has a set of twenty comprehensive standards. They employ a scorecard, and nonprofits know how score is being kept.

Watching the Watchdogs

Unfortunately, any group can hang out a shingle and call itself a nonprofit watchdog, whether it is qualified or not. The many new watchdog groups have begun to create more confusion than value. With the important exception of the Wise Giving Alliance, most watchdogs use mathematical formulas, which are easily manipulated and do not always conform to generally accepted accounting principles (GAAP). They make additions and subtractions to certain assets or liabilities before they run certain ratios, or they might categorize expenses differently or use a different methodology to calculate reserves. This means that the same nonprofit can receive an "excellent" rating from one group, a "good" from a second group, and a "fair" from another. Such ratings are confusing to the public and to us as nonprofit leaders.

My recommendation to nonprofit leaders is not to focus on meeting the conflicting demands of these agencies (except the Wise Giving Alliance), but instead to be more proactive—as a sector and as individual organizations—in defining success and holding yourselves accountable. Your financial data should be public knowledge, and you should make sure you are proactively submitting information to the Wise Giving Alliance and meeting its published standards. For more information, visit www.give.org/standards.

Increased oversight of the nonprofit sector could lead to a variety of outcomes. It could result in fewer nonprofit organizations overall, which may not necessarily be a bad thing. More nonprofits can mean more duplication and increased overhead costs. However, increased oversight could lead to more sharing of resources among nonprofit organizations—such as combining office space, consolidating administrative functions, or combining office supply orders to receive bulk rates. As an example, the American Heart Association and the American Cancer Society are currently exploring joint management of donation processing, cash processing, and bequest administration under one management function.

A big negative of increased oversight is that it could lead to overwhelming red tape that, for example, would make it a pain in the neck for a group of parents to form a 501(c)(3) to build a Little League baseball park. Ideally, the ultimate result of increased oversight would be a happy medium between self-regulation and government oversight that encourages good governance without overburdening social sector organizations.

COMBINING THE NONPROFIT MISSION WITH FOR-PROFIT MANAGEMENT

Clearly, the time has come for us to take a good, hard look at the way nonprofits are managed and use all the tools available to achieve our missions.

What kind of for-profit approaches have benefited nonprofit organizations in achieving their missions? Here are some examples:

- The American Cancer Society recently spent $15 million on paid advertising to increase awareness of the need for universal access to health care to achieve its mission of reducing deaths from cancer by 50 percent by 2015.

- Kiva.org invites charitable givers to loan money—as little as $25— to entrepreneurs in the developing world. Kiva's partnerships with existing microfinance institutions help connect people who want to make a difference with poor, hardworking entrepreneurs. Lenders receive e-mail updates about the business's progress and

> ### Recommended Resource
>
> According to Independent Sector, the Panel on the Nonprofit Sector's ***Principles for Good Governance and Ethical Practice: A Guide for Charities and Foundations*** represents the first time that charities and foundations from a broad cross section of the American nonprofit community have come together to develop principles of ethical conduct, accountability, and transparency that they aspire to and encourage all organizations to follow.
>
> In the first six weeks following the report's release, more than 200 foundations and charities endorsed them, and over 43,000 copies were ordered or downloaded. Most important, the nonprofit community is using the *Guide* to elevate individual and collective commitment to the highest standards of ethical practice. Umbrella groups are integrating the thirty-three principles into existing best-practice programs, foundations are providing the *Guide* to their grantees, and organizations—large and small—are using the *Guide* to evaluate and update existing governance practices.
>
> For more information and to download a free copy of *Principles for Good Governance and Ethical Practice: A Guide for Charities and Foundations* Guide, visit www.nonprofitpanel.org/final/Panel_Final_Report.pdf.

> ### Lesson Learned
>
> The nonprofit sector has a responsibility to self-regulate. It is up to each one of us as leaders to make sure good governance and ethical practices exist sectorwide.

when a repayment is made. Entrepreneurs repay the funds, which lenders can then withdraw or reloan. To date, 23,660 loans have been made through Kiva.org, with a total value of $15,277,460. According to Kiva, their loan repayment rate is 99.76 percent.

- The Susan G. Komen for the Cure Breast Cancer Foundation sells and cobrands commercial products, with a portion of the sales of its own products (such as T-shirts and hats) and product promotions with for-profit organizations (such as handbags and cereals) going to support its charitable operations.

Corporate contributions are also being directed more and more to help causes that directly relate to a for-profit's operations. In the past, corporate donations for the most part went to good causes unrelated to the business of the company—such as a financial firm donating to children's health or a manufacturing company donating to an orchestra. Many companies still do this. However, more and more corporations now support causes that are directly related to their line of products. For example, Home Depot supports KaBOOM, a nonprofit that builds playgrounds, and the Kellogg Foundation supports many nutrition programs. This means that nonprofits are getting not only charitable dollars but marketing and advertising dollars as well.

Nonprofits must act accordingly and think like for-profit marketers and advertisers in soliciting sponsorships and large gifts. As an example, if your organization wants corporate sponsorship for a charity walk, you need to be prepared to provide demographic information about the people who will be walking. The corporation will want to know whether that is a market they also want to reach. Here we once again see the blurring of nonprofit and for-profit lines.

ETHICS

You cannot talk about the use of for-profit tactics in nonprofit organizations for very long before the issue of ethics arises. Unfortunately, in the eyes of the public we are not doing so well in this area. Only 58 percent of respondents in a 2006 survey agreed that most charitable organizations are honest and ethical in their use of donated funds.[4]

Before you even consider taking any cause-related income from a corporation, you need to establish policies up front about the kinds of relationships you will and will not enter. Although your policies might change a bit over time, you should never change them just to allow for funding of a specific proposal. That change could be construed as selling out for the money. Your policies must be guided by what you will or will not do, regardless of the money involved. Even with these policies in place, you have to make some judgment calls. Some things are black and some things white—those are the easy ones. Inevitably, there are some gray areas that are challenging, but be true to your principles and core values.

My barometer is this: There is not any amount of money that is worth tarnishing the reputation of the America Heart Association. It is really that straightforward. If we start getting into a gray area—and occasionally we do—here is my litmus test: Are we comfortable seeing this decision on *60 Minutes* or on the front page of the *New York Times*? If we are not comfortable, then we just say no. On more than one occasion we have refused funds from a potential donor who did not meet this *New York Times* test.

Organizations like the American Heart Association that rely on scientific credibility cannot do anything in terms of corporate relationships that does not meet their scientific standards. Otherwise, they risk undermining the public's trust. For other nonprofits the issue might be legal credibility, academic credibility, or something else. Whatever the crux of your moral authority, do not compromise it. Ever. Many for-profits have recovered from ethical breaches or loss of the public's trust. A for-profit can undergo a product recall or make a mistake or endure a scandal, and oftentimes the public is back out there buying the product a short time later.

It is not the same for nonprofits. If the CEO of the American Heart Association got arrested for embezzling, it would take a lot longer for the American Heart Association to recover than if it had been the CEO of a for-profit. I'm even careful about what I order at restaurants—what would you think if you saw the CEO of the American Heart Association eating a triple bacon cheeseburger, large fries, and a milk shake? Because we operate on public trust, we are held to a higher level of ethical accountability. If we got the facts wrong in our science recommendations, it would do our organization irreparable harm. People expect

Lesson Learned

If you are not comfortable seeing a decision featured on the front page of the *New York Times,* then do not do it. Public trust is among a nonprofit organization's greatest assets.

more of nonprofit organizations. The public believes we should be better and do better. There is a sacred trust when people donate their hard-earned money. Part of our core values is to maintain this trust, and that must be top of mind in every business decision we make.

PUTTING IT ALL TOGETHER: MISSION, MANAGEMENT, AND ETHICS

What practical steps can you take to stay true to your organization's mission, be effective and efficient in the current environment, and maintain your ethical standards? Here are some top-line strategies, which integrate for-profit management techniques with the nonprofit sense of mission and ethical responsibility.

- **Define your mission clearly.** If you have not already, make sure that your organization's mission is concise, clear, and specific. Change or update it when necessary. The American Heart Association's mission is "Building healthier lives, free of cardiovascular diseases and stroke." We updated our mission at our annual meeting in April 2007. Prior to that, our mission was to reduce disability and death from cardiovascular diseases and stroke. The AHA mission statement undergoes a formal review process every third year but is changed only every few decades. The environment changes and the organization changes, so a periodic review is important to ensure that there is alignment of purpose and reality. A good mission statement elicits heartfelt participation and redefines objectives and tasks; it evolves to acknowledge progress and encourage participants to continue to think bigger and achieve more.

- **Keep your finger on the pulse of what is happening in the external environment and adjust accordingly.** Look for external benchmarks to help you track your organization's or operation's success and serve your constituencies in the most effective way possible. For instance, the American Heart Association implemented aspects of the Sarbanes-Oxley law, even though nonprofits are generally not required to do so. We comply on a voluntary basis where it makes sense and is cost-effective. This gives the organization greater transparency and accountability and holds us to a high ethical standard. I predict that more large nonprofits will voluntarily comply in the future. We also began a supplier diversity initiative—a mandate for government agencies and a best practice in many of America's top corporations—to develop commercial relationships with minority- and women-owned businesses that provide products and services to advance our mission. Evaluate your organization's or operation's performance by looking at key performance results and comparing them to those of other organizations, both nonprofit and for-profit. Then develop a plan to reach the benchmarks you find.

- **Be flexible.** As Jim Collins, author of *Built to Last* (Collins Business, 2004) and *Good to Great* (Collins Business, 2001), says, if an organization is built to change, it is built to last. Think about how quickly change is happening and then realize that this is probably as slow as it will ever be. The world just keeps getting faster and faster. Windows of opportunity open and close more quickly, but if your organization is fluid and flexible it can capitalize on these opportunities. Do not be afraid of change.
- **Bring people into your organization who have fire in their bellies.** If someone is a quick study, is willing to learn, and has drive and determination, then he or she may be able to do the volunteer or staff job you need done. The right people for a nonprofit organization are not only competent but also have passion about your mission. They have a sense of a greater calling and are willing to keep their self-interest in check and make decisions for the greater good of your organization. Employees of the American Heart Association were actually willing to give up their jobs in a restructure in order to advance the mission of the organization. Drive, grit, determination, and fire in the belly can sometimes offset a lack of full credentials and track record as long as the raw talent is there.
- **Show people how their role contributes to the bigger picture.** This begins with a clear mission and a bold goal. The American Heart Association hired an internal communications person to ensure that everyone in the organization knows what is going on. Every volunteer and staff member needs to know how his or her job is helping to save lives. Every single employee of FedEx, from the receptionist to the cafeteria worker to the CEO, will tell you that his or her job is to deliver packages on time. Even if you can't afford a dedicated staff person to focus on internal communication,

you can make sure the employees and volunteers at your nonprofit know how building a student group on Facebook is helping to save endangered species or why upgrading the organization's computer servers ultimately contributes to the goal of reducing poverty. Think about how you drive in a dense fog: cautiously, slowly, tensely, uncertainly, seeing only what is directly in front of you. Now think about what happens when the sun comes out and you can see your surroundings and you have a context. You drive faster and with confidence. We need to "lift the fog" for all of our volunteers and staff.

- **Make your customer service consistent with your mission.** What experience do people have when they call your office, search your website, send a letter or e-mail, or phone your call center? Customer service is a strong business practice and cannot be an afterthought. These days, people expect friendly, efficient, customized service from their local pizza shop, so imagine the expectations they have from an organization working toward a cause they believe in! People will not—and should not—cut you slack because you are a nonprofit. Make sure your staff and volunteers are knowledgeable, courteous, and genuinely helpful.

- **Require full disclosure.** Every researcher who stands up and makes a presentation at one of our American Heart Association science meetings must first declare where there is a potential conflict of interest in his or her research—for example, a grant from a pharmaceutical company. Then the presentation begins. When you foster a daily environment of transparency and disclosure, it becomes a habit and ethical issues become less likely. At the national level, the American Heart Association posts on its website donations from the major pharmaceutical and medical device companies.

- **Stay in close touch with the people you serve.** It is too easy to get caught up in meetings, e-mails, and conference calls. Whenever you feel disconnected from your organization's mission or have a difficult decision to make, spend some time getting reconnected with the people you serve. I read e-mails and handwritten letters every day from people whose lives have been saved by our work. You might visit patients in a hospital, deliver meals to the homeless, play with abandoned dogs at an animal shelter, or answer phones for your twenty-four-hour hotline.

The mission of your organization must be at the front of your mind every minute of every day. It guides your decision making and fuels your innovation. It keeps you moving forward. It keeps you out of trouble. And it truly changes the lives of the people you serve. As one who has spent the majority of his career working with a sense of mission, I know that not only does the work we do improve the lives of our constituents, it enriches our own lives as well.

CHAPTER 1 TAKEAWAYS

- **A mission statement is not the same as a true sense of mission.** Nonprofit organizations must have a pervasive sense of mission. Without a cause that resonates with volunteers and donors, nonprofits will ultimately fail and die off.

- **Good intentions are no longer enough.** Nonprofit organizations must apply some businesslike, bottom-line mentalities to maintain their credibility with increasingly skeptical and results-oriented donors. There is no other viable option if our organizations are to survive and thrive in the twenty-first century amid nonprofit sector growth, blurred lines between profit and nonprofit, and increased oversight.

- **More opportunity means more accountability.** The billions of dollars pouring into charities and nonprofit organizations have created enormous opportunities for all of us but also have resulted in intense media, government, and consumer scrutiny—and in growing calls for nonprofits to become more disciplined, more efficient, and more effective. We must rise to the occasion.

- **Mission is crucial in a blurry world.** There is nothing less than a competition for mindshare going on between and among for-profits and nonprofits today. The more the lines blur between nonprofit and for-profit, the more crucial it is for us to stay true to our missions and our ethical standards.

- **The public expects more of nonprofits.** There is a sacred trust between the American public and nonprofit organizations. Part of our core values must be to maintain this trust, and that must be top of mind in every business decision we make.

CHAPTER 2

WHEN EVERYONE POINTS NORTH

Developing a Clear Decision-Making Framework and Business Model

As crucial as a sense of mission is to the success of a nonprofit organization, too many nonprofits try to do anything and everything that relates to their missions. They pursue every proposal and idea that comes in from volunteers, staff, donors, and constituents. Each idea you receive may have merit and relate to your mission, but how do you decide which ones to pursue? And how do you take action in a manner that is consistent from proposal to proposal and minimizes the potential of people being disgruntled if their proposal is rejected?

The key to successful decision making is to focus on the highest-impact areas that will provide the greatest results, which requires focus, alignment of resources, and the discipline to say no. This is all easier said than done, of course. How do you decide when to say yes to projects and when to say no? First, you need to establish an internal framework to help define what you will and will not do. Then you must get your organization to agree to this framework. Once agreed upon and communicated throughout your organization, a clear decision-making framework will help everyone make better decisions at every level.

This chapter focuses on the three actions to take to establish this clear decision-making framework:

1. Define your organization's **core values**.
2. Select and be true to a **strategic driving force**.
3. Assess your **business model**.

In this chapter, you will develop a clear understanding of each of these three important concepts, and you will arrive at a place where everyone in your organization considers the following questions before making a decision at any level:

- Is "x" consistent with our organization's core values?
- Is "x" in line with our strategic driving force?
- Does our business model enable us to fund "x"?

When you have such clear parameters and everyone embraces them, your organization is less apt to zigzag on a whim and there will be fewer conflicting agendas. When someone asks "Which way is north?" everyone points in the same direction. People proposing ideas understand how decisions are made and learn to propose ideas based on the aforementioned criteria. Volunteers and staff understand why various decisions are being made. You minimize any suggestion of favoritism or that a particular initiative has come out of left field.

At the American Heart Association, we undertook the process of clarifying our core values, defining one single strategic driving force, and assessing our business model so that we could have a framework to make better decisions. The results have been extraordinary in terms of the clarity with which we make decisions, the unity of our people in embracing those decisions, and the results we have achieved because we've made excellent decisions. Because we have a clear decision-making process, we have reduced the hours of meeting, debating, and hemming and hawing that can take place when you struggle with decisions in your organization. Decisions make things happen.

Note that if your organization is not quite ready to undertake the activities in this chapter, or if you are a leader of a team or division within a larger organization, you can still apply many of the tools we discuss here. Even a little bit of attention to values, strategic driving force, and business model can go a very long way toward achieving any goal, large or small. It is crucial for an organization or team of any size to know where it is going and how it is going to get there.

> **Recommended Resource**
>
> For small organizations seeking additional support, the **Center for Nonprofit Management** has networks across the country to provide consulting at no or low cost for small nonprofit organizations. To learn more, go to www.cnm.org.

DETERMINING YOUR CORE VALUES

An improved decision-making process begins with identifying your organization's core values—your ethical standards: Values guide your decision making to ensure that your actions are in line with your ethical beliefs. These may include honesty, fairness, justice, environmental sustainability, faith, equality, aesthetic beauty, peace, or any number of other values. Your organizational success depends on individual commitment to your values from each person in your organization, at every level.

When determining your core values, ideally you should include in the process people from various constituencies in your organization. The participants raise the level of discussion, are committed to the outcomes, and hold each other accountable. They also have an opportunity to more solidly connect to your organization and bond among themselves. The process of determining core values is often as important as the values themselves.

> **Recommended Resource**
>
> On its website, **Independent Sector** offers its Statement of Values and Code of Ethics, which the group uses for its own work (http://www.independentsector.org/members/code_ethics.html). The organization encourages all nonprofits to use this document either in drafting and adopting their own statements of values and codes of ethics or, for those who already have codes, to revise them as necessary. The code is available on Independent Sector's website in an easy-to-edit Microsoft Word document.

The American Heart Association's core values are:

- **Integrity**: We pursue our mission with honor, fairness, and respect for the individual, ever mindful that there is no right way to do the wrong thing.
- **Inclusiveness**: We serve responsibly as members of all the communities in which we live and work, fueled by diversity of thought and action.
- **Dedication**: We remain dedicated to our customers and our cause, and committed to discovery and continuous improvement.
- **Excellence**: We strive to be the best in our work, our relationships, our ideas, and our service. This is the greatest demonstration of our pledge to customer satisfaction.
- **Sensitivity**: We operate in a climate of openness and trust in which each of us fully grants others respect and cooperation.
- **Vision**: We are willing to take prudent risks as we strive to be proactive, innovative, and creative in all we do.

Our core values are posted on our website exactly as stated here, along with a comprehensive ethics policy. Everything is transparent and easily accessible to all of our staff, volunteers, and donors. Many corporations post their core values in every common area or provide each employee with a laminated wallet card listing the company's values. Individuals sometimes define their core values to help guide them through life's ups and downs. Although your organization's mission, strategic driving force, and business model can change over time, your core values are constant. They are the ethical grounding of your orga-

---

Lesson Learned

Values are not just about the culture of your organization. Values are part of a framework that defines how your organization makes decisions. Making your values highly visible helps hold everyone accountable to the organization's ethical standards.

nization and become particularly important in times of turmoil. They are crucial to everyday decisions as well, such as determining what partners to work with, where to spend funds, and how staff members interact with volunteers. Our core values drive our actions.

THE POWER OF A STRATEGIC DRIVING FORCE

The second factor in establishing a clear decision-making framework is to select and be true to one strategic driving force. As you will see from the American Heart Association's story, determining one—and only one—strategic driving force for your organization ensures that everyone agrees on the major product or service provided by your organization and the market you serve. In other words, what do you do and for whom do you do it? If you do not clearly define a single strategic driving force, various people in your organization may try to go in multiple directions simultaneously. When everyone is pulling in the same direction, you can make better decisions and achieve your goals more quickly and efficiently. No organization can do everything related to its mission, so your strategic driving force helps you focus in order to have the greatest impact and not be fragmented.

The American Heart Association started with one strategic driving force and then changed it as the organization and the environment changed over the years. The organization was founded in 1924 as a professional medical society. The purpose of the six founders—all doctors—was to answer a single question: Can people ever return to work after a heart attack? It is amazing how far we have come. Today, people have bypass surgery or angioplasty and not only return to work afterward, but return to work in mere days.

As the organization has evolved and grown and science and technology have changed, we have reviewed and adapted our business. This happens to all organizations: You acquire new information, new people, and new strengths that you want to leverage; the external environment changes and presents you with new challenges and opportunities. (Those in the horse-and-buggy business in the 1800s had to adapt to being transportation companies once automobiles came along.) This can take a few years or a few decades. The AHA's first transformation took place twenty-four years after its founding, in 1948, when the organization transitioned from a professional medical society and became a voluntary health organization.

Forty-seven years later, in 1995, my predecessor, Dudley Hafner, and David Ness, a dedicated volunteer from Minneapolis, took the organization through its second major transformation. With the help of the management consulting firm Kepner-Tregoe (KT), they defined the organization's strategic driving force. According to KT, who invented the concept of a driving force in the 1970s, an organization's strategic driving force is "the primary determinant of the products and services an organization will and will not offer and the markets (customers, consumers and geographies) it will and will not serve." To date, I have found KT's description to be the most helpful in thinking about what a nonprofit organization—or any organization—must define about itself in order to achieve its mission effectively. Essentially, your strategic driving force is the method through which you achieve your mission. Equally important, it defines what you will *not* do to achieve your mission. Remember, the strategic driving force is a decision-making tool. In all likelihood, you do not have the resources to implement every idea, so you must have a framework that helps you focus on where you can have the greatest impact.

A strategic driving force helps you make short-term and long-term decisions by clarifying and providing the following:

- Your organization's overall focus and direction
- An understanding of where your organization adds significant value
- Guidance on the scope of products or services you offer and the people you serve
- An indicator of must-have key capabilities among volunteer leaders and staff members
- A way to describe exactly what you do
- A means of evaluating competitors' strategies[1]
- A filter for new growth opportunities as they appear
- A guide for phasing out products and markets that no longer make sense
- A means for determining the fit of new opportunities, joint ventures, and alliances

DETERMINING YOUR ORGANIZATION'S STRATEGIC DRIVING FORCE

A strategic driving force is your organization's statement of what you do and for whom you do it. It defines your core strategy in exploiting opportunities (what you do) and minimizing the risk of spreading yourself too thin (what you don't do). It provides focus to your mission and core values. It keeps you from trying to be all things to all people. It is an overarching definition of the basic type of business you are in. It is the core action that propels your organization forward.

When it comes to strategic driving forces, there are four that most commonly apply to nonprofit organizations (see www.Kepner-Tregoe.com for a list of a few other possible driving forces). As you decide which strategic driving force fits your organization, be aware that there is no right or wrong choice. What matters most is that everyone in your organization agree on a single strategic driving force. This ensures that everyone is clear about exactly what you do and don't do and can make decisions accordingly.

Here are the four most common categories of strategic driving force for nonprofit organizations.

- **Strategic driving force #1: products and services.** An organization that chooses products and services as its strategic driving force focuses on creating a superior line of products or services, such as educational materials, tool kits, programs, events, or counseling. To grow, this type of organization takes existing products or services into new markets. The key competencies required include product and process development, sales, and customer service.

    Examples: General Motors, Coca-Cola, American Heart Association

- **Strategic driving force #2: user/customer markets.** These organizations focus on a key market segment (the people you serve) and strive to satisfy a range of needs. Their products and services are not unique; they differentiate themselves by the population(s) they serve. To grow, they offer new products and services to their particular user/customer. Organizations with this strategic driving force have key competencies in market research and customer loyalty.

    Examples: Johnson & Johnson, American Hospital Supply, AARP, most professional associations

- **Strategic driving force #3: distribution.** These organizations have unique ways of interacting with their customers through their distribution method. They differentiate themselves by the process through which they get products or services from the manufacturer to the end user. Key competencies required for this strategic driving force include constant process improvement and a strong sales structure.
  Examples: Avon, Amway, AT&T, Arthritis Foundation
- **Strategic driving force #4: technology.** Organizations with technology as their strategic driving force invent hardware or software and create new markets with new applications. Key competencies required are innovation and technical knowledge.
  Examples: Google, Yahoo!, Kiva.org

It is likely that your organization currently falls into more than one strategic driving force category. To begin to figure out what single strategic driving force will best move your organization forward, ask the following questions:

- What external market(s) (people) do we service?
- How are we different from other organizations in our niche?
- What do we do best?
- What are our weaknesses?
- For what do we receive the most positive feedback?
- Where do we add the most value (to our cause, our community, the world)?

Here is an analogy to further stimulate your thinking. Let's say you want to go from City A to City B and there are four different routes to get you there. Which one do you take? To determine the best route, you might ask: Do we need to get there in the fastest time, or do we want to travel the shortest distance? Do we want the safest route? Will we be traveling alone or with passengers with special needs? Will we be traveling on public transportation (bus, train, plane) or private (walking, car, bicycle, etc.) transport? Are there other stops we need to make en route? Do we need to be concerned about lodging, auto repairs, fuel, medical facilities, and so on?

Each of the four routes will get you to your destination, but depending on your objectives there might be one route that will get you there more efficiently and effectively. The same goes for an organization's strategic driving force. You can serve your mission in a variety of ways, but think how much more effective and efficient you can be if you focus all of your efforts on the one type of work that your organization is best at or can become best at. Think how much more effective you can be if there are no backseat drivers—people in the organization who would prefer that you take a different route. That is when the most amazing results are possible—and, to continue our driving analogy, that's the way to best enjoy the journey. As with any journey, as the external environment changes and your organization changes, you need to reevaluate your course. Once you determine a strategic driving force, you should revisit it regularly to make sure it is still the best course of action.

When we began to ask these types of questions at the American Heart Association over a decade ago, we had a problem. Our leadership team got together, and, no matter how hard we tried, we just could not narrow down our strategic driving force to fewer than three out of the eight or nine we considered. Three! This was scary because we realized we had spent many years with no clear strategic direction—at the very least, we were heading in three different directions that at times were in conflict with one another. Our KT consultants told us that such lack of agreement is quite common. They told us that most organizations are not unified in their strategic driving force.

Perhaps you're wondering why it is so important to decide on one single, solitary strategic driving force. What's the big deal if you are pursuing several routes? What if you want to be the best at product development and the best at distribution? Here is the answer: Every organization has limited resources—money, time, and people—and nonprofits, especially, face such limitations. You *could* aim to pursue multiple directions, but you are much more likely to be successful if you focus. If things are okay in your organization but you know they could be better, focusing on one strategic driving force might be the action that takes you to the next level.

The leadership team at the American Heart Association (I was chief operating officer at the time) took part in a yearlong process of determining a strategic driving force. It did take one full year, but as a result we were able to focus on one specific direction and we had a strong commitment throughout the organization. The process resulted in the decision that our strategic driving force would be products and services (strategic driving force #1). Specifically, we defined our products and services as *cardiovascular and stroke knowledge and information*.

In practice, this means that we use our strategic driving force (producing cardiovascular and stroke knowledge and information) to achieve our mission (reducing disability and death from cardiovascular diseases and stroke). It means that we see our products and services — cardiovascular and stroke knowledge and information — as our biggest strength and differentiator. We specialize in the products and allow other organizations to help us with market outreach, distribution, and technology.

You are probably thinking that this is not rocket science. Isn't it obvious that the American Heart Association produces information about heart health? Well, today it is. But prior to determining our strategic driving force, our organization's strategy looked very different, and our effectiveness suffered because of it. Prior to 1995, although we had never consciously made the decision, we were, de facto, a distribution-driven organization (strategic driving force #3). We produced heart health information and then distributed it to more than fifty essentially state-level American Heart Association affiliates, who then distributed it to 2,000 local chapters, who then distributed it to intermediaries (health-care sites, work sites, and school sites), who then distributed it to the ultimate customers: patients, employees, and students.

To give you a visual image, our distribution channel looked like this:

National Center → State-Level Affiliates → Local Chapters → Intermediaries → Customers

Prior to 1995, we relied primarily on this single, internal channel of distribution. We didn't necessarily develop the best products; we developed the best products that our internal channel was capable of delivering. Once we clarified our strategic driving force and shifted from distribution to products and services as our strategic driving force, we focused on developing the very best information and then using multiple channels (not just our own) to distribute it.

When we decided to make products and services our strategic driving force, we knew other changes would be necessary, but the impact would be huge. Imagine how many more people we could help by distributing our information through huge organizations like health maintenance organizations (HMOs) rather than just through our internal channel. We had to develop the competencies necessary to create the very best products and services. To determine where we needed to change and improve, we began by identifying five main ways we would use our strategic driving force (products and services, specifically cardiovascular and stroke knowledge and information) to achieve our mission (reducing disability and death from cardiovascular diseases and stroke):

1. Produce credible information services and products on heart disease and stroke.
2. Develop multiple distribution channels (instead of one internal channel) to distribute our products and information to meet customers' needs.
3. Prioritize our research efforts and development of new products (guidelines for doctors, reports, books, website content, events, online tools, etc.) based on areas of highest risk for cardiovascular disease and stroke. This would ensure that we were best in class and cutting-edge in our field.
4. Emphasize science and community mobilization as the foundation of our work, because stellar research and community strength are the basis for our strong products and services.
5. Restrict our market to the United States, so we would not spread ourselves too thin. (We decided to develop the very best products and services for the national market before venturing to other countries.)

As we clarified our strategic driving force, we were able to make additional decisions about where we could add the most value and differentiate ourselves from other organizations in our space. The more specific you can be about exactly what your organization does, how it does it, and for whom, the better you can achieve your mission and differentiate yourself from other organizations.

DETERMINING COMPETENCIES REQUIRED FOR YOUR STRATEGIC DRIVING FORCE

Of course, you can't just wave a magic wand and change your strategic driving force. You need to develop skills and competencies for the specific strategic driving force you have selected. Competencies are those skill sets that are essential to successfully execute your strategic driving force. You probably have many of these in place or in development already, which is why you selected that strategic driving force in the first place!

> **Lesson Learned**
>
> Once your organization is focused on a single strategic driving force, you must ask: What competencies do we need in place to make this a reality?

At the American Heart Association, we determined that to produce and distribute the best cardiovascular and stroke knowledge and information (our products and services), we had to do some new things and we had to stop doing some old things—especially the things that related to our previous strategic driving force of distribution. And, of course, we had to continue doing some things we had always done. After much discussion, debate, and research into other organizations' best practices, here are the four competencies we determined were necessary for us to achieve our mission through our chosen strategic driving force:

1. **Discover and interpret science.** This has always been a competency since the original founding of the American Heart Association by medical professionals. We needed to maintain our strong research and science base. Remember, you don't want to throw out the baby with the bathwater when you are focusing your organization.
2. **Communicate appropriate messages to medical audiences and the general public.** For our knowledge and information to have any impact, people need to receive, digest, and apply it. And we need expertise in working through other channels of distribution, such as hospitals, medical practices, and HMOs.
3. **Advocate.** We had always done some advocacy, but we decided our advocacy work needed to become far more sophisticated for our products and services to get into the hands of key decision makers who could change entire health-care or government systems.

4. **Generate resources for all of the above.** To have resources to develop new products and services, we needed to raise money and generate support for our new area of focus.

Once we determined the competencies we needed, other decisions followed naturally. For instance, we determined that we needed more volunteers and staff who possessed these competencies. We began to define the new talents we would need in staff members, volunteers, board members, and strategic partners to implement our new strategy. In our case, this meant recruiting people with experience and expertise in marketing, sales, advertising, communications, and advocacy.

> **Lesson Learned**
>
> Your strategies define the skills and competencies you need, not vice versa.

IT AIN'T EASY, BUT IT'S WORTH IT

Although the American Heart Association's decision to clearly define its strategic driving force was by all means the right thing to do, it was nowhere near easy. By changing our strategic driving force from distribution to products and services, we essentially had to redesign our entire operation from one of distribution through internal channels (essentially passing information down the line from the national organization to local chapters and then to the public) to one of product development, whereby we would distribute our products and services to the public through multiple channels and form new strategic partnerships. This was an enormous undertaking.

The best parallel I can think of for the enormity of this change is to picture what would happen if cosmetic company Mary Kay told its 80,000 sales consultants (a single internal channel of distribution) that the company was going to focus on developing new makeup products, which would now be sold through Nordstrom, Target, and Amazon.com in addition to Mary Kay's network of sales reps. Imagine the cultural changes that would have to take place—that's what happened in the

American Heart Association. In the past, our focus was on feeding products (primarily heart health information, events, and tools) through a single internal channel. Now, if we were going to focus on developing the very best products, we would need to develop new channels. Our single channel of distribution was significantly overloaded and just not strong enough to handle all of the new products we wanted to offer. Nor were we really experts at distribution of all products. We wanted to continue feeding appropriate products through our single channel in areas where they were doing a great job, but we also needed resources for creating the very best products and services and then distributing them through other channels. (Our products had been very good, but we wanted to make them extraordinary and cutting-edge.) By switching to a products and services strategic driving force, we changed our entire philosophy about what we would do and how we would do it.

Refocusing our strategic driving force led to reorganization of our national committees and staff structure. It was a large endeavor, but it went quite smoothly. Because our staff and volunteers knew that our distribution channel was being overloaded, and they could see how this change would extend our reach and save more lives, they embraced it. Of course, as with any change, it took a few years for us to fully adapt, since we were all doing business and interacting a bit differently. The biggest impact occurred a couple of years later when our fifty-plus field and state affiliates were restructured and consolidated into fifteen regional affiliates. As you will see, because the vast majority of people in the organization believed so strongly in the AHA's mission, most people supported and even embraced this change when they understood why it was necessary. Here is how it happened.

> *Every act of creation is first of all an act of destruction.*
> — PABLO PICASSO

In 1997, I became CEO of the American Heart Association, following the dedicated and visionary leadership of my predecessor, Dudley Hafner, who had been at the helm for seventeen years. Dudley led us through substantial changes, including the process of defining our strategic driving force. The preceding year had been spent studying how we could streamline our organization to be more effective. Our national and affiliate leadership concluded that we needed to make some significant changes to the organizational structure to allocate more resources to research and educational programs and fulfill our mission of saving lives. After much discussion and debate, we ultimately determined that if we restructured, we could reduce administrative costs, provide greater support to the 2,000 grassroots chapters, and funnel more of the donated dollars directly into our mission, our new strategic driving force, and the associated competencies (as previously cited). This determination was a direct result of our laser focus on mission and the new strategic driving force.

What happened was nothing short of remarkable. In some of the most selfless acts I have ever witnessed, all of the fifty-plus affiliates voted to consolidate into fifteen affiliates, dissolving their nonprofit corporate 501(c)(3) tax-exempt status and enabling the American Heart Association to become a single corporate structure.

The only explanation for this stems from the kind of people who dedicate their lives to nonprofit work and believe in a purpose beyond profit. The affiliate leaders, both volunteers and staff who were willing to give up their positions, made the decision based on their passion for the cause, their agreement with our decision-making process, and their sense of a greater calling. They were willing to see beyond their self-interest in staff jobs or being volunteer officers to better serve the mission of the larger organization: saving lives. They voted not on what was best for them individually or as an affiliate but on what was best for the people they were dedicated to serving. They determined this because our decision-making process and rationale were highly visible and tightly connected to our mission. Lots of organizations have mission-driven people, but the American Heart Association had the mission-driven people combined with a clear rationale for how resources could be reallocated from back-office administrative operations into more programs to save lives. They understood that because of the new strategic driving force, we were trying to streamline to get more resources moved into research and lifesaving programs. They were engaged in the process and the conclusion that if we streamlined the organization we could redeploy 150 new staff to frontline mission and fund-raising work. However, this meant consolidating fifty-plus separately incorporated affiliates into fifteen unincorporated regional affiliates.

I am often asked how in the world the organization was able to make this happen. People generally want a quick synopsis, but in reality you would have to see the full-length movie to completely understand how we built a consensus and succeeded. It is difficult to describe massive organizational change without lots of context. But, for the purpose of brevity, I've distilled the process into five key elements:

- First, we brought in outside eyes in the form of a consulting firm to help us see what we couldn't see and to bring more objectivity.
- Second, we were data-driven, making a strong case for how the restructuring could accelerate our growth as an organization and keep us focused on achieving our mission.
- Third, we engaged all affiliate volunteers and staff over the course of a year, and we listened, listened, listened.
- Fourth, we did not draw a map of what the fifteen new, consolidated affiliates would look like. We owe this to the brilliance of volunteer board member Marilyn Hunn (whom you will meet in a moment). Rather than drawing a geographic map to determine how the consolidation would occur, we instead established criteria for what it would take to qualify as a new regional affiliate. Affiliates could then choose their partners. This was one of the best decisions we made. It dramatically increased each affiliate's commitment to making the consolidation work. Affiliates also had input into what the criteria would ultimately be.
- Fifth, we focused on the mission, on funding more research and education, and on saving more lives. We never strayed from the fact that every decision we made was based on our mission.

We could not have done any of this without dedicated, mission-driven people. I could write about many staff members, board members, donors, and volunteers who played a part in this massive effort, but Marilyn Hunn stands out most strongly in my mind. At the time of this transition, Marilyn had her own busy consulting business, and at times I would speculate about where she put in more time—her organization or the American Heart Association. Marilyn is one of the 22.5 million volunteers and donors who keep me humble. It takes a great team of staff members, but we cannot be effective and successful without our volunteer partners. I am constantly humbled by the dedication and generosity of people like Marilyn, as I am sure you are with the supporters of your organization. In my opinion, dedicated, skilled volunteers are worth more than all the venture capital in the world.

Marilyn came up through the volunteer ranks as a leader of her local and state affiliate organizations of the American Heart Association. She eventually became chairperson of the national board, where she has been a passionate and incredibly wise leader. Marilyn bravely chaired the group that streamlined our affiliate structure. It was a task that required the skills and tact of a United Nations diplomat. I am afraid to even suggest how many hours a week of *volunteer* work she committed in addition to her day job.

Thanks to those like Marilyn, we not only completed the consolidation but also accomplished this massive task in record time. Once the decision was made, we were given two years to complete the transition, and we accomplished it in half the time. That is the power of mission and focus. To give you some perspective on the size of this endeavor, the consolidation of our fifty-plus affiliates into one corporate entity is the largest merger in the history of the State of New York (where the American Heart Association is incorporated). Never before or since have that many corporations—for-profit or nonprofit—come together as one. Through this consolidation we accelerated our fund-raising growth from 2 to 3 percent annually to double-digit growth. A few years ago, we consolidated even further, from fifteen regional affiliates down to eight.

My purpose in sharing the details of how and why the American Heart Association consolidated is threefold:

1. It demonstrates the amazing things that are possible when an entire organization is aligned toward a single goal. People were so committed to the American Heart Association that they understood why we were restructuring and accepted the elimination of their own jobs because they knew the new structure would better serve the organization's mission.
2. It emphasizes the mission-above-ego mentality that is present in so many dedicated nonprofit volunteers and employees. Beyond the American Heart Association, the American Cancer Society and the American Diabetes Association successfully achieved comparable reorganizations to their internal structures.
3. In recent years, many other large, national nonprofits—including the Girl Scouts of the USA, the American Lung Association, and the Arthritis Foundation—have made, or are making, a similar decision to consolidate. I believe this trend will continue. In fact, many organizations have asked us for guidance, and we have happily provided it.

Defining—or redefining—your organization's strategic driving force is one of the most powerful actions you can take to guide your nonprofit organization to the next level. It serves to focus you, identify the needed competencies, and align all of your efforts to the achievement of your mission. As a last step toward helping your organization make the right decisions, it's time to add a final element: money.

SHOW ME THE MONEY: ASSESSING YOUR BUSINESS MODEL

After clarifying your values and strategic driving force, the third and final element in establishing an internal framework for making decisions within your organization is a clear business model. In my experience, many nonprofits do not think of themselves as having business models, and that can be a huge flaw. In fact, it can be fatal. Every nonprofit needs a clearly defined business model: You need to be 100 percent clear about how your organization brings in money to sustain itself and how funds are allocated. Even if you do not like your existing business model (perhaps you have inherited a flawed one), you must know what it is and understand how it might be helping you or holding you back.

What is the precise definition of a business model? The definition is twofold, specifying the following:

1. How you are going to acquire financial resources to sustain the future of your organization (how you make money)
2. Who gets to decide how these financial resources get allocated and expended (who gets to spend that money and for what purposes)

First, let's discuss the acquisition of resources. How does your organization get money to operate? Here are some questions to help you assess your organization's business model:

- **How does your organization acquire its revenue?**
  Possible sources include small individual donors, large donors to specific restricted projects, special events, direct-mail solicitation, corporate employee giving, corporate sponsorship of special events,

fee for service, licensing, foundation grants, product sales, endowments, bequests, trusts, cause marketing, seminar fees, publishing fees, membership fees, and government grants.

- **Who acquires the dollars?**
  Your national office? Local chapters? Fund-raising consultants? United Way? If you have multiple bodies or events seeking funds, do these bodies or events compete for the same donors?
- **At what cost do you acquire these dollars? What are the margins from each income source?**
  How much does it cost you to fund-raise or develop the products and services you sell?
- **What is your mix of revenue streams?**
  Are you overly reliant on some sources?
- **Are your revenue streams sustainable and diversified for the future?**
  What changes could occur in the world that might affect your sources of revenue?
- **What is your strategy for revenue *growth*?**
- **Are some income streams retained by the generating function, territory, or department?**
  For instance, are seminar proceeds retained by the seminar department or do they go into the general fund? Do local affiliates or chapters retain a certain percentage of what they raise?
- **Do policies require that a certain percentage of revenue be allocated for certain functions?**
  For instance, does a percentage of each dollar raised need to be spent in a certain way, such as going for funding research or going directly to scholarships?

Second, who are the decision-making bodies that determine how and for what your financial resources are expended?

- **Who decides who pays for what and out of which revenue stream(s)?**
  What is decided by your board, the executive director, local chapters, regional affiliates, and/or a national organization?

- **If your organization has local chapters, how is each chapter's budget determined?**

    For instance, who pays for the audit? Is it the national organization or do affiliates and chapters pay a prorated share? How are decisions made to align resources to specific priorities or launch new initiatives? Are the processes streamlined and timely or bureaucratic and costly?

The answers to all of these questions make up your business model. If you are unclear about your business model, answer these questions in the broadest way possible, and pay attention to what is working and what isn't. Business models are flexible and often need tweaking. Many nonprofit business models have evolved organically—for better or worse—without much strategic thought. Many nonprofit leaders have inherited the business models they are currently using. Even if a particular business model was once relevant, it may no longer suffice in today's environment. Some organizations just accept the fact that things are the way they are, without recognizing that the question of who pays may, in fact, be holding them back from success.

Once you have completed this analysis of your current business model, ask yourself or your leadership team, "If I were starting a nonprofit from scratch, is this the model I would use?" Take a fresh look at your business model and see if it could be improved. It might be a good model or a not-so-good model, and you may or may not be able to change it, but it is important to be in touch with how it affects your ability to achieve your goals.

Although every organization is different, here are some aspects of business models that are problematic:

- **Not sustainable:** Revenue streams need to be sustainable in the long run, and if they aren't, you need to plan for them to wind down. As an example, many nonprofit organizations currently have concerns about the future of direct-mail fund-raising.
- **Too much decentralization:** If the funds raised are placed into too many predetermined functional or geographical buckets with independent decision-making power, you may have a challenge in aligning resources. Also, it may be difficult to put together the funds for a major initiative, since no one funding body has the

resources to launch it. If that is the case, very few big ideas can be accomplished without having to pass the proverbial hat.
- **Too little diversity**: In short, don't put all of your eggs in one basket. Too many nonprofits become reliant on two or three revenue streams, and if adversity strikes one, the organization can be hurt significantly.

Overall, the best business models have diverse, sustainable revenue streams and give the decision makers maximum flexibility in terms of how resources are allocated. This ensures that you can change and evolve over time.

> **Lesson Learned**
>
> A flawed business model prevents your organization from achieving its full potential.

THE POWER OF ESTABLISHING A CLEAR DECISION-MAKING FRAMEWORK

Now let's look at the cumulative power of having clearly defined core values, a single strategic driving force, and an effective business model. Clarifying and assessing each of these factors can take a lot of time and effort, but the results are immeasurable. When you are clear about where you are going, you can much more easily decide what will and won't help you get to your desired outcomes. With each decision, large and small, you are able to ask:

- Does it fulfill our mission?
- Is it in line with our core values?
- Is it in line with our strategic driving force—the business that we've agreed we do best?
- Where applicable, does it make sense with our business model, bringing in revenue in the way that is most effective and efficient for our organization?

Many of these topics are covered in more detail in later chapters. Here is a list of some of the American Heart Association's major efforts during my tenure, each of which we decided to pursue because they met the preceding criteria with a resounding *yes*:

- Launching Go Red For Women, an award-winning national campaign (something we consider a product) to raise women's awareness of heart disease, their number one killer.
- Partnering with the William J. Clinton Foundation and Arkansas governor Mike Huckabee to create the Alliance for a Healthier Generation (another product) to fight childhood obesity.
- Introducing Get With The Guidelines, a program to help hospitals improve care and survival rates for heart and stroke patients (product).
- Introducing the Heart Profilers, an interactive online tool that helps patients evaluate treatment options, possible side effects, and success rates, and also provides questions for them to ask physicians (product).

These results demonstrate the power of becoming extremely clear about your direction and aligning your entire organization. Every one of these projects does the following:

✓ Helps the American Heart Association achieve its mission of building healthier lives free of cardiovascular disease and stroke

✓ Aligns with the organization's core values (integrity, inclusiveness, dedication, excellence, sensitivity, and vision)

✓ Aligns with the organization's strategic driving force of focusing on products and services in the form of cardiovascular and stroke knowledge and information—and distributing those products and services through multiple channels (our partnerships)

✓ Is sustainable based on the AHA business model

We have only pursued projects, partnerships, and opportunities that fulfill all of these criteria. Could we have achieved all of these goals without this clearly defined decision-making framework? Maybe. But we could not have achieved them as quickly, as efficiently, or as thoughtfully. Mission is powerful, but mission plus a clear decision-making framework and a streamlined business model is virtually unstoppable. This is where the rubber of your mission meets the road. Having a laser focus makes all the difference.

One final word of caution: Don't rest on your laurels. Regularly look at each element of your decision-making process and make sure each is still relevant and powerful, especially in this time of rapid change. Your core values should remain constant, but every few years, it is a good idea to revisit your strategic driving force and business model to make sure that they are still relevant and serving your organization's mission.

READY FOR THE FUTURE

The ultimate goal of all of this attention to mission (in Chapter 1) and developing a clear decision-making framework (in this chapter) is to create an organization that not only achieves its goals today but also positions itself for the future. You have just read about the major transitions we have gone through at the American Heart Association to set us up for long-term success and sustainability to accomplish our mission. The present and the future must be always be on your mind simultaneously.

As technology develops, globalization evolves, baby boomers retire, and Generation Y workers assume leadership positions, we must continue to adapt and evolve in order to do the crucial work the world needs. All nonprofits need to become more virtual, fluid, boundaryless, value-driven, nonhierarchical, and quick responding; less bureaucratic; more open to new growth opportunities; and able to constantly reform and change in order to survive and thrive—not to mention the new distribution networks, new audiences, and new issues that we cannot even imagine today.

Throughout all of this change, leaders can embrace this constant: the importance of focusing on one clear mission and a clearly defined decision-making framework. Chapter 3 explores how this laser-like focus can help you achieve results beyond your wildest imagination.

CHAPTER 2 TAKEAWAYS

- **Determine core values and stick to them.** Your organization's core values are your ethical standards: what is important to your organization and how you will do business. They are the ethical grounding of your organization and become particularly important in times of turmoil.

- **Every nonprofit needs a strategic driving force.** A driving force is "the primary determinant of the products and services an organization will and will not offer and the markets (consumers and geographies) it will and will not serve." It is the direction in which the organization is moving.

- **Have one and only one strategic driving force.** No one strategic driving force is necessarily right or wrong, but an organization's leadership must agree on a single strategic driving force—one and only one—so that every staff member, board member, volunteer, and other stakeholder is moving in a unified way. Your volunteers and staff should understand the route you are taking and the seven routes you are not taking—and why.

- **Know your business model and change it if necessary.** It's not second nature for nonprofits to think of themselves as having a business model, but it is an issue that should be examined. Your business model is the process by which you acquire financial resources and how (and by whom) those resources are expended. Be aware of how it helps or hinders you in achieving your mission.

CHAPTER 3

THE POWER OF A BREAKTHROUGH GOAL

Once your organization has its mission, core values, and strategic driving force in place, and you have analyzed your business model, there is no limit to what you can accomplish. When you are focused and strong internally and clear about your decision-making criteria, you can begin to achieve what you may previously have thought to be impossible.

Throughout the 1990s, the American Heart Association set strategic goals each year by increasing numerical targets for fund-raising and for the number of people its programs reached with its lifesaving messages. We made incremental improvements with that method, which was great, but we needed more of an adrenaline rush. To pump up the organization, we launched a new strategic-planning process featuring a bold breakthrough goal that challenged us like we had never been challenged before.

My belief in the importance of a breakthrough goal was inspired by the work of Bob Waterman and Tom Peters in their classic business text *In Search of Excellence*, published by HarperCollins in 1982, and, of course, John Kennedy's famous breakthrough goal to land a man on the moon by the end of the 1960s.

The American Heart Association's breakthrough goal is this: to reduce coronary heart disease, stroke, and key risk factors by 25 percent by 2010 among the *entire* population of the United States.

It is a big, *big* goal.

The American Heart Association is by no means the only nonprofit with a breakthrough goal. Here are some others to inspire you and your organization:

- **UNICEF Millennium Development Goals:** By 2015, reduce by half the proportion of people living on less than a dollar a day, reduce by half the proportion of people who suffer from hunger, and other goals. *Learn more at www.un.org/millenniumgoals.*
- **Make Mine a Million $ Business (a program of Count Me In for Women's Economic Independence):** Inspire 1 million women to build their own businesses with $1 million or more in revenue by 2010. *Learn more at www.makemineamillion.org.*
- **American Cancer Society:** Achieve a 25 percent reduction in cancer incidence rates and a 50 percent reduction in cancer mortality rates by the year 2015. *Learn more at www.cancer.org.*

WHY YOU NEED A BREAKTHROUGH GOAL

Without question, every nonprofit organization should have a breakthrough goal. It provides accountability and a point around which everyone can rally. It energizes and focuses the organization on success. It builds passion and excitement among your employees, volunteers, board members, donors, and the public. Too many nonprofits focus on process goals and not end results. A breakthrough goal forces you to think about the long-term impact of your good work. It also forces you to get serious about being the best you can be. When you set a breakthrough goal you have to be willing to hold your organization's feet to the fire and risk failure. The thing about setting a clear goal like "reducing coronary heart disease, stroke and risk by 25 percent by the year 2010" is that everybody knows whether you have achieved it or not.

Here is the thing about breakthrough goals: They are such an adrenaline rush, providing such excitement and passion and discipline in an organization, that it is easy to get carried away. I am guilty of this. Several years ago at an American Heart Association staff meeting to discuss strategies for the Heart Walk fund-raiser, I threw down a major challenge. We were raising $12 million in the annual Heart Walk, and the question I asked was "What would it take to raise $30 million?"

At first there was no adrenaline rush . . . because everyone's heart stopped. There were also plenty of howls and a great deal of gnashing of teeth. Initially, the responses consisted of all the reasons that it could not be done. But, I persisted, saying that there must be some way to do it. Once we focused on going after that breakthrough goal, staff eventually came up with not only a plan but also a slogan: "30 in 30"—thirty million in thirty months. We achieved the goal—and we did it in eighteen months! Then, as we drew a bead on the $30 million goal, I raised the ante, asking, "What would it take to raise $100 million?" In 2007, we raised $106 million in the Heart Walk, our signature fund-raiser, which includes over 600 events across the country.

HOW TO CREATE A BREAKTHROUGH GOAL

How did the American Heart Association determine its breakthrough goal and then execute it? Here is a step-by-step explanation of how we did it and how you can, too.

Step 1: Brainstorm

Begin by taking a look at your mission and your strategic driving force and asking: "What do we want our situation (our constituency, our community, our issue) to look like that is different in X period of time versus the way it looks today?" At the beginning, all you need to do is focus on the *what*; don't yet worry about the *how*. This is about brainstorming and thinking big—dreaming dreams. If it makes you more comfortable, you can even include blanks in your thinking. For instance, at the American Heart Association we started by saying that our breakthrough goal was to reduce coronary heart disease stroke and risk by *blank* percent.

Eventually, however, you need to have an indisputable measure so people know how success is defined. Each of us is often challenged to define success, but you achieve the most when you have some form of measurement and time period. Remember, at this point you can always adjust your goal. Step one is simply about the free flow of dreams, hopes, and aspirations for the world you want to see. Have a big tent at this stage—many diverse voices, experiences, and perspectives.

If you get stuck, the simple question "What would it take?" is an extraordinarily powerful tool. I have found that once the initial resistance fades, this question stirs innovation and overcomes barriers that people had not thought it possible to surmount. It often produces amazing results. It shifts everyone's mind-set. Fair warning: Most people start out telling you all the reasons something cannot be done. Simply respond that there must be some way, and ask "What would it take" as many times as needed to turn the tide of objections. This mentally removes a person's unconscious barriers to thinking about possibilities. If you still get resistance, ask this question: "What would you recommend we attempt if you knew we could not fail?"

Step 2: Do Your Homework

Try to be as data-driven as you can by performing an environmental scan to test the reality of your goal. You need quantitative data on markets, customers, competitors, and trends in your field, based on the size and location of your organization. You need to perform an analysis of the strengths, weaknesses, opportunities, and threats (SWOT) affecting your organization, or you are just guessing. It is not enough to think that you have your finger on the pulse of your issue or the community you serve. Do not guess. Get data to determine whether your goal is possible (e.g., you can't increase the size of your Little League program to 1,000 children if there are only 600 appropriately aged children in your town!).

Our research at the American Heart Association involved looking at the trends in death rates and risk factors over the last five, ten, and fifteen years and projecting what they might be in the future. We looked at our projected revenue streams. We tried to anticipate the changes in the external environment that might affect us, such as possible medical breakthroughs. We thought about new programs that we could introduce to alter the projected trends in a positive way. And then we took a step of faith and went for the 25 percent number.

If your organization is large, you might conduct primary research with the communities you serve. If you run a small organization, doing your homework may mean finding existing market data or conducting an e-mail survey using a low-cost online program such as SurveyMonkey.com or Zoomerang.com. Remember, we don't know what we don't know.

Step 3: Be Specific and Unique

When creating your breakthrough goal, make sure you are setting your sights on a goal that is significant not only quantitatively but also qualitatively. Furthermore, make sure your breakthrough goal is unique. Otherwise, you may be duplicating the efforts of another organization and diluting the potential impact of your work. Be sure to ask the following:

- Is anyone else doing this?
- If so, how can we do it more effectively?
- If not, is anyone else better positioned to do this?
- Where can we provide added value?

A church might have goals for increasing membership and the number who tithe, as well as for the satisfaction level of church members. A financial counseling organization might look beyond the number of people they serve to the number of those people who are living within their means and with debt reduction a year later. Groups serving youth might focus on reducing absenteeism, drug use, or dropout rates or measure the movement of at-risk students becoming more active in school activities. Organizations providing temporary housing might set a breakthrough goal to increase the number of people they serve who live on their own within a year of moving into temporary housing. Organizations providing social assistance might set a goal to increase the number of people living above the poverty level a year later. A Little League team might set a goal to increase retention of players year over year. When creating a breakthrough goal, think beyond your immediate work to the broader implications it has. Add emotion to the numbers.

Step 4: Test Your Theories

To avoid setting a breakthrough goal that is also impossible to achieve, your next task is to do some reality testing. When we adopted the 25 percent goal, we had to sit down and look at some modeling. Think of this as being similar to creating financial models in a business plan: In a business you are predicting profit; in creating your breakthrough goal you are measuring impact. Your aim is to create a stretch goal—an adrenaline rush—but the goal should also have a good chance of coming to fruition!

For instance, we had data saying that 250,000 people were dying each year because of electrical problems in the heart (sudden cardiac arrest). We looked at the limited access that the public had to automated external defibrillators (AEDs), then we forecasted what might happen if we introduced a new program that significantly increased the number of AEDs placed in local communities. Based on this number, we calculated the number of lives we might save by providing greater access to AEDs. Remember, at this point we were not making final decisions, but we were at the beginning stages of developing a real plan for achieving our breakthrough goal. We were developing ideas and doing some general estimates. (As it happened, we did ultimately decide that increasing the number of AEDs in public places would help us achieve our breakthrough goal.)

Step 5: Add Flesh to the Bone

Now that we've done some brainstorming and estimating, it's time to get more specific. At the American Heart Association, we looked at other indices connected with cardiovascular disease and stroke and set goals related to these factors. Think of these as mini-goals inside the breakthrough goal. Here are the four indicators that we determined would help us monitor our progress:

- Reduction in the death rate from coronary heart disease and stroke by 25 percent
- Reduction in the prevalence of smoking, high blood cholesterol, and physical inactivity by 25 percent
- Reduction in the rate of uncontrolled high blood pressure by 25 percent
- Elimination of the growth of obesity and diabetes

We determined that if we could reach these very specific mini-goals, then our overarching breakthrough goal would be in our sights. What mini-goals can your organization set to make sure you are on track to achieve your big goal?

THE NONPROFIT LEADERSHIP TRIFECTA

Now that we have discussed how to determine a breakthrough goal, let's see where the breakthrough goal fits with the other concepts we've discussed. In the last two chapters we walked through the process of homing in on your organization's mission, core values, strategic driving force, and business model. Clarity about these factors provides a discipline with which to allocate resources and make decisions. Your breakthrough goal is the final factor you can use to help make important decisions.

Together, a mission, a strategic driving force, and a breakthrough goal constitute the Nonprofit Leadership Trifecta. Run any potential decision through this three-pronged filter as a way to evaluate potential strategies, programs, or projects. This test can also help you prioritize the ones you ultimately choose. Here are the questions to ask. I have customized the questions to the American Heart Association for the purpose of example:

- **Does it align with our mission** of building healthier lives free of cardiovascular diseases and stroke?
- **Does it align with our strategic driving force?** Note that the American Heart Association's strategic driving force, as of 2007, is to focus on developing cardiovascular and stroke knowledge and information products (such as books, reports, and heart-healthy guidelines) as needed and to work through partnerships and influence to impact multiple levels of society.
- **Will it do the most to help us reach our breakthrough goal** of reducing coronary heart diseases, stroke, and key risk factors by 25 percent?

There are many good opportunities and excellent programs we might consider, so we make those difficult choices based on our analysis of which opportunities receive an emphatic *yes* in answer to the preceding questions. Think of the breakthrough goal as a tiebreaker. As an example, if there are three projects competing for limited funds, all of which meet the requirements of your mission and strategic driving force, but you can fund only one, ask this question: "Which project will bring us closer to our breakthrough goal?"

EXECUTING YOUR BREAKTHROUGH GOAL

Besides being a good test, your breakthrough goal needs a specific execution plan. Every organization's processes and resources are different, so here are some tips for developing and executing a strategic plan to reach your breakthrough goal in an efficient, effective way:

- **Don't reinvent the wheel.** Remember that you have selected this breakthrough goal because it is aligned with your mission and your strategic driving force. Look to past successes and best practices, internally and externally, and apply past learning.

- **Develop a detailed execution plan with target dates.** Determine the strategies to achieve each mini-goal: who is responsible, what financial resources are required, who is accountable for the execution, and what the timetables are to get there. When possible, identify quick hits of "low-hanging fruit"—the opportunities where you can have an immediate impact. And remember the Pareto principle (the 80/20 rule): 20 percent of your initiatives and 20 percent of your customers give you 80 percent of your results. Or, stated negatively, if you focus on the wrong 80 percent, you will get only 20 percent of your desired results.

> **Lesson Learned**
>
> Remember the 80/20 rule. You must focus the majority of your energy, attention, and resources on high-impact initiatives—and be able to tell the difference.

- **Align resources.** Look at any programs that you are currently conducting that are not contributing as much to the breakthrough goal as a new initiative would. Then redeploy the people and financial resources from that project to the new strategies. All involved parties must be held accountable to explain how their performance standards will contribute to the achievement of your new goals.

- **Address systems and attitudes that don't reinforce new behavior.** As much as you need to develop new strategies and practices to achieve your breakthrough goal, you likewise need to eliminate things that do not advance you on this new path. You should assess and change formal processes such as staff performance standards and criteria for what will be funded. Ask yourself: "Is there anything in our current culture that is holding us back from achieving our goal?" Ruthlessly purge the activities that do not move the needle to make way for innovations.

- **Anticipate and address resistance.** In all of us there is a natural resistance to change. I've found that resistance to breakthrough goals generally falls into three categories:
  1. **Reluctance to change.** This is natural for all of us, but we need to overcome it to remain relevant and fresh. Remind people that change is necessary for an organization of any shape, size, or mission to keep progressing. Engage them in focusing on solutions rather than comparing the possible future to the present. Get them excited about participating in improving your organization and achieving extraordinary results. Solicit their opinions. Ask, "What do you think it would take to accomplish X?" Get their concerns out in the open, and then help define what's in it for them.
  2. **Complacency.** Some people resist a big goal because your organization is "just fine the way it is." With these resisters, emphasize that the bar is constantly being raised by others in the community and that you need to keep up. What used to be a great, cutting-edge idea is commonplace now. Even very good organizations can always become better.
  3. **Lack of unanimity.** You will never achieve unanimity, and sometimes you have to accept that that is okay. But you can achieve a consensus (generally 70 to 80 percent agreement), so be careful to strike a balance between listening to naysayers—who may have legitimate concerns—and waiting for unanimous support. Don't let a few people hold you back from an amazing accomplishment.

- **Communicate early and often.** Just as you need to communicate your mission and strategic driving force to every person associated with your organization, you must shout your breakthrough goal from every rooftop. Define the principles, philosophies, and concepts for achieving your breakthrough goal up front; engage people in putting flesh on the "how"; and update people frequently on your progress. Remember, people support what they help create.

Give them a paintbrush and a shot at painting part of the canvas. All participants, including donors, board members, staff, and volunteers, need to see their role in a broader context and understand how they are contributing to the achievement of the bold goal.

- **Build in accountability.** What you measure and make highly visible gets the attention. Your breakthrough goal will be achieved with millions of behaviors and individual actions. Staff will know what behaviors and actions contribute to the goal by what they own and are held accountable for. Task forces, committees, and boards also have to be accountable. Monitoring, reporting, and discussion are essential—not for the sake of bureaucracy, but because that is what keeps all the oars rowing in the right direction.

- **Add talent to your team.** Oftentimes, executing a breakthrough goal requires some competencies that your organization has not needed previously. You may need to recruit experts in communications, market research, Web technology, or other areas to help you. In Chapter 4, you will see how our breakthrough goal led us to one of the biggest changes in American Heart Association history when we hired a commercial advertising agency to help us increase public awareness about heart disease and what people can do to prevent it.

- **Make the most of technology.** Many organizations have implemented technology to streamline their organizations internally, but nonprofits also must use technology to achieve their missions in the external world or risk becoming irrelevant. I cannot think of a breakthrough goal being achieved today that would not include a strong technology strategy.

- **Recruit partners.** When we established our breakthrough goal at the American Heart Association, we realized that we would need to form strategic alliances to pull it off. To interest those needed allies, we took measures to make our organization a more attractive partner—the partner of choice in a crowded field. At the American Heart Association, we made a serious effort to increase our visibility with the general public and provide rock-solid execution in all that we did. We made sure the AHA was a good, reliable partner in the relationships we had established so that word would spread. My colleagues and I networked and built relationships with local leaders in the community, corporate, and nonprofit sectors so we might be top of mind for potential partners.

As you think about partnerships and forming meaningful, high-impact alliances, approach the world with a mentality of abundance not scarcity. You cannot worry about who gets credit for every accomplishment. You must focus on your objectives and go after them. Don't go it alone. There is an old saying: "If you want to walk fast, walk alone. If you want to walk far, walk together." Chapter 5 discusses one of the most significant partnerships we have formed—with the William J. Clinton Foundation—to help us on the way to our 25 percent goal.

- **Overcommunicate.** Changes like the implementation of a breakthrough goal can be disruptive and create uncertainty. If you do not think you're overcommunicating, chances are you're not communicating enough. An e-newsletter does not cut it. Talk up your goal in formal speeches, informal chats, and group meetings with volunteers. Include it as a topic of discussion in performance reviews with staff. Post it prominently on your website. Information is power, and it inspires people to achieve great things. Do not hold it close to the vest. Open up and share, and you will energize the organization. Everyone wants to be in the know—or at least feel as if they are.

Lesson Learned

In times of change, overcommunicate. If you do not think you are overcommunicating, chances are you are not communicating enough. Try to address the WIIFM question that all of your constituents will be wondering: "What's in it for me?" Everyone needs to see how what they do fits into the big picture of the bold goal.

PROMOTING A BREAKTHROUGH GOAL WITHOUT DIRECT AUTHORITY

If you are not a leader or decision-making person in your organization, the strategies in this chapter are nevertheless applicable, but you need to be more strategic about getting buy-in for your goal. For instance, let's say the breakthrough goal you would like to present to the college scholarship committee on which you serve is to triple the scholarship amount over the next five years. To gain support, focus foremost on building trust with your fellow committee members (i.e., listen, listen, listen). Make sure you have data to answer all of their questions, so you are not simply relying on your own excitement or work ethic to determine what is possible. Depending on your organization, you might need to talk to staff, volunteers, major donors, partners, and/or constituents. Develop a strategy for each audience, which may include one-on-one up-front visits, ongoing communications, or appointing certain people to an oversight committee to guide the recommendations. You must make sure you are actively working to influence the influencers.

No matter who constitutes your audience, remember that breakthrough goals need facts to support their validity. No one wants to jump on board with an idealistic but impractical dream. Show people that your breakthrough goal is attainable, and provide them whatever data they need to see your vision of what is possible for your organization.

OUR RESULTS

All this talk of breakthrough goals would be meaningless if it did not lead to the better world we desire. I am exceedingly proud to report that we are making excellent progress toward our breakthrough goal. As of June 2008, age-adjusted death rates from heart disease are down 30.7 percent. Death rates for stroke have declined by 29.2 percent. Uncontrolled high blood pressure has been reduced by 14.5 percent, high cholesterol by 24.5 percent, and smoking by 15.8 percent. What do these percentages mean? Thanks to these improvements, 190,000 more people will be having dinner with their families tonight—people who wouldn't be here had the rates remained unchanged. But the American Heart Association, and its many partners who have made this success possible, still has its challenges in the areas of diabetes, obesity, and further reduction in the other risk factors. Otherwise, these death rates could be completely reversed in the next several years.

Why am I so obsessed with breakthrough goals? It is because of the nature of our business. In the nonprofit world, big goals are not about becoming brand leaders or increasing earnings per share. They are not about selling more widgets or winning awards. In the work we do, achieving big goals means improving the quality of life.

CHAPTER 3 TAKEAWAYS

- **Every nonprofit needs a breakthrough goal.** It provides accountability and allows you to make difficult decisions about the allocation of limited resources. It provides excitement among your employees, volunteers, board members, donors, and the public. There is no reason that we should not challenge ourselves every day to do more and have a greater impact on the world.
- **Creating a breakthrough goal follows a four-step process:** (1) Brainstorm, (2) do your homework, (3) test your theories, and (4) add flesh to the bone.
- **A bold goal is meaningless without rock-solid execution.** It is not enough to have a bold goal if you do not have the discipline to align the resources and reward systems in your organization to achieve it. When you set a breakthrough goal, you have to be willing to hold your organization's feet to the fire.
- **Shout your goal from the rooftops.** Just as you need to communicate your mission and strategic driving force to every person associated with your organization, you must shout your breakthrough goal from every rooftop. Everyone, including donors or members, board members, staff, and volunteers needs to see their role in a broader context and understand how they are contributing to the achievement of the bold goal. There is no such thing as overcommunication.
- **Ask, "What would it take?"** This deceptively simple question stirs innovation and inspiration and, often, amazing results. It mentally circumvents a person's unconscious barriers to thinking about possibilities.
- **Breakthrough goals change the world.** In the nonprofit community, setting and achieving big goals mean nothing less than making the world a significantly better place.

CHAPTER 4

BREAK OUT THE BIG BRASS *BRAND*

> Nothing great in the world has ever been accomplished without passion.
>
> —G. W. F. HEGEL

In February 2006, a red tide flooded American cities. The Empire State Building gave off a stunning red glow. Niagara Falls ran red for the day. Television anchors wore red dresses, and thousands of companies distributed red dress pins to their female employees around the country.

Sounds like a marketing campaign for Coca-Cola, right? Or perhaps a campaign by the clever marketers from Target, trying to make their red-and-white bull's-eye logo ubiquitous? It was not. The red tide was part of a grassroots campaign to put women nationwide on alert that their number one health risk is from heart disease.

The American Heart Association's Go Red For Women campaign was created by marketing agency Cone Inc. for $1.5 million over a two-year period. It returned $40 million in contributions and drew participation from more than 11,000 companies. By March 2006, Go Red had generated more than 3 billion media impressions. It has permeated the online social networking world as well, with active groups on Facebook, MySpace, and other popular online communities.

This level of exposure for a nonprofit effort is virtually unprecedented. And it all began with a simple question. A number of people on our team had asked the question: "Why can't nonprofits create big, exciting marketing campaigns just like for-profits?"

This question did not come out of the blue; within the American Heart Association and among my colleagues at other nonprofits I had already been known as the guy who always jabbered on about marketing and referred to our constituents as "customers."

That's right, customers. I am well aware that the words *marketing* and *customer* do not sit well with some nonprofit leaders. I remember that during the first year I was CEO I was cautioned not to use the term *marketing* in a department title, and when I said it in a meeting I was chastised by an officer for using a dirty word! I am happy to take some criticism, but in this day and age nonprofits have no other choice but to think of their constituents as customers. If we do not embrace the notion that we have customers, we will lose out to the many for-profits and nonprofits that do. (Remember that blurring line between for-profits and nonprofits.) According to business guru Tom Peters, 70 percent of customers stop using a product or service not because of price or product quality issues but because they did not like the human side of doing business with the provider.

Nonprofits must think in terms of branding, customer service, and lifelong customer relationships. We must think and act like marketers so that we can compete for *mindshare*, a key concept to embrace in your marketing efforts. Mindshare is the awareness that a particular brand has in the minds of consumers. When someone starts to cry, we think "Kleenex." When a natural disaster occurs in the United States, we think "American Red Cross." When a college student tells us that she wants to give back by teaching for a few years, we think "Teach For America." When someone wants to learn about heart health, I hope they think "American Heart Association." This is why we put serious effort into advertising and branding.

How does your current mindshare with the people you want to reach compare with that of other nonprofits in your field? In today's competitive environment, your organization must be top of mind with funders, volunteers, and the people you serve. If you want to improve your organization and do as much good as you can, you have to actively work on your visibility. Some people seem to feel that it is inappropriate for nonprofits to use marketing techniques, but that is simply not true. Marketing efforts can be effective in boosting image, driving education, extending reach, and increasing income. In other words, they help you achieve your mission. Not only are they acceptable, they are essential.

> **Lesson Learned**
>
> You must have a significant portion of the public's mindshare to advance your mission and achieve your breakthrough goals. Otherwise, people's attention—and dollars—will go elsewhere.

Think of the pursuit of mindshare as breaking out the big brass *brand*. You can do this in a small, local way by advertising in a local newspaper or community blog, putting up flyers, or handing out brochures and balloons outside the grocery store, or you can pursue mindshare on a national level. Our goal with Go Red For Women was to create awareness in the minds of women that heart disease is their number one killer. This is a hugely important issue, so we wanted to build a marketing campaign that would treat it as such.

We succeeded. *BusinessWeek*, a publication that usually reserves its coverage for companies trying to turn a profit, has hailed the National Wear Red Day for exhibiting "marketing hustle worthy of a new car rollout." The magazine reported that the American Heart Association's Go Red For Women campaign used big-name endorsements and flashy events and "all the tricks of a big ad campaign for a shampoo or an SUV." Some nonprofit leaders might have cowered at this characterization. I was thrilled, because the more people who know about women's heart health, the more lives we have a chance to save. And the campaign for mindshare worked. We increased women's awareness that heart disease is their number one health threat from 35 percent to 57 percent in three years. That increase in awareness and mindshare will save lives.

WHAT IS YOUR ORGANIZATION'S BRAND?

Enhancing your organization's image is one of the most important things you can do to ensure its future success and attain your breakthrough goals. At any given moment, many organizations and messages are competing for the public's attention. Your image—or brand—can help consumers quickly cut through this clutter and make the choice to listen to your message rather than that of someone else.

Let's define this concept of brand. Famous advertising copywriter and ad agency founder David Ogilvy defined *brand* as: "[t]he intangible sum of a product's attributes: its name, packaging, and price, its history, its reputation and the way it is advertised." Brand can apply to an entire organization or to individual products. Brands are so important that they can be given a dollar value when companies are up for sale. It is important for you to know what your brand is and to make sure it is the brand you want to project. Control your brand; don't let it control you.

Whether you have ever thought about it or not, your nonprofit has a brand. Your brand includes tangible elements, such as:

- Organization name
- Logo
- Tagline
- Color scheme
- Letterhead and brochures
- Website

It also includes intangible elements, such as:

- Perceptions
- Beliefs
- Emotions

Marketing and advertising efforts are ways to affect people's perceptions of your brand.

Traditional advertising, marketing, and branding techniques are the most efficient and effective ways to spread a message to the public. That's why for-profit businesses use them. Techniques such as print ad campaigns, rebranding efforts, website redesigns, billboard advertising, radio public service announcements, e-mail blasts, and direct mail allow you to affect the public's perception of your organization or the importance of your cause. Think of branding and marketing as ways for your organization to crawl into the public's mind, determine how to get their attention, and get them to take action to advance your mission. After all, what is the point of offering meaningful products or services if nobody knows about them?

No matter what your budget, you can apply marketing and branding techniques to help you gain mindshare. Here are some suggestions.

Define Whom You Are Trying to Reach and Where They Are

First, determine your target audience. Are you trying to recruit volunteers, solicit donations, convince people to sign up for your services, or educate them to take action? Where are you most likely to reach these people? If you're not sure, see whether you can find data about where these people are or what messages resonate with them. Look to other brands or organizations that appeal to your audience and see where they target. For instance, if you are reaching out to teenagers, you may find that most teen-focused brands have a strong marketing presence on social networking sites like Facebook or MySpace. Then that's where you should be, too.

Define Your Brand Elements

When large companies hire branding consultants, those consultants usually begin with a *brand analysis*—a series of questions that help to define the organization's brand—and find language, images, and emotions that relate to it. You can do the same for your organization. You don't need a big budget to have a strong brand. Here are some questions to spark your thinking. You will likely notice that the words, phrases, and emotions that came up in previous chapters to define your mission, values, and breakthrough goal come to mind in determining your brand.

- What do people think of when they hear your organization's name?
- What are the benefits your organization offers to the people it serves?
- What do you offer that no other organizations offer, or what do you do better than other organizations in your field?
- What makes you unique?

- What promises does your organization make? Do you deliver?
- How would you describe the personality of your brand?

Some words that might define your brand include: *leading, exclusive, largest, cutting-edge, trusted, community-based,* and *expert.* Keep thinking and researching until you find words that resonate with you and your organization's leaders. Your brand is the constant message beneath any marketing efforts you undertake.

Address Concerns or Fears

Another issue to think about is what concern or fear your organization can resolve for people. How can your brand put people at ease? This can come through in your overall branding efforts or in particular marketing or branding campaigns. As an example, with the escalation of gasoline prices in 2008, Meals On Wheels was having a crisis in recruiting volunteers. They decided they needed to reach out to the public through a marketing campaign, and they were smart about it. They didn't just go to the media and ask for public service help to announce that Meals On Wheels needed volunteers. Instead, they thought about a concern of their constituents—high gas prices—and they created a marketing campaign that addressed that fear while still staying true to the Meals On Wheels brand, which I would describe as trust, safety, and quality. Meals On Wheels asked the media for public service appeals that would promote the idea of three "ones"—the first appeal would ask for people to volunteer with Meals On Wheels one a day a week, the second would ask for one hour a day, and the third would ask for one gallon of gas. Think about how much more effective this well-thought-out program was compared to just a panic appeal to the media that the organization needed more volunteers because of the gasoline crisis. Meals On Wheels tried to think through what would appeal to the potential volunteers, and they wanted to provide clarity in the message of exactly what would be expected of people.

Develop a Positive Tagline

An organization's tagline is a key phrase that captures the essence of its mission, promise, and brand in a concise and memorable way. For many years, the American Heart Association's tagline was "Fighting Heart Disease and Stroke." This tagline served its purpose for a long time, but research both formal (paid market research) and informal (a casual survey of volunteers, staff, and donors) indicated that it had become stale and was no longer resonating with the public. We decided that we wanted to energize our positioning. Our review of other large nonprofits' marketing efforts showed that their positioning was more action-oriented, more hopeful, and more applicable to a wide variety of programs. Take a look at some examples of energizing and compelling nonprofit taglines:

- American Diabetes Association: Cure. Care. Commitment.
- Arthritis Foundation: Take control. We can help.
- Big Brothers Big Sisters: Little moments. Big magic.
- March of Dimes: Saving babies, together.
- Susan G. Komen Breast Cancer Foundation: For the cure.
- United Cerebral Palsy: Life without limits for disabled persons.
- YWCA: Eliminating racism. Empowering women.
- American Cancer Society: Hope. Courage. Answers.

In 2004, under the guidance of Robyn Landry, executive vice president of communications, and Dave Josserand, volunteer chair of the communications committee, the American Heart Association adopted a new tagline: Learn and Live. This new tagline addresses both heart disease and stroke and functions as a symbolic umbrella that can be used in a variety of programs, applications, and advertising campaigns. It provides yet another way for internal and external audiences to connect with and embrace our brand, and to know that our end goal is about saving lives.

Does your organization's mission have a hopeful, action-oriented tagline? Does it have any tagline at all? Particularly if your organization has a long, unwieldy, or old-fashioned name—or a name that is too similar to that of another organization—a tagline is an essential differentiator. It may be time for you to develop a new tagline. For ideas, solicit feedback on your current tagline, if you have one, and research other organizations you admire.

A NONPROFIT PAID ADVERTISING CAMPAIGN: THE PASSION PROJECT

What happens when you decide that not just your tagline but your overall brand needs an update? This happened at the American Heart Association a few years ago. Through extensive market research, we learned that the American Heart Association had significant recognition with the public. This was good news, right? You could take the heart and torch symbol and stand on any street corner in America and about 90 to 95 percent of people would recognize this as the American Heart Association. However, if you asked those people what the organization does, for the most part people would say, "Well, I am not sure exactly what they do, but I think they do it pretty well."

Hmm.

Through this market research, we also learned that the public image of the American Heart Association was as an organization that is pretty conservative, cautious, and uncomfortable selling itself—perhaps the legacy of its professional medical society heritage. This image tended to make the organization seem aloof, clinical, even disconnected.

The public was not seeing our passion—the passion of the staff, volunteers, donors, leaders, survivors, and all those who had been helped by the knowledge and information provided by the AHA. Particularly for an organization with the word *heart* in its name, this was a serious concern. We realized that we needed a way to make the outside world aware of the passion we have inside the organization. We needed to arouse passion among the populations we were trying to reach. We needed to build more of an emotional connection. We knew we were doing great work, but we were communicating this primarily through facts and figures. Heart disease has a real human side, but we were not putting a face on it with the public. We needed a more compelling way to talk about the human suffering caused by heart disease and stroke.

This led to the creation of the Passion Project, our initiative to build more passion into the organization's image in the public eye and to share the true stories of our work. We knew this campaign could succeed because we had created an organization with a clear mission, a single strategic driving force, and a breakthrough goal. The internal tools were in place, so we could focus on boosting our external image.

Remember, you must clean up your act internally before you can focus externally.

We selected paid advertising, focused more on the human story of our work, as the primary medium by which to spread our passion to the public. Because we are a large national organization, we were able to hire a large national advertising agency. In 2003, after distributing a request for proposals (RFP) to various ad agencies, we selected Campbell-Ewald, an agency that was best known for handling Chevy cars and trucks. There are, of course, smaller agencies across the country, some of which specialize in working with nonprofits. Some nonprofits even work with local college and business school advertising departments to receive pro bono services. As with most professional services, referrals are the best way to find a vendor.

The theme of the first campaign for the American Heart Association was It's Personal to increase public awareness that heart disease is the number one killer and a serious health problem. The campaign launched with a judicious and yet comprehensive media buy, which was large for a nonprofit (several million dollars) but pencil dust compared to what a consumer products company like Procter & Gamble would spend. We had to make every penny count. We set out to achieve our awareness goals, and we also decided it was important to use the ads to drive the public to our call center and our website for information on what they could do to educate and protect themselves and their families.

The investment paid off. The It's Personal campaign helped put a face on cardiovascular disease and created an emotional connection with consumers and patients. Overall, the campaign provided lifesaving information via the Learn and Live Quiz on our website and helped improve consumer awareness in key areas. The campaign ran in national media from February 2004 through January 2007 and generated 1,309,053 customer engagements directly from the advertising via phone calls, website visits to the Learn and Live Quiz, and business reply card responses. Additionally, 59 percent of those who completed the Learn and Live Quiz took some type of health action. In early 2007, we launched a second three-year campaign.

The American Heart Association was not the first nonprofit to go to paid advertising. The American Cancer Society had been doing this for a few years. From 1999 to 2001, the American Cancer Society increased its spending on paid advertising by more than 900 percent. In conjunction with paid advertising, they distribute print, TV, radio, and online public service announcements through the Ad Council. In 1998, the Partnership for a Drug-Free America launched a $195 million campaign that involved television, radio, print, billboards, and interactive media designed to decrease the use of illicit drugs among teenagers.

IS PAID ADVERTISING RIGHT FOR YOUR ORGANIZATION?

Advertising is a very big investment no matter what the size or scope of your organization. Is it worth it? What is the return on investment (ROI) if you choose to take this path? I would argue that it is nothing less than a larger share of your customers' minds and hearts. In addition to increased awareness among the public about who you are and what you do, paid advertising can lead to a residual ROI in increased volunteerism, membership, fund-raising, and corporate relations.

There are definite pros and cons that you must consider when deciding whether advertising is right for your organization.

Pros of a Paid Advertising Campaign

- Unlike in public relations efforts, in an advertising campaign you control every aspect of the message. Through advertising, you decide which people will hear about your organization, who will get your message, and when they will hear it. More control also means you can communicate with a consistent call to action throughout the organization using the same tone and graphic look.

- As a nonprofit, you also can negotiate the lowest rates for media and secure more added value—free advertising spots. If your nonprofit operates on a national level, negotiating a media buy nationally versus locally also means savings. You may be able to save up to 50 percent by purchasing ads nationally compared to making separate regional media buys if your organization has regional affiliates. Some media outlets also offer leftover space at a discounted rate for nonprofit organizations.

- You will have more opportunities for exposure. Many nonprofits rely on free public service announcements, but as a result of the increasing number of 501(c)(3)s, competition for the shrinking pie of free ads has become fierce.

- Instead of benefiting only one or two programs or communicating one or two key messages, an overarching branding campaign resonates across all of your initiatives. All other marketing efforts, from news media relations to direct marketing and promotions, are more relevant to a consumer who has been exposed to your branding message.
- You can include a call to action, through the promotion of a phone number and/or Web address. Paid advertising campaigns do not have to be about general branding alone.

Cons of a Paid Advertising Campaign

- **Expense.** You may have other priorities that contribute more to achieving your mission at this point in time. If you don't invest enough to hit the public with repetitive messages, you may not achieve your goals. You also need to make an investment in some sort of evaluation.
- **Expertise.** You need volunteer and staff expertise to manage any advertising program.
- **Bandwidth.** A paid advertising program has the potential to attract large numbers of people to your organization. You must be ready to handle this influx if it occurs.

The bottom line is that every nonprofit needs to embrace branding and marketing to best serve its constituents and keep the organization flourishing into the future. Make sure your message or call to action reaches its intended audience. Even if you cannot afford a paid advertising campaign, you need to pay attention to your organization's brand elements, think through strategically the image you want, and start working proactively to achieve it. The American Heart Association built a strong brand even before it started paying for advertising.

MARKET RESEARCH

People often ask me how the American Heart Association came to the idea of the heart-check seal of approval found on over 800 products on grocery store shelves. This program is a significant piece of the American Heart Association brand, and it is a good example of how we do things in nontraditional ways. There is a certain amount of risk in any program, and in this case we ran into quite a few roadblocks. I believe that in every crisis lies an opportunity, and that was certainly the case with the AHA's food certification program. Here is the story.

It all began with market research. No for-profit marketer worth his or her salt would ever begin a campaign of this magnitude without comprehensive market research. Not that this always saves a company from a big mistake (New Coke or Crystal Pepsi, anyone?), but it is a standard, respected practice. In the mid-1980s, the American Heart Association was among the first nonprofits to conduct market research in its sector. My major in college was advertising, so it made sense to me. After all, you don't know what you don't know.

The work of the antitobacco movement is a good example of the importance of market research. Decades ago, antitobacco advocates thought it would be effective to tell kids the plain facts about the risks of smoking and how smoking could ultimately kill them. These messages didn't work as well as expected. When they surveyed teenagers, they found that, in some instances, the messages were actually *encouraging* kids to smoke. Kids were seeing smoking cigarettes as a form of rebellion and a rite of passage. Research later showed that the more effective messaging was to focus on how kids were being manipulated and exploited by tobacco companies. They also succeeded with messages that focused on popularity and how uncool it is to "kiss an ashtray."

We wanted market research to guide us when a food manufacturer approached the American Heart Association to do a line of food products together. At the time, we were an exceptionally conservative, risk-averse organization. We realized there could be a negative emotional reaction when we were considering the creation of a food product line. We needed to test this idea before creating something that would go into people's mouths and stomachs. We wanted market analysis data to help us decide whether or not this was a good idea.

We convinced the board and the leadership team that we needed to test the food manufacturer/American Heart Association food product idea with the public. To be candid, I wanted a positive response from the market research. I thought it was a tremendous opportunity to generate revenue, increase our visibility, and serve a healthy purpose. And that is exactly why we do market research—because I was totally wrong. The focus groups were unanimous. They said, "Food products by the American Heart Association and this food manufacturer? They will taste awful!"

In my excitement about the potential for providing heart-healthy options, brand exposure, and revenue, I had forgotten about consumers' perceptions of the taste!

Besides saving you from a big mistake, the other advantage of market research is that your customers might give you better ideas than you came up with yourself. That is just what happened in this case. The focus groups said, "Don't manufacture food products; just tell us which existing products meet your standards. We are confused, and you can be helpful." If you have a limited budget, you can conduct focus groups informally by setting up panels of staff, volunteers, constituents, and/or partners. Remember to include the kind of people who are the target audience for your product or campaign and as diverse a group of such people as possible. Encourage them to be brutally honest and to share all of their ideas, suggestions, and feedback. Doing this type of research *before* you invest in any new product or campaign prevents potential problems later in the process.

Lesson Learned

Customer research is essential. It helps you avoid mistakes, and it may also provide you with innovative ideas. Remember: You don't know what you don't know.

A year later, the American Heart Association decided to launch a food certification program with the heart-check on food products that met the organization's heart-health criteria. We called the program HeartGuide. We conducted market research with health-care providers, the general public, and trade associations, as well as the food industry. Our research indicated that some sort of labeling program, provided by a trusted organization, would benefit consumers. The food industry was very much in favor. However, the interest in our program shifted when it became clear that federal regulations on food labeling were not being strictly enforced. Instead of using the heart-check, food companies found they could use other promotions not previously allowed, with lesser criteria and fewer restrictions. New products making health claims—such as "low cholesterol," "low fat," and "light"— became so prevalent that by 1989 they accounted for 40 percent of new product introductions. The food industry could use other symbols to promote these new products.

The HeartGuide program became, well, a debacle. The FDA did not like the program. The USDA did not like it. To give just one example of why, they were concerned that the AHA seal on selected food products could not convey the importance of the total diet being balanced, and consumers might believe they could eat the HeartGuide-approved foods in any quantity. Then the National Food Processors Association started to protest that we would generate public confusion, although they never had any data to support this notion. There was concern that the American Heart Association would, in effect, become a quasi-regulatory body. Then, in advance of our launch, Stouffer's rolled out a program that looked much like our HeartGuide certification. Kraft was angry that we refused to work with a company owned by tobacco companies. The FDA threatened to seize products that had agreed to implement the program, even though our legal counsel and outside counsel agreed that our program was within legal boundaries. Although the American Heart Association was prepared to go to court, the food companies did not want to be in a prolonged legal fight. Ultimately, we withdrew the program in April 1990, two months after it had launched. The program shut down and is now, of all things, a Harvard Business School case study!

Partly as a result of the spotlight that HeartGuide put on the issue of the confusing food labels, a few months later the Health and Human Services secretary was quoted as saying that food labels had become the Tower of Babel and were totally confusing to consumers. Eventually, Congress passed legislation that created a new food label and specifically allowed a food certification program. Senator John Chafee, of Rhode Island, was quoted as saying that the legislation would never have passed had the American Heart Association not put a spotlight on the issue. In the end, although the HeartGuide program did not succeed, the American Heart Association did feel satisfied that it had helped to enact food labeling reform.

As a result of the new legislation specifically allowing certification programs, the American Heart Association shortly thereafter reintroduced its Food Certification Program to help consumers make better food choices from among the ever-widening array of options. For this program, any food that the AHA certifies must first comply with the existing FDA or USDA requirements for making a heart-related health claim. Products featuring the program's heart-check mark meet the American Heart Association's criteria of being low in saturated fat and cholesterol for healthy people over age two. Today, more than 800 products participate in the American Heart Association's Food Certification Program. What is more important, the heart-check is helping consumers make healthier food choices.

Remember, no matter what your organization's mission, you need to conduct research to find out what your customers want, what the larger market wants, and what environment you are operating in. You can do this through surveys, focus groups, formal market research, research that has already been published, information surveying and polling, and keeping up to date on trends in your field and your region. You must have information, data, and research to back up your ideas.

GO RED FOR WOMEN

Let's go back now to the blurring lines between for-profits and nonprofits. That fuzziness is another major argument for nonprofits to embrace marketing and branding strategies. Throughout the 1990s, many for-profit organizations began what is now known as cause marketing. *Cause marketing* is generally defined as a company's agreeing to donate a portion of the proceeds from every product sold to a nonprofit. The company may also include some logo or mark on the product to indicate the donation. Other companies expanded the definition, engaging in even deeper relationships and campaigns to tie their brands to good causes. Here are some examples of various ways corporations have worked with nonprofits, along with the impressive results they have achieved:

- **Avon Products:** The Avon Breast Cancer Crusade, launched in 1993, was designed to appeal to the hearts and heads of Avon's 400,000 sales representatives and female customers. Within the

first six months, the crusade reached more than 100 million women. It has gone on to raise more than $400 million since 1993.
- **Reebok:** Human rights issues resonated with Reebok's major customers, the youth segment. The company sponsored Amnesty International's Human Rights Now! concert tour through international media relations, promotions, and the creation of the Reebok Human Rights Award. Through the award, Reebok achieved worldwide recognition for its contributions to human rights causes and built long-lasting associations with the human rights community.
- **ConAgra Foods:** ConAgra, the second-largest food company in the United States, developed the Feeding Children Better program in 1999, aimed at ending childhood hunger. The program included national partnerships with organizations fighting children's hunger, public awareness campaigns, and after-school programs providing wholesome meals to needy children in safe and caring locations. As a result of these efforts, more than 1 million meals are served annually to children in need.

Are for-profits detracting from the work of nonprofits? My opinion is no. Our country has monumental challenges being addressed by an often inadequately funded nonprofit sector. More effort and resources moving to good causes is a real plus. It also helps draw more attention to the good work that we all want to accomplish.

All of the campaigns mentioned here were big and impactful and were created by the marketing agency Cone, Inc., which pioneered the concept of cause-related marketing. To compete successfully for mindshare, we made a decision at the American Heart Association to get Cone working for us. This led to one of the most successful national marketing campaigns in nonprofit history.

At first, Cone resisted working with the American Heart Association, saying that they only worked with for-profit corporations. But Kathy Rogers, the AHA's vice president for corporate relations, persisted, and eventually Cone took us on as a client. Cone conducted some initial assessments and found one glaring issue: While the American Heart Association was doing a lot of work with women in awareness and educational programs, there was a huge gap in their efforts. As one research study put it, women walked and raced and cooked to fight breast

> **Lesson Learned**
>
> When possible, work with leading experts. Even a small amount of their time can be enormously valuable. You need outside eyes to give you different perspectives and help you see things you otherwise would not see or consider.

cancer, but few understood that it was actually heart disease that was their number one killer.

Cone proposed Go Red For Women, "a nationwide movement celebrating the energy, passion and power we have to band together and wipe out heart disease." The overall vision for the initiative is for women to adopt or improve heart-healthy habits and to support the cause in a way that is relevant to their lives.

Like many issues, women's heart health was not necessarily easy to explain in a quick sound bite. Cone vice president Kristian Darigan, who led the American Heart Association account team, summed it up in a subsequent Harvard Business School case study about the program:

> When we began working with the American Heart Association, the prevalence and misunderstanding of heart disease in women was well known within the American Heart Association and within certain scientific communities. It was, however, known to a much less extent among healthcare providers and among women—who were both critical in raising awareness and saving lives. Therefore, we needed to use systems-thinking and develop multiple short- and long-term opportunities and vehicles for action to propel women's heart health to a top-of-mind subject among these key audiences.[1]

We had a lot of great programs targeted to women such as corporate sponsor promotions with the Power of Love around Valentine's Day in February, a women's behavior change program called Choose to Move, research on women's awareness levels, and local fund-raiser luncheons, but Cone convinced us that we had to pull them together under one strongly branded umbrella.

The Go Red For Women campaign is among the most far-reaching, comprehensive marketing campaigns in nonprofit history. Looking at each element of the campaign is instructive for nonprofits of various shapes, sizes, and missions. Don't be intimidated by the size of this program. As several of the following examples demonstrate, many of this program's branding and marketing strategies can be replicated by even the smallest nonprofits.

National Efforts

- **Viral/buzz/word-of-mouth marketing:** As social networking and the Internet dominate marketing and branding efforts today, it is just as important to have your customers talking about you as it is to talk directly to them. Word-of-mouth campaigns are among the most effective, particularly when it comes to good causes. Nonprofits are at an advantage in this realm because of their volunteer networks. In fact, viral marketing is one of the best strategies for an organization with minimal funds. Any organization can coordinate viral e-mail campaigns, Facebook groups, or ribbon or plastic bracelet efforts. For Go Red, the effort included red lighting on office buildings, landmarks, and courthouses; the distribution of red dress pins; and, of course, the simple act of people wearing red. Any organization can build a profile or fan page on Facebook.com or run a viral e-mail campaign.
- **Collateral materials:** The American Heart Association produced extensive collateral materials to support Go Red, including bookmarks, posters, screen savers, and e-cards. For the medical community, we created the Physician's Toolkit, containing patient reports, a summary of new heart-health guidelines, and wallet cards, to support patient and provider education. Between 2005 and 2006, over 4 million patient education materials were distributed through Physician's Toolkits and via health plans. Any organization can design and distribute low-cost collateral pieces, such as flyers, informational one-pagers, lapel pins, pens, and e-cards.
- **Media relations:** Go Red was supported through extensive media coverage—on television and in print (approximately one-third of media impressions were national and two-thirds were local). To reach the medical community, we also conducted a national science news conference announcing the first-ever guidelines for the prevention and treatment of heart disease in women. *Woman's Day*

magazine has also been a tremendous early and ongoing supporter of the Go Red movement.

- **Paid advertising:** To further promote Go Red For Women, we bought advertising with a focus on publications from three categories—women's fashion, epicurean, and women's lifestyle. This includes magazines such as *Glamour, InStyle, Cooking Light, More,* and *Redbook.* Additionally, we developed a major online program to promote the Go Red Heart CheckUp with popular sites such as Glam, Everyday Health, and Revolution Health. Additionally, a separate buy to reach the Hispanic/Latino audience includes ads on the Telemundo TV network, on the ABC Hispanic Radio network, and in *Selecciones* and *Siempre Mujer* magazines. As mentioned, local media outlets offer public service announcements and free advertising spots to nonprofit organizations. Community calendars, websites, and blogs provide other opportunities to promote events.

- **Corporate sponsor activations:** Securing Macy's as a national sponsor for Go Red was a major breakthrough for the American Heart Association. Eighty percent of the company's workforce is female, as are 80 percent of its customers, not to mention the fact that Macy's shopping bags are red! This sponsorship also led to the fun element of fashion shows at Macy's flagship store in New York City as well as in local markets. In addition to Macy's, Go Red's national corporate sponsors have included Pfizer (for the first three years of the program) and Merck (beginning in 2007).

- **National Wear Red Day:** National Wear Red Day was a collaboration between the National Center and regional affiliate organizations, with the National Center being responsible for concept development, collateral materials, and the affiliates executing the program on the ground. Each year on the first Friday in February, participating companies encouraged their employees to wear red-colored clothing to work. They also asked employees to donate $5 each to the American Heart Association. With that donation, participating employees received a red dress sticker. The American Heart Association supported the participants' effort with how-to activation kits that included posters, a newsletter, tax receipt forms for contributions, and flyers to include with employee paychecks.

In 2006, more than 11,000 companies participated in National Wear Red Day. (Note that National Wear Red Day is now jointly sponsored by the National Heart, Lung and Blood Institute, an agency of the federal government.) Many organizations declare an official day or week—either nationally or in their local community—which is an excellent way to rally media attention, volunteer participation, and other support.

Local Efforts

- **Organizational partnerships:** Fortunately, the AHA already has 22.5 million volunteers and donors, but we also reached out to nonprofits that were concerned about women's health and wanted to share the message.
- **Local Go Red Luncheons:** The American Heart Association's local chapters hosted fund-raising luncheons that promoted heart health. These local lunches proved an important source of both fund-raising and momentum for Go Red. In 2004, the first year, American Heart Association chapters hosted 52 lunches raising almost $3 million. In 2006 there were about 170 lunches that raised $10 million.
- **Cities Go Red:** In the second year of Go Red, we created the Cities Go Red strategic platform for attracting local corporate sponsors. The plan, devised by the National Center, allowed regional affiliates to seek local sponsorship for Go Red as another fund-raising channel. Sponsorships were sold around the individual city's efforts/activities, and guidelines were included for creating local branding (Boston Goes Red, Indianapolis Goes Red) that added to the overall impact of the day. Local sponsor benefits included recognition at area events, inclusion in press outreach, the ability to promote/fund-raise, and the use of a local logo.

With each year, the red tide expanded on the national and local levels. By the third year, morning talk show hosts wore red and spoke about heart disease in women, New York City's Fashion Week hosted the Rhapsody in Red gathering at the New York Public Library, and more than 150 landmarks (including Graceland!) were illuminated with red lighting. In the first two years of Go Red, roughly 10 million red dress pins were distributed and 300,000 women joined the movement online.

CORPORATE PARTNERSHIPS

Thirty years ago, a nonprofit working with a for-profit corporation in a marketing relationship was virtually unheard of. The American Heart Association came to corporate relationships quite slowly and carefully. As you can see, strong corporate partnerships have been a big component of the success of Go Red for Women. There is no doubt, however, that nonprofit/for-profit relationships are a tricky business. A conflict of interest, or even the perception of a conflict of interest, can damage a nonprofit's reputation and its moral authority. The key to avoiding this is to have an appropriate firewall in your decision-making process.

In the 1980s, the American Heart Association was among the first nonprofits to establish a corporate relations operation. But we did this in a very specific way: Rather than going out and saying, "Here is something we want you to fund"—although we had those arrows in our quiver—we took the approach of saying, "Let's sit down with members of your senior team and our senior team and get to know each other. We will each talk about our priorities and see if there are areas where our objectives overlap, thus creating opportunities to work together."

Corporate money can be very enticing, so you must stick carefully to your mission and strategic driving force. It does not matter how much money a corporation is willing to offer; an organization must be true to its mission and strategic plan for a relationship to make sense and provide results for everyone involved. For instance, it clearly would not make sense for the American Heart Association to receive funding from a tobacco company or a restaurant chain that specializes in high-fat and high-cholesterol products.

We have had to turn down big sponsorship dollars because they did not align with our mission and strategic driving force. In one case, I got a phone call from a major potential sponsor, who offered a large amount of money to work with us on a campaign around smoking cessation. They approached us because smoking is a significant cause of cardiovascular diseases. I told them that the American Heart Association was really honored to be approached, but we just do not have significant competence in that area. We do not deal with smoking cessation. I told them that the American Legacy Foundation and the American Lung Association do work in that area and offered to make referrals. Looking back, it was actually pretty easy to turn down that money. Smoking cessation is an important cause, but it is not one of our priorities because other organizations are already working on it and doing it quite well. We would simply duplicate their efforts and not add real value. It is a slippery slope if we start changing our organization every time someone whips out a checkbook.

In my dealings with for-profits, I have always found a genuine desire to help the nonprofit be successful. But—and this is a big but—when you are receiving marketing dollars you must be acutely aware that you are getting dollars that could have been spent on ads or direct marketing the company would have used to reach its target profit. So if you're receiving marketing dollars, the corporation likely wants to see some return on investment that also meets its objective; the two can be complementary. This is very different from receiving a charitable grant because real business needs are part of the equation. If you are going to get these marketing dollars—and make no mistake, they are marketing dollars—you have to be able to identify the company's objective that overlaps with your organization's objective. Then you have to be able to communicate this in a language that the for-profit world understands.

Above all, you need to provide data about what—and, often, whom—you bring to the table. When we sit down with a corporation to talk about sponsorship of a Heart Walk, for example, we definitely talk about our mission and the excitement of the day. That is nice and warm and fuzzy. But we also come armed with data outlining the demographic makeup of the people the Heart Walk reaches—how many are male, female, kids; what age groups and socioeconomic categories they come from; and so on. Rule number one for working with corporate marketing departments is this: To be taken seriously, you must have credible, meaningful demographic data. You need to show exactly how many people a sponsor will reach.

Through all of this, of course, you must keep an eye on how this corporate sponsorship aligns with your organization's mission and core values. It can be challenging to maintain an appropriate firewall, but it is essential. In establishing a firewall, first look at standards and guidelines for nonprofits provided by Independent Sector (www.independentsector.org). You may find ethical guidelines for your field as well. The American Heart Association is also guided by the standards of the National Health Council. In general, a good firewall should consist of the following:

- Clearly established policies addressing what you do and do not accept from sponsors and what would potentially represent a conflict of interest
- Criteria by which you evaluate sponsorship proposals
- Provision for a written agreement with the corporation prior to a sponsorship initiative being launched
- Mandates for financial disclosure of the relationship
- A detailed description of how your organization reviews sponsorship proposals, how decisions are made, and by whom

Even if you are comfortable that all of these issues have been addressed, you also must think about public perception of any sponsorship. Might anyone perceive a conflict of interest? At the American Heart Association, there are extensive policies, guidelines, and protocols around corporate relationships. There are two different review groups that look at all proposed corporate relationships and have to sign off on them. It is not an easy process to do business with the American Heart Association, but that is intentional and creates the firewall necessary to protect the brand. Well-defined policies and protocols also ensure that you are consistent in your relationships with corporations.

Lesson Learned

When it comes to corporate partnerships, be careful to avoid even the perception of a conflict of interest.

CUSTOMER FOCUS

During my tenure as CEO I insisted that the American Heart Association measure customer satisfaction. In this day and age, when every organization, including the local pizza shop, measures customer satisfaction, we need to do the same.

Within the past five years, we have placed a greater emphasis on understanding the needs of our customers and designing programs, products, and services to meet their needs. This is a shift from our historical focus on the development of products as a primary focus. Previously, we tended to think about customers as a secondary factor. Part of this transition in thinking has included defining six broad markets that represent our key customer segments:

- Patients
- The general public
- Researchers and scientists
- Health-care providers
- Public officials
- Donors

The staff who are assigned to each market have worked to build a profile of their customers that describes their key attributes and interests. Of course, there are submarkets within each of these markets. Focusing on these profiles helps us develop strategies attuned to the needs of each market. It is very important for an organization to be data-driven in its decision making. There is no area in which it is more important to monitor and collect data than your key customer groups. Doing so helps you identify problems if you have them, as well as come up with new ideas. Then you can work to overcome the problems and capitalize on the opportunities. It is the problems that you *do not* know about that can do significant damage to your organization, such as the dissatisfaction of a particular audience you are trying to serve or a group of volunteers.

At the American Heart Association, we annually survey our key market groups, their subgroups, and our intermediaries (such as health-care providers and employers). As an example, we survey not only the participants in our annual walk, but also the companies (the intermediaries) through which the walkers are recruited. What do we look for when we survey? Our goal is excellence. In today's environment, it is not enough to just have "satisfied" customers (4 on a 5-point scale); you need to have "very satisfied" customers (5 on a 5-point scale) to really achieve customer loyalty.

We also survey our employees using the Gallup organization's twelve key questions to evaluate *employee engagement*, which is directly related to providing superior customer service. This is another example of a for-profit strategy that we have employed successfully. The underlying premise of the Gallup survey is that if you score well on these questions, chances are greater that the same employees who have high morale are treating your customers well.

We survey annually on such topics as volunteer satisfaction, customer satisfaction, and employee morale, and we develop appropriate action plans to continue to improve. If your organization does not have the resources to do extensive surveying, you can use an online survey program such as Zoomerang.com or SurveyMonkey.com, or hand out hard-copy surveys at meetings or events. Ask the people you serve or your volunteers what your organization does well, what you could improve upon, what additional services they would like, and what ideas they have to offer. Feedback is always helpful, and it also shows your constituents that you care about their opinions.

> **Lesson Learned**
>
> It is no longer enough to have satisfied customers. To keep people's loyalty in a crowded market, you need *very* satisfied customers. Survey your key customer segments regularly to gauge their satisfaction level.

To ensure that we maintain our customer focus when we work alone or with partners, we have established a major objective to increase customer loyalty. To this end, we are now annually measuring the level of satisfaction of our customers and partners. We have established specific goals to improve that level of engagement and are holding ourselves accountable for improvement. Our focus is on 100 percent customer engagement and increased customer loyalty. To increase engagement and loyalty, we believe we must:

- Build confidence with customers by improving trust and delivering on our promises.
- Treat all customers with respect, and swiftly resolve any problems that occur.

- Build passion in customers so that they cannot imagine the world without us, and create the feeling that we are the perfect organization for them.

We are developing strategies to address the factors that have the greatest influence on customer loyalty, such as the quality of our programs and services, our level of customer service, and the degree of stakeholder engagement that we have. We are also increasing the urgency of our efforts to reach audiences that are culturally and ethnically diverse and who suffer disproportionately from heart disease and stroke.

Because of the overlap among our customer markets, we also spend a lot of time on integration and collaboration internally. We want to be sure that we are taking all possible steps to eliminate duplication of effort while providing the best possible experience for our customers. To that end, we are creating a set of *customer pathways* to better define how we bring customers into the organization and increase their involvement with us over time, based on their needs and preferences. For instance, we are exploring how an initial customer contact with the AHA, such as visiting the website, can turn into a call to the call center, which can turn into participation in a Heart Walk, which can turn into a lifelong relationship. It is important to us that each customer feel that he or she is having a consistent customer experience with the organization in every instance. Making the most out of these interactions is also being good stewards of our donor dollars.

If you really want to be customer focused, in addition to the regular assessments I suggest that your senior team regularly test your organization's customer service. Phone your own call center and sign up for the products and services your organization provides. See what problems and opportunities you encounter when you, as a customer, receive them. This should be done on a regular basis throughout the organization at all levels. At one point, I tried using the Kintera software that we provide to Heart Walk participants to raise money. The first challenge I encountered was transferring e-mail addresses from my Outlook contacts into the Kintera database. I knew that if I had this difficulty, many of our customers would as well. So we came up with a helpful strategy for transfers from other databases.

Ultimately, marketing and branding efforts are about differentiating your organization today and sustaining it into the future. Many of us

> **Lesson Learned**
>
> To become more customer focused, become a customer of your organization's products and services. Regularly spot-check your website, call center, programs, and products to check for problems or opportunities to do a better job.

complain about our media-saturated world, but instead of criticizing the messages we see on TV, the Web, and magazines, why not introduce the good work of the nonprofit sector to this realm? Even with a small budget, marketing savvy can reap big dividends.

CHAPTER 4 TAKEAWAYS

- **Marketing is not a dirty word.** As long as a nonprofit organization's marketing is effective in boosting image, driving mission, extending reach, and increasing revenue, not only is it acceptable for a nonprofit, it is essential. This is about targeting your resources most effectively in achieving your mission. Marketing is one way the American Heart Association saves lives.
- **Any marketing effort must link to your organization's mission and strategic driving force.** To work for your organization, a paid advertising campaign—or any marketing effort—must be in line with your organization's mission, core values, strategic driving force, and business model.
- **Tell your personal/human story.** We were very factual in our messages but too sterile. Put a human face on what you do. That is what the public will remember—the stories of the people you serve.
- **Create a memorable tagline.** The most effective nonprofit taglines are action oriented, hopeful, and applicable to a wide variety of programs. Create a tagline or revise an existing tagline to meet these criteria. Stay in touch and update your tagline when it gets stale and no longer resonates with your customers.
- **To create a big campaign, start with word-of-mouth marketing.** As social networking and the Internet dominate marketing and branding efforts today, it is just as important to have your customers talking about you as it is to talk directly to them. Word-of-mouth campaigns are among the most effective and least expensive. Any organization can coordinate viral e-mail campaigns, Facebook groups, or ribbon or plastic bracelet efforts.
- **Measure customer satisfaction.** Your good intentions do not make much difference if you are not serving the needs of your customers. Take a lesson from the local pizza shop or online shopping site and ask customers how you are doing. Anticipate their needs and rising expectations. Better yet, become a customer yourself and test your organization's products and services.

CHAPTER 5

BOLD MOVES AND BEST PRACTICES

At the American Heart Association, we have incorporated dissatisfaction with the status quo into our corporate culture. We continually challenge ourselves to do more. We need to keep reassessing our structure, our volunteer and staff talent, our fund-raising goals and procedures, and our impact. People are suffering and dying every day from heart disease and stroke, and we must do all we can to save them.

I know that you have the same passion for the work you do and the people you serve. This is why the status quo is not good enough. Taking bold, innovative action and adopting best practices in your organizational management are an absolute mandate for any nonprofit organization that wants to be the best it can be.

In this chapter, you will read about some innovative moves and best practices of the American Heart Association. With each initiative described, think about how the concept can apply to your organization. The world is moving fast, and it is not enough merely to keep up. Just like for-profits, we must stay ahead of the curve to survive and thrive. There is no reason that nonprofits cannot be early adopters, innovators, and best-in-class practitioners. All you need are big ideas and smart strategies. This chapter offers both.

When it comes to being bold and innovative, confidence and optimism are key. When I see a possibility and start working toward a goal, I really do not ever think that we will fail. I always assume that we can accomplish something, even when it has never been done before. And even if things do not go as planned—as occurred with the HeartGuide program—we are always moving forward. That is not being naïve and it is not saying that you do not need to prepare, do contingency planning, and work incredibly hard. Just go into things with a positive attitude, believing that you are going to make it happen and be successful.

Begin with the belief that anything is possible, and then think about what big goals you want to achieve with your organization. Where can you be more innovative? More creative? More tech savvy? More appealing to the next generation of donors and volunteers? Here are several examples from which you can gain insight and ideas to apply to your organization.

BIGGER, BOLDER FUND-RAISING

It is a plain fact that most big goals need big funding. And just like for-profit organizations, nonprofits are always thinking about increasing revenues. The key to the American Heart Association's success in fund-raising is its focus on a few areas where the organization is able to execute extremely well. For instance, we conduct three special events across the country, which raised almost $200 million of the $800 million we generated in 2007—a large percentage of our diverse fund-raising activities. Over the years we have developed competencies in certain areas, shed activities at which we could not be first-rate or where there was not significant upside potential, and continued to build our capacity in the things we do best. The trick is to keep successful annual events consistent and reliable for donations, but not to let them become stale, boring, and predictable. Here are some dos and don'ts for bold fund-raising:

- **Do have long-term fund-raising goals.** Each fund-raising event should have goals, and these goals should fit into a longer-term plan. I recommend planning your fund-raising over a three- to five-year period to match your strategic plans for that same period. Make your fund-raising plan a living document—keep it updated and modify as necessary.
- **Don't be conservative.** Reach out and stretch with aggressive goals. If you reach for the stars and fall a little short, you will

probably still set new records for your organization. As you learned in Chapter 3, the American Heart Association adopted a target of $30 million in thirty months for the Heart Walk and reached that goal in just eighteen months. This occurred because every person involved in that effort felt a sense of accountability and connection. When we reached such a big goal, everyone got excited about wanting to achieve even bigger goals. Success breeds success. Do not let your team down by slowing your organization's momentum. Keep raising the bar.

> **Lesson Learned**
>
> When a CEO, executive director, or any leader raises the bar, the staff and volunteers can realize successes that they did not know they were capable of achieving.

- **Don't spread your organization too thin.** Focus on a few fund-raising initiatives or events at which you think you have the competence to be best in class. It's better to continually improve a successful fund-raising dinner or event that you do every year than to try new fund-raisers that are out of your comfort zone.

- **Don't be afraid to phase out lower-potential events.** Phasing out of events can be a tough decision both because it is hard to say no and because you are reducing an income stream in the short term. However, you're better off focusing on a few successful events. (Of course, don't put all your eggs in one basket; make sure you have a diversified and sustainable revenue stream.)

- **Do explore new opportunities for generating revenue.** Nonprofits no longer rely on donations alone. Many organizations have developed additional revenue streams by selling products that have a strong tie-in with their mission. Often such products can provide the personal involvement that many of today's donors seek. The best example of this is the phenomenally popular LiveStrong wristbands used as a fund-raising item for the Lance Armstrong Foundation, which raises money for cancer research. The bands were developed in 2004 by Nike and its advertising agency, Wieden +

Kennedy. The bands, which are yellow in honor of the yellow jersey worn by winners of the Tour de France, the premier cycling event that Armstrong has won seven times, sell for $1 each. As we all know from seeing those yellow bracelets everywhere, those dollars can add up. To date, the Lance Armstrong Foundation has sold over 70 million of them. Not only does this raise money and awareness, it also creates a massive database of donors for the foundation's other fund-raising efforts.

- **Do enable your fund-raising with technology.** All nonprofits should take advantage of fund-raising opportunities enabled by technology. The American Heart Association uses a contact management system created by Kintera (www.kinterainc.com) that allows fund-raisers to create a Web page, transport their personal contacts into the Kintera system, and generate solicitation letters with a click of a mouse. You can send those contacts a solicitation letter with a link that allows them to go to your personal donation page, where they can contribute by using a credit card. Then you can automatically generate a thank-you e-mail. This is easier not only on the volunteer but on the contributor. We have found that if a participant in the Heart Walk uses the online tool, he or she raises about three times more money than a walker who does not use the online tool. Just think: If each walker used this tool, the American Heart Association's income could skyrocket and its costs would decline.

- **Do apply the Rule of Three.** In small organizations and large, you can always assume that one-third of the volunteers you recruit will do the job superbly. One-third will do the job, but you are going to have to push them and encourage them and really stay on top of them. And the final one-third are simply not ever going to do what they have been asked to do. If you accept this Rule of Three as a fact, you can plan accordingly. How? By overrecruiting volunteers. Plan for one-third of your recruits not to meet their goals. If this occurs, you will still meet your fund-raising numbers by applying the Rule of Three. If they pleasantly surprise you, terrific!

- **Do make sure every volunteer responsible for fund-raising has a very specific job description so each person knows what is expected and in what time frames.** Provide all fund-raisers with a one-pager outlining what that person is responsible for and how his or her role fits with the big picture. Vague directions produce vague outcomes, and people like to understand the difference they are making.

- **Do follow up with volunteers before their deadlines.** For every fund-raising target date you set, follow up with your volunteer fund-raisers in advance of the date. As an example, if you have ten volunteer leaders who are responsible for securing $500 in donations each, don't wait until the fund-raising deadline to follow up—work with them in advance of the deadline to ensure they are on schedule, and support their efforts if necessary. Identify potential problems early so you can take corrective action.

- **Do provide training for every volunteer involved with fund-raising.** Every level of person involved in the fund-raising process, from high-level corporate executives to the teenagers volunteering at a charity fun run, needs training. Even a small amount of training—a thirty-minute bagel and coffee meeting—makes a difference. The purpose of training is threefold: (1) It provides nuts-and-bolts information about the fund-raiser's job and how it fits into the big picture, (2) it gives volunteers the opportunity to meet one another and build a supportive community, and (3) it puts a personal face on your organization. This is a golden opportunity to start bonding each person to your organization's mission.

If you have not updated your fund-raising strategy in a while, now is definitely the time. In the next few years, we will be facing changes in fund-raising that will require us to stretch again. Trends in philanthropy and different generational attitudes about giving will affect how we raise funds. For instance, many Generation Y philanthropists (born after 1980) are giving away large amounts of money in their twenties and thirties instead of waiting until retirement. Increasingly, donors of all ages are demanding that organizations provide evidence of tangible results. Many also want to have hands-on involvement in creative solutions that improve the quality of life for their fellow citizens. Our challenge is to demonstrate that we can deliver in the face of these expectations. If we cannot, we risk becoming irrelevant to our own donors and volunteers, who will take their energy, efforts, and commitment elsewhere.

BEST PRACTICES IN LEVERAGING NEW TECHNOLOGIES

You cannot talk about best practices in any organization today—for-profit or nonprofit—without talking about technology. Nonprofits must maintain their relevance in a world where, according to a November 2007 Harris Interactive poll, 80 percent of American adults are online. Although we cannot always fund extensive high-tech initiatives, we can certainly access existing technologies and use them to extend the reach of our organizations and reduce our fund-raising costs. Virtually all initiatives at the American Heart Association include a Web component. Here are some best practices in Web-based initiatives for you to consider applying in your organization:

Streamlined Donation Web Pages

The American Heart Association raises a lot of money from its website. However, when we analyzed how people used our website—data available to any organization through a free service like Google Analytics—we found that many people were logging in and clicking on the donations page but never making a contribution. People would start down the path but not complete it. We learned what the problem was from some informal interviews and analysis of click-through rates: Donating required too much clicking. Once we understood this, we streamlined and simplified the number of steps a potential donor was asked to complete. Contributions soared.

How can you optimize online giving to your organization? In 2007, American Express, in partnership with the Center on Philanthropy at Indiana University, released the results of the American Express Charitable Gift Survey, which provided some helpful answers. The study uncovered a surprising finding regarding online donations—although nearly two-thirds (65 percent) of Americans in the study gave to a charity in the past year, only one in every ten donors took advantage of the convenience of giving online.

When asked why they did not give online, the single largest reason people offered (after not having a computer) is that they were unaware of online contribution options. More than one-quarter (28 percent) of offline-only donors said that they did not give online because they could not find an online giving site, they did not know they could make a gift online, or they did not think of giving online. How easy is it to reach the donation page on your website? Are you driving people to your site with e-newsletters and e-blasts? You may have an untapped pool of donors just waiting for a link to your online donation page, and, statistics say, their gifts will be larger than donations sent by mail.

User-Created Content

The term *user-generated content* is hot these days, and it is beautifully applicable to the nonprofit sector. The American Heart Association has applied this trend to memorial gifts by offering people the opportunity to create memorial Web pages. If you have a loved one who has died of cardiovascular disease or a stroke, you can create a memorial Web page. Other people can visit your page, make memorial gifts, or write a remembrance about that person. This is a tremendous use of technology. It is a meaningful way to pay tribute to a loved one, and it raises money for the organization.

Social Networking

I will admit that I did not know much about Facebook until a younger friend encouraged me to check it out. Here is how she convinced me: by running a search on "American Heart Association" and coming up with hundreds of Facebook users who included the organization in their personal profiles or began groups to support our efforts. Particularly when it comes to younger donors and volunteers, it is crucial to follow social networking and the way users are interacting with their favorite causes through sites like Facebook and MySpace.

If you are a large national organization, you'll likely find—as I did—that some of your supporters have already started profiles, groups, or fan pages for your organization. Facebook and MySpace are great places to promote events, recruit volunteers, spread your brand image, and post photos and news articles about the good work you do. You or a designated volunteer can also leave a comment or note on your supporters' profile pages to show that you are aware of and appreciate their efforts. Yes, this does involve giving up some control, but in my experience, positive content far outweighs the negative. It is, however, a good idea to have a volunteer or staff member regularly monitor your organization's online reputation.

Webcasts

If a picture is worth a thousand words, then how much is a video worth? Many people—because of schedules, money, location, or whatever—might not be able to attend a specific event. You can get more mileage out of every event you produce by letting people attend virtually, during or even after the event, with stored webcasts downloadable from your website. Webcasts are a relatively inexpensive way to expand the reach for any particular event you have.

Visitors to the American Heart Association website can watch doctors discussing innovative rehabilitation techniques for persons who have suffered a stroke or interviews with patients who discuss their feelings about rehab and offer advice for others going through it. AHA national spokesperson Dr. Clyde Yancy walks visitors through the major cardiovascular conditions and their effects. These videos are also posted on the popular video-sharing website YouTube, where thousands of people see them as well. If you are not videotaping your workshops, seminars, events, and speeches, you are missing out on an enormous—and free—opportunity to spread your message to new audiences through online viral videos.

Podcasts

In 2005, the American Heart Association piloted a podcasting effort, offering six podcasts of major news stories related to cardiovascular diseases. These podcasts are several minutes long, feature interviews with spokespeople, and can be downloaded from the news area at

---

Recommended Resource

Technology is expensive, but it is essential to our work. Fortunately, there is an organization called **CompuMentor** (www.compumentor.org), a nonprofit that helps other nonprofits enhance productivity and build sustainable technology systems that support their missions. TechSoup.org is CompuMentor's resource website for nonprofits, featuring how-to articles, online discussions, and donated and discounted technology products.

www.americanheart.org. Since February 2006, more than 26,000 people have listened to podcasts on the American Heart Association website.

Blogging

Many nonprofit websites offer people the opportunity to write blog posts or comment on the organization's blog posts to share their opinions on issues, fund-raising ideas, and related current-event news. Any organization can launch a blog for free through a provider such as www.blogger.com or www.wordpress.com. Women who participate in the American Heart Association's 2007 Choose To Move Challenge campaign, a free physical activity program for women, have been maintaining blogs since March 2007. Consumers from across the country have followed these women through their blog entries, interacting with the bloggers and asking questions about the success and struggles of the individual women. This is a great way to build public awareness of your organization in a personal, fun way. You'll also discover that people who never came across your organization's work in the offline world will find you online and become involved. Blogging expands your reach, your brand, and your mindshare.

BEST PRACTICE IN DIVERSITY

Focusing on diversity is not just the right thing to do, it is a critical business strategy for any organization to achieve its mission. You would be hard-pressed today to find a major corporation without a diversity initiative, and nonprofits need to follow suit. At the American Heart Association, we understand that employing individuals and recruiting volunteers with diverse attributes and backgrounds and reaching out to customers with similarly diverse characteristics is vital to achieving our mission.

For today's younger donors and staff members, diversity is an expectation and an absolute imperative. One in three members of Generation Y (those born after 1980) is a person of color. This generation feels uncomfortable with homogeneity and will abandon organizations that do not reflect the diversity of the world.

At the American Heart Association, we know that cardiovascular diseases and stroke afflict people of all races, ethnicities, genders, religions, ages, sexual orientations, national origins, and disabilities. We are committed to ensuring that our workforce and volunteers reflect America's diverse population. We know that such diversity enriches us with the talent, energy, perspective, and inspiration we need to achieve our mission.

Here are some best-practice diversity strategies that have helped us keep our organization vital and better serve our mission.

External Research

A good way to begin any diversity initiative is to gather research and experiences from other organizations. This includes attending conferences and other types of sessions that focus on contemporary diversity practices.

> **Recommended Resources**
>
> Good resources for diversity information and event listings include **DiversityInc** (www.diversityinc.com) and Georgetown University's **National Center for Cultural Competence** (www11.georgetown.edu/research/gucchd/nccc/).

Diverse Partnerships

As a health organization, we are acutely aware that people of different cultural backgrounds have greater or lesser risks for certain diseases. For instance, the incidence of stroke among African-Americans is two to three times greater than that for Caucasians. We started the Power To End Stroke initiative to try to reduce the risk of stroke in this community. Yolanda King, daughter of Martin Luther King, Jr., agreed to be the volunteer chair of this initiative. She was an extraordinarily active and effective volunteer—always right there on the front lines. In July 2007, we had the second annual Power To End Stroke gathering in Atlanta, and everyone loved Yolanda. She made a huge difference in our recruiting efforts and in getting the public engaged in this issue. Everyone wanted to have a photo taken with Yolanda. She and I stayed for about forty-five minutes after the event and posed for photos with every single person who wanted one. She would not leave until everyone had a picture. I said good-bye to her that evening, looking forward to the next opportunity to work with her. Tragically, she died of a heart problem shortly after that event, taken from us far too soon.

I was honored to be asked to speak at the celebration of her life. My being asked had nothing to do with being Cass Wheeler, of course. It had everything to do with being CEO of the American Heart Association. The Power To End Stroke soared under Yolanda's brief leadership. We simply would not be where we are today with this campaign were it not for her leadership. Few people could say no to Yolanda. She was an incredibly energetic, yet self-effacing, leader.

In addition to working with Yolanda, the American Heart Association has expanded and strengthened its base of diverse partners to fight heart disease and stroke in minority communities. Here are some examples, to demonstrate the depth and breadth of such partnerships:

- The National Minority Health Month Foundation launched the Power To End Stroke initiative with us.
- The Indian Health Service partnered with us to reduce the impact of heart disease and stroke among Native Americans at the national, state, and local levels.
- Delta Sigma Theta, Inc., one of the largest African-American sororities, is a partner in Go Red For Women and serves as a vital link for American Heart Association affiliates in local communities.
- The U.S. Department of Health and Human Services, Office of Minority Health, is working with us to develop a pilot initiative to reduce disparities in health care for minority populations.
- To reach the Hispanic population, we provide ongoing heart disease and stroke information for Univision Network's online health section. We recently began providing Spanish-language media with translations of relevant research news from our scientific journals.

With whom could your organization partner to reach a more diverse group of donors, volunteers, staff members, and beneficiaries for your good work? If you find that your organization is too homogeneous, you might consider networking with diverse organizations in your community, such as professional associations, clubs, or religious organizations.

Supplier Diversity

This initiative aims to build business relationships with diverse suppliers and simultaneously expand our pool of qualified suppliers. A supplier diversity program helps to raise an organization's profile while building trust in the communities it seeks to serve, promoting economic growth, and, ultimately, improving effectiveness in reaching all people. If you are serving diverse people and raising funds from diverse donors, then it makes sense to source your office supplies and services from diverse vendors.

> **Recommended Resource**
>
> For more information on how for-profit organizations set up and run supplier diversity programs, refer to the **National Minority Supplier Development Council** (www.nmsdc.org) and the **Women's Business Enterprise National Council** (www.wbenc.org).

Internal Affinity Groups

If you run a large organization, you might consider the formation of internal affinity groups. An affinity group is a self-sufficient support system inside your organization made up of people who identify with or support a certain issue. Corporations have affinity groups for a wide variety of issues, such as working mothers, Latinos, lesbian/gay/bisexual/transgendered people, and technology workers. The groups provide opportunities for networking, mentoring, socializing, and advocating on behalf of the group within the organization. Beginning in January 2007, four affinity groups formed within the American Heart Association: Moms @ Work, Amigos Haciendo Amigos, Going and Growing Through Grief, and Book Buddies. These groups create a friendly place to work and help employees on the job, as well as helping them deal with the everyday stresses of life.

Annual Diversity Report

In 2006, the American Heart Association developed and published its initial annual diversity report. The full report is available to the public at www.americanheart.org and includes information about our consumer initiatives (such as the Power To End Stroke and culturally specific programs related to Go Red For Women) and our internal initiatives. It also tracks our progress toward diversity goals, including more strategic alliances with diverse organizations on the regional level; more diversity among our national board of directors, high-level committees, and metropolitan boards; and increased news media coverage of our cultural health initiatives.

Formation of a CEO Diversity Advisory Cabinet

This is a group of staff members that meets quarterly to research, support, and implement diversity-related best practices. This includes all of the aforementioned topics and such special events as the annual Diversity Week and applying for awards and recognition for our diversity efforts. Note that such awards exist at national and local levels. If you are a leader in the diversity arena, such awards can be a nice boost for your supporters and your overall brand.

A BOLD MOVE: CREATING A NEW DIVISION

Perhaps the most difficult innovation to make is a major organizational realignment. Chapter 2 discussed the American Heart Association's decision to consolidate the number of regional affiliates and develop multiple channels of distribution. Both of these massive changes took place because they served the AHA's mission: building healthier lives free of cardiovascular diseases and stroke.

Let's focus on the "and stroke" portion of that mission. The American Heart Association began funding stroke research and stroke-related programs in the 1950s. Years later, we created a scientific journal and began to sponsor an international stroke conference of scientific and medical experts. However, a 1994 market study revealed that most people still did not associate stroke with cardiovascular disease and therefore didn't necessarily realize that the American Heart Association was doing anything to combat the disease. We decided that we needed to ratchet up our efforts in this area.

Initially, we formed a stroke division to help increase the focus on stroke prevention in all of our programs, products, and services. Our board of directors also considered changing the American Heart Association name to include the word *stroke*. Instead, we decided to take the unprecedented move of creating a new division—the American Stroke Association (ASA). The goals of this bold move were to:

- Showcase our commitment to stroke prevention.
- More closely integrate our existing stroke activities with the American Heart Association's newly established goals and strategies—namely, our bold goal to reduce coronary heart disease and stroke by 25 percent by 2010.
- Make stroke prevention a greater public priority.
- Increase awareness that the American Heart Association is the organization to turn to for information about stroke. Without the word *stroke* in the organization's name, people didn't make the connection. Now our official logo includes the traditional heart and torch image with both "American Heart Association" and "American Stroke Association" appearing with it.

Today, the American Stroke Association is the division of the American Heart Association focused exclusively on reducing disability and death from stroke through research, education, fund-raising, and advocacy. If you think this sounds like a corporate spin-off, you are exactly right, from a branding perspective. We took the move directly from the for-profit playbook, and for the same reasons: focus, resources, and impact.

Of course, the move opened fund-raising opportunities. In 1999, the Bugher Foundation committed $7.5 million over eight years to the AHA for stroke research, and it recently renewed its commitment. The new American Stroke Association developed or revised more than forty programs, products, and services. One product, the Acute Stroke Treatment Program, was launched to give hospitals the tools needed to create primary stroke centers.

The creation of the American Stroke Association also opened the doors for new strategic alliances with the Centers for Disease Control and Prevention; the National Heart, Lung and Blood Institute; and the National Institute for Neurological Disorders and Stroke. In 2002, the Ad Council (www.adcouncil.org) agreed to do a multimillion-dollar public service awareness campaign with the American Stroke Association. This resulted in significant advances in the recognition of stroke as a major-emergency 9-1-1 problem. According to a series of tracking surveys conducted in 2005, 2006, and 2007 by the AHA as part of its national public service advertising campaign, there have been significant increases relative to general awareness of stroke. From 2005 to 2007 there was an increase (from 60 percent in 2005 to 65 percent in 2007) in the percentage of respondents who reported that they would specifically respond to symptoms of stroke by calling 9-1-1 immediately. Confidence in recognizing the warning signs of stroke significantly increased from 20 percent in 2005 to 30 percent in 2007.

In another major thrust that holds the promise of saving thousands of lives, the ASA has joined with the Joint Commission on Accreditation of Healthcare Organizations in creating the voluntary Primary Stroke Center Certification Program. This program enables consumers and emergency medical professionals to identify hospitals that are equipped to treat acute stroke according to nationally recognized standards. The National Institute for Neurological Disorders and Stroke, the American Academy of Neurology, and the ASA have a free online training tool to teach critical stroke assessment skills to hospital-based professionals. The American Stroke Association also works with the American Academy of Neurology and the American Academy of Family Physicians on a series of stroke prevention self-assessment tools that primary care physicians can provide to their patients. None of these tools existed previously, but the existence of a dedicated division within the AHA's organizational structure now ensures that stroke receives the full attention and resources it deserves.

The ASA publishes *Stroke Connection*, a magazine with a circulation of 112,000 for stroke patients, their families, and caregivers. The ASA also operates the Stroke Family Warmline, which offers support for stroke survivors and their families. The ASA's International Stroke Conference draws 4,500 scientific experts, physicians, and other healthcare professionals to share the latest scientific information. Establishing the American Stroke Association as a brand gave us the opportunity to focus our resources and to be more accountable to our goals for the prevention of strokes.

The branding also provided us with the opportunity to preserve the long-term equity and capital that we had in the American Heart Association's name, while making a clear public statement about our commitment to the area of stroke. Since creating the American Stroke Association, we have been approached by other large nonprofits faced with similar situations. For instance, the Leukemia Society, as it was then called, approached us for advice, and we gladly sent a team to meet with them to talk about what we had done. They seriously considered the branding option, but, after careful consideration, decided to change the name of their organization to the Leukemia & Lymphoma Society in order to highlight both issues. Their decision was more in line with their mission and strategic plans. There is no "right" decision in this case, but we were pleased that they asked for our input. As nonprofit leaders implementing more for-profit strategies, we are essentially writing our own playbooks and can all benefit by comparing notes and sharing best practices with each other. This book, of course, is one step toward that goal. Although your organization may not be large enough to create a separate division, it is important that you regularly assess whether your organization's name and brand are fully expressing the important work that you do.

MAKING ROOM FOR INNOVATION AND IMPROVEMENT

Having shared all of these ideas for bold moves and best practices, it is time for the caveat: Beware of doing too much. Particularly in the nonprofit sector, where you have a broad constituency (diverse people and audiences) and a lot of demands, you have to make sure you do not take on too much. This is an easy trap. After all, it is much more fun to invent than to execute. It is easy to brainstorm lots of cool Web initiatives and partnerships, but without a clear plan of execution the likelihood of failure is much greater than the chance of success.

So how do you make room for all this exciting innovation? Out with the old! I call this a *purge mentality*: You should declutter your closet before buying a new wardrobe. When you look at your organization with this mentality, you begin to see practices, projects, and even small administrative tasks that are no longer necessary. Becoming aware of them is the easy part, however; eliminating them is much more of a challenge. Organizational inertia is a powerful thing. Both staff and volunteers become wedded to favorite projects and ways of doing business. It takes a systematic process and discipline to declutter. Every year or so, each department looks at the functions it provides and identifies all the things it does, asking what it needs to be doing that is innovative and new and what it can actually stop doing.

Often, the answer is "reports." During a purge, one AHA department decided to publish its report twice a year instead of quarterly. Other departments simply cut out some reports entirely. Here was their strategy: "Let's see if anyone even asks about the report if we do not publish it next quarter." No one did, so they stopped! In another department, they decided to forgo comprehensive meeting minutes and instead only distribute a list of action steps required after a meeting. Of course, some reports are essential, so there are a few questions to ask before eliminating a report. What decisions are made based on this report? Is it "just" information? The important lesson is not about the specific decisions made but the process of taking a fresh look.

> **Leadership Lesson**
>
> Declutter projects and processes regularly, to make sure you are not being held hostage to the way things have always been done.

Technology also provides an opportunity to streamline processes and free up time to pursue new projects. Perhaps a process that used to take twenty-three steps can now be accomplished in fourteen steps. At the more strategic level, what products are nearing the end of their life cycle and need to be dropped? What initiatives used to be successful but do not now have quite the return on investment? Nothing lasts forever. You have to stop periodically and make sure that what you are doing is showing a return, and not just any return but the best return against your strategic goals using the resources available. Otherwise, you are wasting resources, even if you are doing so with the best of intentions. It is one thing to come in new to your position and kick over someone else's applecart. The real challenge is to kick over your own.

CHAPTER 5 TAKEAWAYS

- **The status quo is not good enough.** We must continually challenge ourselves to do more. There is no reason that nonprofits cannot be early adopters, bold innovators, and best-in-class practitioners. Where can you be more innovative? More creative? More tech savvy? More streamlined? More appealing to the next generation of donors and volunteers?
- **To improve your volunteer fund-raising efforts, follow the Rule of Three.** One-third of the volunteers you recruit will do the job superbly. One-third will do the job, but you are going to have to push them and encourage them and really stay on top of them. And one-third are simply not ever going to do what they have been asked to do. If you accept this Rule of Three as a fact, you can plan accordingly and overrecruit a fund-raising team.
- **Leverage new technologies.** All of your initiatives should involve a comprehensive Web strategy. Think social networking, blogs, webcasts, podcasts, and user-generated content. If you are not ahead of the curve with technology, you will quickly fall behind. Technological competence should be on every organization's list of best practices.
- **Incorporate diversity into your efforts.** Diversity is not optional. Your organization must reflect the diversity of your constituents to serve them most effectively. Look to partnerships, local networking opportunities, supplier diversity, and affinity groups to learn about best practices and ensure equal services and opportunities for all.
- **Remember to declutter.** The only way to have room for innovation is to let go of programs, activities, and products that no longer produce a return on investment. Regularly take a fresh look at your efforts and purge what is no longer necessary. Just because you have always done something does not mean it is still a good idea.

CHAPTER 6

BUILDING THE BEST STAFF

One of the most important things we do for our organizations is make hiring decisions. It is crucial that we find and retain employees who are qualified, skilled, and experienced. In the nonprofit world, we have an additional qualification: commitment to our mission.

Successfully building and leading any team is, in some ways, like being the head coach of a sports team. You have to evaluate the talent you have, train team members to achieve their maximum potential, and bring in new players that have different or better skills than players currently on your roster. And since we are talking about living, breathing human beings, you have to be flexible and deal with the inevitable curveballs.

Whether a sports team or a nonprofit community organization, we cannot reach breakthrough goals without having stellar people. That takes well-thought-out and carefully executed strategies to recruit, develop, and retain them. We cannot expect people to perform to our standards if we do not set clear performance expectations. If this language sounds straight out of the for-profit playbook, it is. When it comes to recruiting, hiring, managing, motivating, and leading employees, there are many techniques developed in the for-profit business world that work equally well in a nonprofit culture. As you will see in this chapter, the American Heart Association and other nonprofits have demonstrated that these for-profit people strategies also work for nonprofits.

In nonprofits, of course, the workforce includes both staff and volunteers. This chapter and the next focus on best practices for leading and managing paid staff. Chapter 8 focuses on leading and guiding your volunteers.

NONPROFITS AND THE LEADERSHIP DEFICIT

The competition for top talent is tough now and will only get tougher in the years ahead. Every year, seasoned performers retire or leave our ranks and must be replaced. Across the board—in government, nonprofit, and for-profit organizations—there is going to be a shortage of talented employees as the baby boomers retire. According to the Bridgespan Group, a nonprofit management support organization, the number of new senior managers needed in the nonprofit sector will increase from 56,000 to 78,000 between 2006 and 2016. The group's 2007 report, "The Nonprofit Sector's Leadership Deficit," projects a cumulative total of 640,000 senior positions that will need to be filled.

One example of this impending deficit can be found in the museum management field. At the time of this book's writing, several of the most prominent museums in the United States—the Metropolitan Museum of Art, the Guggenheim, and the Philadelphia Museum of Art—are all seeking new directors. According to Millicent Gaudieri, quoted in a *Newsweek* article on the topic, "We're facing a generational shift right now."

> **Recommended Resource**
>
> **"The Nonprofit Sector's Leadership Deficit,"** a report by the Bridgespan Group, is available for download at http://www.bridgespangroup.org/kno_articles_leadershipdeficit.html.

The good news is that many of today's young people seem attracted to careers in the nonprofit sector. Volunteerism rates are way up among teenagers and college students, more young people are voting, service programs such as Teach For America are more popular than ever and, according to *The Chronicle of Philanthropy*, there has been a large jump in the number of colleges offering courses in nonprofit management—up to 250 colleges and counting.

I believe that we, as nonprofit leaders, have an obligation to encourage more young people to enter nonprofit work. We can speak at colleges and write op-eds and media articles about the fulfillment of working for a nonprofit organization. Just as it is our job to make nonprofits well-run and great places to work, it is also our job to attract the best and the brightest to our field.

The most important accomplishment we can achieve as managers at any level is to ensure the future success of our operations—by leaving the reins in capable hands once we are gone. Creating a culture with an abundance of high performers—who have maximum impact on advancing your mission—is the legacy we should all aspire to leave.

CAN NONPROFITS REALLY ATTRACT AND RETAIN TOP TALENT?

The short answer to this question is yes! Nonprofits do face particular challenges to recruiting the best talent, but there are ways to address each challenge. We also offer some significant benefits that for-profits cannot offer to employees. Let's take a closer look.

The Challenges: Lower Pay, Fewer Benefits, and Fewer Advancement Opportunities

For many nonprofits, these are realities that cannot be ignored. Sometimes, the budget is just not there to pay a higher salary and provide top-tier benefits. However, attitudes in the nonprofit community have shifted over the years to the belief that we can be more competitive. There is greater recognition that if we don't have good, capable paid staff it is going to be hard to recruit good, capable volunteers—the two go hand in hand. The American Heart Association has an objective to set its salary ranges at the seventy-fifth percentile of comparable nonprofit jobs and the fiftieth percentile of comparable for-profit jobs (you can research comparable salaries for your industry and region at www.salary.com).

If higher salaries are not possible for your organization, an increasing number of nonprofits are willing to pay lump-sum year-end performance incentives to employees who achieve measurably higher results. If donors are expecting nonprofits to demonstrate tangible results, then we have to pay for more highly skilled staff or at least offer performance incentives. You can also offer nonmonetary perks, such as flexible work hours, telecommuting, and generous vacation policies.

Nonprofits also have a problem with retention. Many people sign on with a nonprofit with the attitude that they will try this kind of work for a year or two and move on. This issue particularly affects smaller nonprofits that have fewer positions overall, but even at a large organization like the American Heart Association, turnover is highest in an employee's first one to three years. However, if we can retain an employee past that three-year mark, he or she is likely to become a long-term employee. This is where onboarding, training, and good management come into play. Ongoing professional development is a major benefit, especially for younger workers who are still figuring out their career paths.

Lesson Learned

Time spent coaching and providing skills training builds loyalty and enthusiasm among your employees. The sink-or-swim mentality won't do your retention efforts any favors.

The Advantages: Mission and Challenge

Yes, we face challenges, but nonprofits also offer some benefits that for-profits cannot. First and foremost on this list is mission. In your recruitment and retention efforts, be sure to emphasize the opportunity your employees have to make the world a better place. At the American Heart Association, we explain to potential employees that they will be an important part of saving lives and changing lives. Meaningful work is an enormous selling point.

Additionally, nonprofits can use a lean operating style as a selling point. We can give employees early and plentiful opportunities to take on challenges and a scope of work that people might not enjoy for years in the for-profit sector.

Finally, think about the selling points unique to your organization's culture. Do you provide the opportunity to spend time with children? To travel to exciting destinations? To work outside? To hobnob with politicians? At the American Heart Association, we highlight the fact that, while we are performance driven, we are informal, team oriented, and a fun place to work, where people genuinely care about one another. Many people would trade a few thousand dollars for a happy work environment.

You Need a People Strategy

Culture, perks, and training are great, but they do not add up to a clearly defined success strategy for hiring the best people. You need to integrate your talent management strategy with your overall mission and long-term strategic plan. We have a strategy for everything else in our organizations, so why wouldn't we have a strategy for our workforce?

If you have never thought about how your talent management fits into your overall long-term strategic planning, you are not alone. A 2008 McKinsey report indicated that too many organizations still dismiss talent management as a short-term tactical problem rather than an integral part of a long-term business strategy requiring the attention of top-level management. They conclude that a lack of talent is a serious barrier to growth.

Hiring and developing great people is not a one-time program to implement; it is a way of being all the time. You need to have a strategy and devote time and resources to build and maintain a top-notch staff. Great teams do not happen by accident, and people are your most valuable asset. You can't achieve your mission without them!

PEOPLE STRATEGY, PART I: ASSESSING TALENT

The American Heart Association has drawn on its own experience, as well as many other resources included in this chapter, to focus on attracting and retaining top talent. Our overall strategy, and the one I recommend to you, is to do the following:

1. Attract and retain *star performers* throughout your organization.
2. Improve or let go of underperforming employees.
3. Decide which positions or roles in your organization have the most impact on achieving your mission and breakthrough goals, then develop a specific plan for putting the right people in those *key positions*.

These strategies apply whether your organization has 5 employees or 50 or 500. This also means that once you have great people at any level, you have an ongoing plan so each person can learn and grow and stay in the organization. If you don't include retention and development in your people strategy, employees become easy prey for recruiters from other organizations. Part I looks at the first two items on the preceding list: attracting and retaining star performers and improving or letting go of underperforming employees. Part II examines the third item.

Identify High-Potential, Potential, and Low-Potential Employees

The people strategy I recommend to nonprofit organizations is based on the concept of *Topgrading*, a process developed by Bradford D. Smart. Topgrading is a process to improve an organization's interviewing, selection, development, and retention. It begins with assessing current employees and placing them in three categories: (1) High-Potential, (2) Medium-Potential, and (3) Low-Potential (Smart uses the terminology "A players," "B players," and "C players"). Begin to think about staff members in your organization and where they would fall in the following categories:

- **High-Potentials:** These are people who perform at an exceptionally high level and have clear potential to assume greater responsibility. High-Potential employees are superior performers who can and will make a substantial difference for your organization. They are your stars. According to a report published a decade ago by McKinsey, these individuals are twice as likely as other staff members to improve organizational growth and productivity. The American Heart Association's criteria for High-Potential status include being productive *and* promotable—someone who is good at his or her job and also wants to advance to a position of increased responsibility.

Clearly, we all want to have as many High-Potentials as possible in our organizations. The more we can focus on recruiting and developing High-Potentials, the better. However, it is important to note that a High-Potential job candidate is defined as the best person for the job *at the salary level available.* Brad Smart advises organizations to seek to hire someone from the top 10 percent of talent available at the salary range you are offering.

- **Medium-Potentials:** These people do their jobs well and have the ability to keep growing as their jobs evolve. A Medium-Potential employee is approaching that top performance level but needs some further development and experience to become a High-Potential player. Although you should strive to have High-Potentials in all positions, you will likely have a group of valuable individuals in this category—those who are good at their jobs but perhaps are not interested in or skilled at moving up.

- **Low-Potentials:** These are people who do not now and likely never will have the skills or emotional makeup to perform their jobs at the high level needed for you to reach your organizational goals. Low-Potentials need to be either moved into a job in which they can succeed or removed from the organization.

Note that there is no forced distribution of High-Potential, Medium-Potential, and Low-Potential employees. However, the goal of this process is to put a plan in place to maximize the number of High-Potential employees and to minimize the number of Low-Potential employees in your nonprofit. As an organization, it may take you a while to reach a common definition and understanding of specifically what is required to be in each category of potential, but it is a journey well worth beginning, knowing that it will evolve over time. The definitions don't have to be perfect to start.

Avoiding Hiring Mistakes

After you have assessed your existing staff, you need to turn to the hiring process. When hiring new employees, do your best to hire only High-Potentials. When you bring in new talent, commit to hiring peo-

> **Recommended Resource**
>
> ***Topgrading: How Leading Companies Win by Hiring, Coaching, and Keeping the Best People,*** by Bradford D. Smart, Ph.D. (Portfolio hardcover, revised edition, 2005). This book includes the full Topgrading interview guide and features a detailed case study on Brad Smart's work with the American Heart Association (www.topgrading.com).

ple who are the very best you can find for that position in the available salary range. This sounds obvious—who doesn't want good employees?—but mistakes are all too common in the nonprofit world. There are a few reasons for this. Often nonprofits believe—falsely, I think—that they can't attract the best people because they can't pay top dollar. Or they are so busy that they hire the best person they can find within a certain time frame, even if that candidate is not ideal. Another common mistake occurs when you are not clear in your own mind about the capabilities you need and, therefore, hire someone who doesn't meet a job's actual requirements.

How do you avoid these pitfalls? It can be challenging, but it is possible if you are truly committed to hiring only High-Potentials. Do not set your standards too low! If you are passionately committed to your mission, then you must have the right people working to achieve it. Here are some recommended practices:

- **Reconsider the *number* of employees you need.** If your funds are limited, then consider this: Would you be better off having fifteen Low-Potential and Medium-Potential employees (at lower salaries) or ten High-Potential employees (at higher salaries)?
- **Hold positions open for a longer period of time.** One of the most important lessons we have learned in our hiring practices at the American Heart Association is that it is often necessary to hold jobs open longer to hire top talent. The pressure can be intense, especially in a tightly run nonprofit, to accept a Low-Potential or Medium-Potential player now rather than continue recruiting for a High-Potential. You might find yourself saying things like "I know that John Doe is not the best candidate we can find for that salary, but a Medium-Potential player now can at least take the pressure

off and get some programs going!" This strategy is a poor one. Leaving a job unfilled for a while requires other people to work harder for a time to cover the extra work, but in the end it's always worth finding the right person. When a High-Potential person finally starts in a position, you know the wait was justified for the longer-term benefits. Think for a moment about the best employee you have ever supervised. Now imagine that your entire team performed at this level—how different your life would be and what a difference it would make to your organization.

- **Make everyone in your organization a recruiter.** Many nonprofits don't recruit the best talent they can because they are not using the best recruiters—their own employees. We can spend money and time with ads, e-mail blasts, and even head-hunting agencies while we miss out on the opportunity to have our own employees—especially the High-Potentials—recruiting from their personal and professional networks. Everyone in your organization should be a recruiter regardless of formal job description. Remind your staff that virtually every person with whom they come in contact could be a candidate for an interview. This is particularly true for the executive team. Recruiting is not just a human resources (HR) responsibility or even a senior team responsibility. The American Heart Association pays a finder's fee to staff members who refer a candidate whom we ultimately hire. This happens frequently, and without question we receive better candidates overall.

Effective Interviewing

If you are going to implement only one piece of advice you read in this book, I recommend that you improve the way in which you interview. Nothing improves your organization—and your ability to reach your goals—more than bringing in the very best people to work with you. As we all know, someone can look like a High-Potential but turn out to be a Low-Potential (or worse!) after a seemingly thorough interview process. The pain of hiring the wrong candidate can range from irritating to catastrophic. Some government studies have placed the cost of a mishire at twice the person's annual salary.[1] In the nonprofit world, we also must consider the impact that a mishire has on our mission and our volunteers.

I can already anticipate the biggest objection to the interviewing process I am about to describe: It's too time-consuming. Yes, it is very time-consuming. As CEO, I have participated in many interviews that have taken two to four hours. You may be thinking, "How can you invest that amount of time?" My response is, "How could I afford not to, especially given the work that we do?" I ask you to read with an open mind, particularly if you do not or your organization does not have the best track record for hiring top talent.

The following suggestions for improving your hiring process and practices refer to an organization with an HR person or department. If your organization does not have an HR department, you can still implement these concepts, or you might find an HR professional with an interest in your organization's mission who would gladly sign on as a volunteer to help.

- **Train people how to interview.** It is essential to train your hiring managers how to interview and hire the very best people for your organization's needs. Even if you have an HR function, your hiring managers need to be skilled in interviewing and selecting job candidates. To consistently hire excellent candidates, your organization needs to have a standard and consistent interview process. This requires training all hiring managers in what to look for, the questions to ask, and how to assess desired capabilities and other characteristics such as attitude, passion, work ethic, and cultural fit with your organization. Too often we assume that managers just know how to interview, when in reality most of us were just tossed in the water and have survived without much formal training and preparation. Consider running two-hour to four-hour training courses to better prepare hiring managers. You can also have inexperienced interviewers sit in to observe experienced interviewers.

- **Require the hiring manager to clearly identify the capabilities needed to do the job.** Make sure that everyone involved in the interviewing process has a sure knowledge of the job description and the capabilities required and that they know how to look for red flags from the applicant's resume, cover letter, career history form, or any other preinterview documents.

- **Conduct behavioral event interviews.** This type of interview—the type that I recommend and that we use at the American Heart Association—involves more than just asking a question and receiving a textbook answer. In a behavioral event interview, you ask the candidate to describe events that reveal examples of his or her work style, skills, and experience. For instance: "Tell me about a time that you had a tough situation with a volunteer and dealt with it effectively." Then, depending on the person's story, the interviewer can probe deeper. You can ask the person to cite examples from various jobs in order to see patterns emerge around certain capabilities such as addressing performance issues, building teams, setting aggressive goals, managing time, managing complex issues, and meeting deadlines.

Rather than asking *whether* the candidate can do X, behavioral event interviewing allows you to hear about *how* the candidate has done X and in what ways it was successful or unsuccessful. This substantially reduces the chances of hiring someone who can talk a good game but doesn't really have the experience and skills you need. If you are not sure how to ask behavior-based interview questions, browse through a book such as *High-Impact Interview Questions: 701 Behavior-Based Questions to Find the Right Person for Every Job*, by Victoria A. Hoevemeyer (AMACOM, 2005).

- **Consider using the CIDS interview format.** The exact behavioral event interview questions we use at the American Heart Association is called the CIDS, or *chronological in-depth structured*, interview. This interview format was developed by Brad Smart as an essential component of the Topgrading process (annual licensing fees to obtain the CIDS interview questions begin at $1,000 for small organizations). The CIDS interview process is the most powerful interviewing tool I have ever experienced. The CIDS format provides behavior-based questions in an order and a format that elicit the most truthful and helpful responses from job candidates.

  The CIDS process begins by asking job candidates to fill out a career history form and submit it prior to the interview. This form should reveal every full-time job the candidate has held. Most organizations ask candidates to fill out such a form, but the CIDS career history document is more in-depth. For instance, it asks for the starting and ending salary for each position, which allows you to form a better picture of how well the person performed in each position.

  In the actual interview, the CIDS format guides you through a series of questions to ask the candidate about each position held. It is behavior based, and by the time you ask the same ten to twelve questions about each position the candidate has held, you begin to see patterns emerge around certain capabilities. Then you close out with some open-ended questions about how the candidate assesses his or her own strengths and weaknesses, followed by probing questions about any capabilities that may not have surfaced in the earlier parts of the interview.

Every organization needs a consistent, disciplined interview and reference-checking process, and following a clear set of guidelines like CIDS ensures that you are thorough in your fact-finding and in the questions you ask each candidate.

- **Conduct tandem interviews.** Ideally, tandem interviews would be done by the hiring manager and another associate in a different position. The reason for two (or more) interviewers is so that everyone is hearing the same thing from the candidate at the same time. The interview is more thorough, and the interviewers play off one another and learn from one another's questions and comments. I have participated in interviews where there have been four of us! In such a situation it is essential to make the candidate feel comfortable, which can be done early on with some friendly social chitchat. The interview concludes with about thirty minutes for the candidate to ask questions of all the interviewers, and that discussion is enriched by having more than just the hiring manager's perspective provided.

- **Encourage interviewers to provide a balanced view of your organization.** Another pitfall to avoid is having interviewers who are too enthusiastic about your organization. You are more likely to encounter hiring mistakes if your interviewers are not pointing out up front what some of the frustrations of the position or the organization are apt to be. Every job has its downsides, and it is better to point these out proactively so that candidates come in with their eyes wide open.

- **Don't forget to interview for a candidate's fit with your mission and core values.** Remember that a job interview does not just assess a candidate's skills and experience but also his or her potential fit with your organization. The clearer you are about your mission, core values, and culture—the way you do business—the easier it is to assess a candidate's fit. For instance, the American Heart Association is primarily a decentralized, consensus-driven organization. Decisions are not simply made and mandated, so decision making is a slower process. Prospective employees need to know, understand, and be comfortable with this reality. No matter what, use the interview process to make sure a candidate will thrive in your organizational environment.

- **Have a consistent process for checking references.** This sounds like a no-brainer, but busy nonprofits can sometimes cut corners to save time and resources. Skipping a candidate's reference check is not the place to skimp. No matter how fantastic a candidate appears to be, reference checks are absolutely crucial. It is also important to approach them with a completely open mind. When checking references, subconsciously we want to prove ourselves right when in reality we need to listen for any subtle clues and try to prove ourselves wrong. At the beginning of each interview, tell candidates that they need to contact all of their past supervisors and arrange for you to check their references. Stated up front, this also helps encourage candor in the interview.

Retaining and Developing Existing Talent

As you begin to focus your hiring efforts on recruiting only High-Potentials, you also need strategies to retain your current High-Potentials and develop your Medium-Potentials and Low-Potentials into better performers.

First, in terms of employee morale and fairness, I believe that we have an ethical responsibility as supervisors to tell people how they are categorized. Even if you don't have a formal assessment process, you have a mental assessment of your staff—and they deserve to know what you think of them. This encourages candor and authenticity in the organization. At the American Heart Association, I have found that the High-Potential/Medium-Potential/Low-Potential process actually serves as a motivator for many people to continue to get better or to make a career change if necessary.

So, first and foremost, tell your High-Potential employees that they are High-Potentials! I want our High-Potential players to know that their managers think they are outstanding performers. The same goes for Medium-Potentials—let them know where they are succeeding and what they can do to excel. By not telling High-Potential and Medium-Potential players their status, people don't know what their future holds. It's important to tell people that they have a bright future with your organization. This simple act alone can help increase your employee retention rates. How often has a nonprofit lost a star performer to another organization because the person didn't think his or her future was very bright there and sought a change? This happens way too frequently. At the very least, opening up a discussion about an employee's future can help foster two-way communication between a manager and employee that can increase the manager's knowledge of the employee's aspirations. It also increases the employee's understanding of the organization and where he or she fits in the larger picture.

Addressing Poor Performers

As you can imagine, it is really fun to tell High-Potentials that they are High-Potentials. It is also encouraging to tell Medium-Potentials about their status and see them rise to the occasion and work hard to become High-Potentials. It is not so much fun to tell Low-Potentials about their status. We all have a natural tendency to procrastinate on some of the unpleasant tasks in life, and fewer things are more unpleasant for a manager than dealing with a performance issue. Remember, though, that there is no forced distribution, so not every manager has Low-Potential employees. However, if you do, you need to address the situation and not just hope the employees improve on their own.

When dealing with Low-Potential performance, you should ask a series of questions to assess where the problem really lies:

- **Does this person know how to do the job or the task required?** Oftentimes we as supervisors oversimplify and think the problem can be resolved with additional employee training, so we look for a quick fix and send that person off to some training course, hoping that will fix the problem. Some performance issues are related to a lack of training, but many—most, I would argue—are not.
- **Does this person clearly understand the results he or she needs to achieve and how to make that happen?** The results are nullified if a trail of arguments, wasted money, or angry volunteers accompany them.

- **Does this person have a plan with interim benchmarks so he or she knows how to get from point A to point B?** Have you provided the tools and resources necessary to accomplish the job you have asked this person to do?
- **Is this person receiving time and coaching from you as his or her manager?** Sometimes the problem lies with the way the person is being managed. If this is the case, the performance issue may really lie with you.

After asking these questions, have a meeting with the Low-Potential performer during which you specifically outline the gap in performance. Work with this person on developing a plan to take corrective action, with interim benchmarks and deadlines such as giving them 60 to 120 days to correct the performance lapse. If improvement is not made, the employee must understand that he or she will be moved to another job or terminated. The corrective plan and timetable need to be confirmed in writing, with a statement that if it is not accomplished the employee will not continue in the current position. I have observed over the years that communicating this last part verbally doesn't have nearly the impact as seeing it in writing. Sometimes people just block out the verbal "moved to another job or terminated," and any subsequent action comes as a shock. Putting your intentions in writing is key. If you work with Low-Potentials to improve their status and they do not meet their interim benchmarks, you have to act.

There is a positive way to think about this: Everyone wants to be in a position where he or she can be successful. Low-Potentials need to know that they are not succeeding in their current roles. Often, they already know or strongly suspect that they are not performing up to expectations. Not only do you owe it to your organization, its volunteers, and its donors to address low-performing staff members, you owe it to the individuals themselves. I deeply believe that everyone wants to be a star somewhere and that everyone can be a star if they can find the right position and organization in which to reach their full potential.

Another reason it is so crucial to address your Low-Potential employees is that they are a drag on the rest of the staff. You cannot retain stars if you don't address poor performers. The stars want to soar and work with a stimulating team of other stars.

> **Lesson Learned**
>
> If you do not address the issue of Low-Potential employees, the Medium-Potentials and High-Potentials will leave because they want the stimulation and challenges of working with true peers. Addressing poor performers helps them find a better fit and also helps you retain the best and the brightest.

Proven Results

How has this process worked in practice at the American Heart Association? Our employees, across the board, have improved their performance since we implemented a version of Topgrading—the assessment and placement of existing staff into the three categories. In 2000, 20 percent of the top 250 managers were judged to be High-Potential. By 2004, 60 percent were High-Potential players. Results certainly vary from organization to organization, but with serious attention to your talent strategy, your organization can achieve such significant results. The rigorous system we now use organization-wide helps ensure that this is not just grade inflation or managers learning to game the system but constitutes measurable improvements in performance.

It is not likely that you will achieve 100 percent High-Potential staff, but large increases such as those at the American Heart Association can make a tremendous difference—helping you improve your daily operations and move closer to achieving your mission and breakthrough goals.

PEOPLE STRATEGY, PART II: IDENTIFYING KEY POSITIONS

There is an additional layer to the American Heart Association's talent strategy that is quite different, and although it is still relatively new there is every indication it will produce extraordinary results. As much progress as we had made in recruiting, hiring, and assessing employees by level of potential, we knew we had to do more to win with talent. We decided to create a task force consisting of members of the senior team and senior HR staff, and we charged them with taking us to the next level in talent retention and development. This resulted in linking our HR strategies more directly to our strategic business plan. In other words, we wanted to ensure that we had as many High-Potential employees as possible, but more specifically we wanted as many High-Potential employees as possible in jobs that most impacted our strategic goals. This resulted in bringing in those outside eyes again in the form of Mark Huselid, a professor at Rutgers University, who led us through a review of our strategic plan to identify all the capabilities that we had to be good at in order to achieve our goals. The capabilities we identified were as follows:

- Fund-raising
- Volunteer guidance and management
- Strategic talent management
- Advocacy/influence
- Public/media relations
- Partnerships/alliances
- Consensus building
- Collaboration
- Communication/education
- Customer relationship management
- Cultural competence
- Training/development
- Organizational agility
- Anticipation/forecasting

Next, we polled 100 of our top performers to ask: Are there a few of these capabilities where we need to be exceptional in order to achieve our breakthrough goals? Here are the questions we asked to ascertain our top capabilities:

- How important is this capability in terms of achieving our strategic goals?

- To what extent would this capability represent a distinctive difference/advantage compared to other nonprofits?
- What impact would this capability have on customer perception of the value of programs/products/services?
- What is the current level of performance for this capability?
- If this capability is underperforming, to what extent would a significant upgrade of talent in this area have an impact?
- Imagine you have 100 investment points to distribute across each of these capabilities. Where would you invest to yield the highest return?

Based on the responses to these questions, we found that three capabilities received the highest rating of importance and therefore have the biggest impact on our potential success. Our three highest-impact capability areas are:

1. Fund-raising
2. Volunteer guidance and management
3. Strategic talent management

We designated these three capabilities as the most important and deemed the rest of the competencies *foundational*—they are the necessary foundation of our success. This then led to the inevitable, and perhaps most important, final question:

- Which positions in the American Heart Association have the greatest impact on our three strategic capabilities?

The jobs at the American Heart Association that had the most impact on fund-raising, volunteer guidance, and strategic talent management were declared *key positions*. We determined as a principle going into the process that the list of key positions might evolve over time. To begin, Mark Huselid advised us to limit our list to, at most, 15 percent of the jobs within the AHA. An important distinction is that we are talking about key *positions*, not key people. Every position in an organization is important, but not every position has maximum impact on fund-raising, volunteer guidance, and strategic talent management— or whatever you determine your organization's key capabilities to be.

Here are the criteria we used to define which jobs at the AHA would be classified as key positions:

- **Strategic impact:** Does this position have a disproportionate impact on the AHA's ability to execute some part of its business strategy related to fund-raising, volunteer guidance, and strategic talent management?
- **Performance variability:** Is the gap between high and low performers in this role substantial? As an example, if you looked at the American Heart Association's top fifty metro markets, are there some that are fund-raising twice or three times as much per capita as others? That is a substantial performance variability that cannot be accounted for based solely on the wealth of the population. Getting High-Potentials in each of these positions could possibly close that variability gap and accelerate growth.
- **Impact of top talent:** Is this a position where top talent would significantly enhance the success in achieving a business strategy related to fund-raising, volunteer guidance, and/or strategic talent management?
- **Difficulty to get:** Is it particularly difficult to attract and retain top talent in this role?

We eventually identified 230 positions as meeting the preceding criteria. What we were ultimately striving for was to have High-Potential players in High-Potential positions that have the most impact on the AHA's ability to achieve its strategic goals. Key positions fall across many departments of the organization, ranging from health strategies to fund-raising to operational areas. A few examples of key positions are the executive director positions of the top fifty metro markets, the communications director positions of the top fifteen media markets, and the nine senior HR staff positions of the eight regional affiliates and the national center. Note that positions that are not designated as *key* are defined as *foundation positions*—because they represent the foundation of our success.

We then took another bold step and decided that we would adopt a philosophy of equity versus equality. With an equality philosophy, all employees are treated pretty much the same. With an equity philosophy, jobs are differentiated for investment of time and resources based on their ability to impact strategy. As an example, we would invest in training for all employees, but we would invest more training dollars and time for employees occupying key positions. All employees are important, and all employees receive training, development, and opportunities to advance, but there is a greater investment in the employees in key positions.

Maintaining Bench Strength: Succession Planning

Now that we have talked about the importance of hiring and developing High-Potential employees throughout the organization and placing them in key positions, you are starting to get a picture of what a first-rate workforce looks like and how to develop one. But as we all know, you have to continually cultivate new talent. Leaders at every level need to make sure their bench strength is adequate. When positions open, you need to know that you have people inside your organization who are qualified and ready to move up.

The basis for succession planning begins with regular talent reviews: Whom do you have now, where are they going, and whom will you need in the future? I recommend splitting your talent reviews into two types: (1) review of all employees and (2) review of successors for key positions. Here is how each one works at the American Heart Association:

- **Talent review for all positions:** We hold meetings annually with functional and regional executive vice presidents (EVPs) to review their classifications of each of their direct reports—High-Potential, Medium-Potential, Low-Potential—and then to identify possible successors within their region or function who are ready to move into these positions either now, in one to two years, or in three to five years. We also review development plans for each possible successor. This process then cascades down through each region and each function.
- **Talent review for key positions:** Quarterly meetings of the senior team are held to look at one-fourth of the key positions and to identify the successors (from all across the organization, not just within their region) who are ready to move into a key position now, in one to two years, or in three to five years. Again, a development plan is reviewed for each potential successor.

Based on these talent reviews, managers help their employees create individual staff development plans. These plans include recommending them for internal and external training courses, including them as observers in internal meetings to enable them to develop a broader perspective, appointing them to a task force to address a specific issue, sending them to travel for a day with an internal expert in a particular job, or even providing them with short-term stretch assignments to encourage them to develop their competencies in a potentially more challenging role. Our investment of resources in these development plans is based on whether the employee is in a foundational or a key position.

If you are at the beginning stages of succession planning, start to think about the strength of staff members who could move up in the future. It is surprising how many organizations do not proactively plan for future staffing needs, especially for key positions. You also should talk to your employees about their desires for the future. We owe it to our employees to know their dreams and hopes and aspirations so that they stay with the organization and are more helpful in achieving its mission. When people are personally fulfilled, they are more productive and creative. Asking your employees where they want to go and what they want to do—and what your organization can do to help— serves both the employee and the organization's mission.

The responsibility for the training and development of up-and-coming staff members is most effective if shared by the organization and the individual:

- **The organization** has a responsibility to help people grow and develop, either through internal programs or by providing reimbursement for external education and development. Although most nonprofits do not have the resources for tuition reimbursement, they can and should offer as many training opportunities as possible. Many training organizations and consultants offer nonprofits a discount or even free training when they have empty slots. Others are willing to provide a discount to nonprofit organizations or provide special nonprofit-based training that is free or underwritten by a sponsor. Another option is to have one of your High-Potential stars give a presentation on a topic in which he or she is an expert.

- **The individual** has a responsibility for his or her self-development as well. The skills required to be successful in a job today may not be the skills to ensure that a person is successful a few years from now. Employees must take it upon themselves to make sure they are keeping pace with changes in technology, management, the overall field or industry, and their positions' specific functional skills. E-newsletters, blogs, social networking groups, and Listservs are all great ways to stay on top of trends. It is also a good idea to encourage your employees to join committees and boards of other nonprofit organizations or professional associations to add to their skill sets and professional networks.

Part of our training and retention strategy is to help employees see a career path for themselves at the American Heart Association. You can discuss a few potential career paths, depending on the size of your organization. These discussions should coordinate with your thinking about succession planning. At our organization, each supervisor discusses one to two possible career paths with each employee and helps to develop a training/experience plan tailored to the person's objective. At a smaller organization, these types of conversations can take place directly with the executive director. They are great for employee morale and for keeping the organization's leaders in touch with employees at all levels.

CHAPTER 6 TAKEAWAYS

- **You must have a people strategy.** Developing your staff is not a program to implement; it is a way of being. To be most effective, your workforce strategy should be driven by and support your strategic plan.

- **Implement an assessment process** for existing staff. Identify the High-Potentials, Medium-Potentials, and Low-Potentials. Then you can construct development plans to help the High-Potentials get even better, to help the Medium-Potentials develop and become High-Potentials, and to move Low-Potentials into positions inside or outside the organization where they can become High-Potentials. All these actions are intended to foster higher performance and better retention for all staff.

- **Have a consistent and thorough interview and reference checking process.** If you do nothing else to improve your organization, improve the interviewing process for new employees. Train managers in behavioral interviewing and make sure you have a rigorous process to hire only people considered to be High-Potential players.

- **Identify key positions that can have the highest impact on achieving your goals and make them the first priority to fill with High-Potentials.** You achieve the best results possible when you have High-Potential players in key positions to accomplish the most important strategic goals of your organization.

- **Retain your best employees to ensure your future success.** Provide ongoing talent reviews, offer training and growth opportunities, define future career opportunities, and assist employees in developing plans to help them achieve their goals. Invest disproportionately in employees who have a greater impact on achieving your organization's goals.

CHAPTER 7

INSPIRING THE BEST WORK

Managing Nonprofit Employees

Once you have a great team on board, how do you inspire, lead, and manage them to achieve all that they are capable of? Managing in a nonprofit environment is an art comprising some for-profit techniques, some personal development on the part of the manager, and some good, solid common sense. The challenge and the opportunity of being a manager lies in the fact that we do this job in a constantly changing environment: people, situations, and outside forces can change on a dime and our employees look to us for consistent leadership through it all.

Unfortunately, many nonprofit workers have fallen into management roles without giving much thought to what that responsibility entails. Or, as is increasingly common today, other nonprofit managers come from for-profit backgrounds and have not adapted their style and skills to the nonprofit environment. Fortunately, management is a skill that can be taught, learned, and improved. The only prerequisite is a desire to improve.

ANATOMY OF A GREAT NONPROFIT MANAGER

Over the years, through my work and observations of staff members at all levels, I have found that one of the most powerful ways to lead is by example. No matter what the size or mission of your organization, you cannot expect others to do what you are not willing to do yourself. And your attitude sets the tone—positively or negatively—for the people you manage. This does not mean that you have to be a superhero and always be perfect. It means that the more attention you pay to your own personal and professional development as a leader, the better your team will be.

Leading—whether you currently have direct management oversight of other people or you aspire to that type of position—means modeling the behaviors you want your team members to have. According to Bill George, author of *True North: Discover Your Authentic Leadership*, "[Authentic leaders] lead with their whole selves—their hearts as well as their heads. They don't get pulled off course by seductions and pressures. Every leader who has failed, that I've seen, has not failed to lead other people, they've failed to lead themselves."[1]

Recommended Resource

True North: Discover Your Authentic Leadership, by Bill George, with Peter Sims (Jossey-Bass, 2007).

Leading by example includes several important elements of inspiring and managing others. Here are the characteristics nonprofit managers need to cultivate and display:

- **Passion.** The more passionate you are about the mission of your organization and the work that you are accomplishing, the more other people will be inspired to feel the same way. Passion is contagious. People can see it, feel it, and perhaps even taste it. They want to see passion and energy on the part of their leaders and coworkers, particularly in nonprofits because they are focused on a cause. Passion can give employees and colleagues a sense of urgency that is required to make difficult decisions and constantly raise standards. Don't be afraid to show your enthusiasm and share your excitement or frustration about issues affecting your organization or cause.

- **Approachability.** In busy, understaffed nonprofits it is too easy for workers to bury their heads in work and not take time to talk to the

> **Lesson Learned**
>
> As a manager, your attitude, whether it be good or bad, creates the environment for things to flourish. Plant the right seeds.

people around them. This is a mistake. Connecting with your direct-report colleagues is a crucial part of your job and of achieving your organization's mission. How often do you drop by your employees' and colleagues' offices just to say hello? How quickly do you respond to voice mails or e-mails from your staff? Some leaders are afraid of informality and approachability because they fear that it leads to familiarity or less rigor among their staff members—or the appearance of such things. It is true that informality may not work for all nonprofit cultures, but at the American Heart Association an informal culture fits well with our core values, particularly our commitment to inclusiveness, trust, sensitivity, respect, and cooperation. I believe that an informal culture encourages communication and candor in an organization. It helps create a team feeling—that we are serving our mission and achieving our goals together.

I set very high standards and I demand that people give 110 percent. But I believe a leader needs to be approachable, open, and responsive. As CEO, I try to foster an environment where people are comfortable and apt to speak up, whether it be to point out a problem or to suggest a new idea. My door is always open, and people feel free to stop by. I listen to staff members and take a personal interest in them. I answer my own phone when I am in my office. I regularly host "chats with the CEO" to engage a small group of five or six people to find out what is on their minds and give them an opportunity to ask questions. I also take small groups from all levels out for occasional informal lunches with no agenda other than to get to know one another.

Every few weeks, I ask my assistant to schedule time on my calendar for *management by wandering around* (MBWA), a concept made popular by Tom Peters and Robert Waterman in their book *In Search of Excellence* (HarperCollins, 1982). MBWA means that I get out of my office and walk around, not knowing whom I will run into. Then I just stop and talk to people about what they are doing, how their work is coming along, or what they're doing outside the office.

If you don't feel comfortable walking around and chatting informally, invite a colleague to come along with you. What is important is that your employees see you, know you, and feel comfortable approaching you. Instead of waiting for them to come to you, go to them. A caveat: You don't want to be perceived as going around grilling people about their projects, so stay with open-ended questions. If you aren't sure of people's perceptions of your management style, it is worth asking a peer for an honest assessment of your professional persona. The main point here is to be visible and let people see that you are genuine.

- **Consistency.** People do not want to work for someone if they never know how that person will react to problems or challenges. Whether they realize it or not, staff members take comfort in the consistency and predictability of their leaders. Being consistent does not mean that you have to be a robot and react exactly the same way to every situation, but your behavior needs to be within a predictable range. For example, I think that in a crisis my staff have come to expect me to be solution-focused, rather than dwelling on the past, a quick mover, and calm. Think about how different it would be if sometimes I acted this way and other times I panicked and became hysterical? The staff would never know what to expect, and they would be afraid to bring me bad news because they could not predict my reaction. They know that I can handle good news and I can handle bad news but that I don't like surprises. Consistency builds trust and stability among your staff.

- **Accountability.** All employees have to hold themselves accountable, admit mistakes, and take their share of responsibility when things go wrong and times are challenging. This is doubly true for managers. People admire and respect a manager who takes responsibility. For example, if a project is late and over budget, the leader has to take responsibility and do so in a visible way. The leader cannot simply blame others. When you have a tendency to point the finger at others, realize that there are three fingers pointing back at you. In my opinion, the best managers take more responsibility when things go wrong and a lesser share of credit when things go well.

> **Lesson Learned**
>
> One of the most effective ways to breed loyalty, hard work, and goodwill in a team is to ensure that they receive praise when it is due.

- **Likability.** I used to say that all I want is to be respected and have people think that they are treated fairly, but I now believe that managers have to be respected, treat people fairly, *and* be liked. People like you in proportion to how you make them feel. For the most part, people put in extra effort if they like their supervisor. Creating a warm and friendly working environment reinforces that "it is not about me; it is about us and our shared mission. Remember this important statement made by Marcus Buckingham and Curt Coffman in their management book *First, Break All the Rules* (Simon & Schuster, 1999): "People leave managers, not companies." But being likable does not mean that you are soft and that you don't hold your staff accountable. It means that you treat them with respect and you genuinely care about them.

- **Sense of fun.** At the American Heart Association, we take our work seriously, not ourselves. Having fun and even making fun of ourselves is a form of reflection and letting off steam from our work, which—let's be honest—involves a lot of talk about disease and death. Even I am willing to risk making a fool of myself for a little laughter. Periodically, during a training conference I am asked to participate in a skit to communicate a message and make the learning fun for the participants. I have dressed as Donald Trump, a character from the movie *Men in Black*, and John Travolta's character from the movie *Saturday Night Fever*. In every instance, the staff loved it and so did I. When was the last time you did something to surprise your staff and make them laugh? Dressing up for Halloween or a company skit can do wonders for employee morale.

- **Focus on self-improvement as a manager.** I am a great believer in continuous learning and encourage all managers to seek educational opportunities that will help them grow, develop, and bring more perspective and knowledge to their jobs. The environment we all function in is constantly changing, and what gets you to a certain point in your management career may not get you to your next destination. We all need to learn new skills and hear new ideas about how we can do our jobs better.

The best nonprofit managers are always reading books, magazines, blogs, and articles about leadership, management, and effective business practices in the nonprofit and for-profit worlds. This does not mean that you should adopt the strategies of every guru-du-jour. Some managers misguidedly try to adopt the management fad of the month. You know how it goes: Yesterday it was the Balanced Scorecard, today it is Six Sigma, and tomorrow it will be something else. This is a mistake. It is helpful to read about new management techniques and apply an idea or two to your job. It is risky and irresponsible to change your style or direction whenever the wind changes.

If you successfully cultivate these characteristics, you will build trust and loyalty among your direct reports and other people in your organization. Think of positive acts of leadership and management as making deposits into an emotional account with each person in your organization. This builds trust. The more people trust you, the more open and honest they are with you about their challenges and problems at work. The more people trust you, the more they seek your guidance on handling their jobs. The more people trust you, the more you will know about what is really happening among your team, which means you can anticipate problems as well as successes. A lack of trust results in resistance, excuses, and fear—all obstacles to achieving great results in your organization.

The more goodwill you have in your trust account, the better positioned you are if you ever need to make a withdrawal. There are times when you need to pick up the phone or walk into someone's office and say, "Here's the situation and I really need you on this." That is an emotional withdrawal. If you haven't made any emotional deposits, it is almost impossible to make a withdrawal. When trust is high, execution is speeded up because there is less resistance. And when the intangible resources of an organization—such as trust, unity, and strong relationships—are in place, you can harness the tangible resources—finances and people—to even greater purpose and effect to achieve your mission. People follow leaders they trust.

> **Lesson Learned**
>
> By leading with transparency, authenticity, honesty, and consistency, you are making deposits into people's emotional accounts, which builds trust. You cannot manage effectively without people's trust.

It is important to cultivate trust among your team members as well. Team members need to trust you and trust one another. Trust is built over a period of time and begins with the leader being trustworthy in dealing openly and candidly with the team collectively and as individuals. Don't talk behind anyone's back, be sensitive to people's needs, praise in public, reprimand in private, treat everyone with dignity, honor your commitments, meet your timelines, don't be late for meetings, and conduct yourself ethically. Building trust comes down to being a good role model and holding others to the same standard. All of these things enable you to create a positive and trusting environment.

PRACTICES OF GREAT NONPROFIT MANAGERS

People in any position, from the most senior to someone who started last week, want to be valued, respected, and able to contribute. Leaders who meet those needs are successful. With that in mind, here are the techniques I recommend for being an effective and successful nonprofit manager.

Great Nonprofit Managers Know Where Their Team Is Going and How They Are Going to Get There

Have a plan for how you and the team are going to get from point A to point B. Make sure that each team member knows what he or she is accountable for and how it fits into the overall plan. Then ensure that each employee has the resources and support to be successful. How do you know if they do? Ask them! Communicate frequently to make sure that everyone knows the goal and what they need to do to help the team reach it. Monitor progress, help remove barriers, and provide feedback every step of the journey.

Great Nonprofit Managers Set Clear Expectations and Have Strong Performance Management Systems

Great managers are straightforward about their expectations for what employees will accomplish and how success will be measured. Here are some guidelines for setting clear, measurable goals for each employee:

- Meet with each team member and mutually agree on five to seven measurable performance objectives they will be accountable for at year-end. Obviously, position descriptions will contain many more things for which employees are responsible, but these five to seven performance standards identify where they can have the most impact and specify how they will be evaluated at year-end. Formal reviews of progress should occur quarterly or semiannually. However, progress toward these standards should be a part of your weekly or biweekly coaching session with each team member to make sure that problems and challenges are being identified and addressed along the way.
- Set goals based on end results not processes. For example, the important thing is not just how many volunteers you recruit to join your advocacy network but what percentage of those recruited volunteers actually take action when asked to do so.
- Minimize subjective aspects of performance. When employees receive a year-end review, they should come in knowing how they performed based on the numbers. Nonprofits often shy away from accountability—primarily because staff members don't have direct control over volunteers—but specific goals are necessary. Salespeople don't control their customers, but they are held accountable for year-end results. Many individuals in the for-profit sector are held accountable for cross-functional projects where they don't have direct control. For instance, an objective performance goal would be to sign up five corporate sponsors for your new Go Green tool kit. Objective performance standards should account for 70 to

80 percent of an employee's annual evaluation. There may be some other, more subjective evaluation measures that account for the other 20 to 30 percent, such as planning effectively, meeting deadlines, and communicating well.

Great Nonprofit Managers Stop People from Spending Time on Things That Do Not Matter

If our mission is moving a huge rock, too often we focus on how hard people are pushing and how much time they spend pushing. We lose sight of whether the rock has moved. Good managers stay focused on whether their employees are accomplishing what really needs to be accomplished, not just working hard for hard work's sake. Regularly pause to make sure that you remain focused on results, results, results—and results that have a high impact. If the work you are assigning to your employees is not helping to push your organization's mission forward and achieve your breakthrough goals, then it might be time to reassess that work. There is no time for busywork in organizations that are trying to make the world a better place.

Great Nonprofit Managers Are Strong Communicators

Information is power, and the more you open up and share, the more you energize your team and the less apt they are to worry about what is really going on. Good communication skills are also necessary to clarify and drive performance. Typically, people come together and communicate—let's say, in a weekly staff meeting—then they all leave the room assuming that everyone is on the same page. As we all know from experience, this is not always the case. We all *think* we are good communicators, but very few people really are. When you participate in a meeting, training session, conference call, or any other communication, you are safer to assume that you have *mis*communicated. Harsh, I know, but true. This means that after any meeting or appropriate conversation, you should confirm all important action items in writing, to clarify and confirm what is going to be done, by whom, and when.

Might this be perceived as overkill? Sometimes. But when an important meeting takes place, even between two people, it is beneficial and helpful to send a brief written review. This may consume some time in the present, but it will save you hours of time and difficulty later on if everyone is on the same page from the beginning. We need to confirm early if we have, in fact, miscommunicated; this minimizes problems and increases the likelihood that things will be done according to plan and schedule.

Good communication also means engaging others. As a team leader, you have to be careful that you don't cut off communication without even being aware of it. In group meetings, your team may have a tendency to defer to you without your getting candid feedback. To avoid this, utilize one of the most powerful statements you can make as a manager: "Here is what I think and here is how I arrived at this conclusion, but I need to know from you what I am not seeing." This encourages candor from your team and enables you to make better decisions. Remember, no one says that you, as the team leader, have to be right all the time. Draw on the brainpower and experience of your team.

Great Nonprofit Managers Allow Some Leeway

Once you and your team members mutually agree on their performance measurements and you have communicated to the best of your ability, give them some latitude based on their individual levels of experience. Employees need and deserve a good amount of leeway in their decision making. Ensure that your team understands the parameters of their responsibilities, then encourage them to feel confident and comfortable using some creativity and taking prudent risks. This does not mean abdication—it means not micromanaging.

Great Nonprofit Managers Give Frequent and Specific Praise

Employees seem to expect more of a human touch in nonprofit environments. To be a great nonprofit manager, make it a priority to give positive reinforcement when your employees do something well. Sometimes there is reluctance among leaders and managers to give positive reinforcement because they are not happy with literally everything that individual employee is doing. Well, nobody is 100 percent happy with everything an employee does. But giving praise is too important to hold back. How do you balance your drive to want people to do better with the reality that human beings need recognition? Make your positive reinforcement very, very specific.

For instance, your compliment might sound something like this: "You did a great job on yesterday's event, and that will really help us achieve this month's fund-raising goal." You are not telling the person that he or she does everything well—you are praising specific accomplishments and actions and putting their success in a context. Notice the emphasis on how this person's work contributed to the organization's goals: It is not enough to say that the event went off very well; you need to say that it will help us achieve this month's goal—a goal that moves us toward our important mission. Nonprofit employees like to know that their work is making a real difference.

The best time to give your compliment is as close to the event as possible. Immediate feedback has a definite impact on motivating more of the same behavior. I particularly like giving praise in the morning after a successful event. I notice that it has me starting my day feeling positive about our work, and it helps others do the same. But don't wait for the morning if you see an opportunity to give specific praise. Find someone doing something well and tell that person you have noticed. That person will be on a roll for the rest of the day.

Great Nonprofit Managers Set High Standards for Ethical Accountability

When there is conflict or opportunity for conflict on your team, work hard to find a win-win situation for everyone involved—this is especially crucial when it comes to an ethical conflict. Take action swiftly. If a staff member, volunteer, or corporate partner commits an ethical or legal breach, that person or organization must go, because you can never sacrifice your ethics. It is simply not right, and it sends the wrong signals to everyone involved. Ethical breaches, such as lies, legal misconduct, or financial impropriety, destroy trust in management, the team, and the organization as a whole. In the nonprofit world, ethical lapses must be treated with the utmost seriousness.

Although there are daily challenges in the life of a manager, it is a truly wonderful feeling to watch your team members succeed and grow. The techniques and lessons presented here ensure that you have many opportunities to do just that. Management is a big responsibility, with equally big rewards.

As a nonprofit manager, you are also tasked with another responsibility: guiding volunteers. Many of the tactics we've discussed apply to your role as a manager of volunteers, but there are also some key differences. Chapter 8 explores the topic of volunteer guidance and management.

CHAPTER 7 TAKEAWAYS

- **As a manager, you set the tone.** A manager's attitude—positive or negative—creates a team's overall attitude. This does not mean that you have to be a superhero and always be perfect. It means that the more attention you pay to improving your own personal and professional development as a leader, the better your team will be.

- **Make deposits in people's emotional trust accounts.** Think of positive acts of leadership and management as making deposits into an emotional account with each person on your team. The more goodwill you have in your trust account, the better positioned you are if you ever need to make a withdrawal, such as asking for a favor or forgiveness for a mistake. If you haven't made any emotional deposits, it is almost impossible to make a withdrawal.

- **Give specific praise.** Make it a priority to give positive reinforcement when your employees do something well. Make your positive reinforcement very specific so that employees understand exactly what they are doing well and will continue the same behavior.

CHAPTER 8

RECRUITING AND GUIDING VOLUNTEERS AND THE BOARD OF DIRECTORS

Now we come to a topic that is unique to the nonprofit world: volunteers. Apart from college interns seeking to build their work resumes, most adults who approached a for-profit company offering to work for free would be met with baffled looks. In the nonprofit world, such generous supporters are a critical component of our success. But how do you recruit, guide, and communicate effectively with people who are not on your payroll?

Nonprofits need to think strategically about volunteers at every level, from participants in small events to members of the boards of directors. We need a plan for recruiting, retaining, and guiding volunteers, just as we need a plan for paid staff. Otherwise, we run the risk of wasting and losing these incredibly valuable resources.

How important are volunteers to the success of nonprofit organizations? According to the Corporation for National and Community Service, four out of five charities registered with the IRS—an estimated 174,000 organizations—use volunteers, and that number does not include an additional 400,000 unregistered organizations. In addition, an estimated 83 percent of America's 380,000 religious organizations have volunteers involved with their work.[1]

You've Gotta Have Heart

As the nation's second-largest voluntary health organization, the American Heart Association has 3,500 paid employees and 22.5 million volunteers and donors. That includes 29,000 science and medical professionals who are members of the AHA's sixteen scientific councils. There is no doubt that the grassroots volunteer force is the backbone of the organization. We would never achieve the results that we have without this massive volunteer base, and as an individual, I could never do my job without their dedication. But we can never take that commitment and loyalty for granted. Remember that volunteers are also customers.

> **Lesson Learned**
>
> Volunteers are also customers. We must treat them accordingly and earn their trust and respect.

However, the fact that some people in nonprofit organizations are paid for their work and most others are not creates a challenging people-management situation. Put simply: Some are required to do their jobs because of their status as employees, while others are not. This is the great complexity of the nonprofit world, and it requires careful leadership to keep everyone functioning together. The challenge for you as a leader is that you are actually managing two organizations simultaneously—your paid staff and your volunteer structure.

VOLUNTEER/STAFF PARTNERSHIPS

The most effective framework to guide this complex interaction is the concept of *volunteer/staff partnerships*—creating a team environment in which the staff members do not feel subservient to the volunteers, nor do the volunteers simply carry out what the staff wants. Volunteer/staff partnerships mean that each group brings different skills to the table and plays a different role, but both groups have responsibility for the same end results. Volunteers and staff are partners on the same team. The partnership is based on mutual respect and the recognition that each group has a job to do and that everyone must work together and listen to each other's views.

The success of any partnership, personal or professional, always comes down to communication and trust. Trust takes time to build and needs to be diligently nurtured. You cannot just take a staff member and a volunteer, put them together on a project, and say, "Presto!" You need to build an organizational culture that values both staff members and volunteers. Building a confident, competent staff and having a successful track record in the community helps a great deal.

Nonprofits tend think of themselves as being either staff-driven or volunteer-driven. This kind of thinking is counterproductive. An organization cannot carry out its mission, adhere to its strategic driving force, or reach its breakthrough goals without staff and volunteers working together. That is the essence of a true partnership.

RECRUITING VOLUNTEERS

The competition for volunteers and volunteer time has never been greater. People have more work and family demands than ever, so the time they might use to volunteer is at a premium. Just as you strive to build an organization full of High-Potential and Medium-Potential staff members, you should seek High-Potential and Medium-Potential volunteers as well. Here are some recommendations for attracting the most skilled, engaged, and dedicated volunteers to your organization.

- **Turn every volunteer into a recruiter.** Just as your current paid staff members are your best resource for recruiting new staff members, your current volunteers are your best resource for recruiting new volunteers. Encourage your most dedicated volunteers to spread the word about volunteer opportunities to their friends, family, neighbors, and colleagues. Be proactive in asking your volunteers to recruit others. Provide them with relevant marketing materials and volunteer sign-up forms. Invite them to help you staff booths at community events where you will be signing up new volunteers. Set up groups on social networking sites such as LinkedIn.com and Facebook.com, so your current volunteers can join these networks, post comments and event announcements, and easily forward e-mails about your organization to their friends.

> **Lesson Learned**
>
> The primary reason people volunteer is that a current volunteer asked them, so provide as many ways as possible for your current volunteers to recruit.

- **Cast a wider net.** Sometimes we get into the habit of recruiting from certain populations and we forget to reach out to new and different types of people. Every organization has different volunteering needs, so consider reaching out to demographic groups you might not be reaching. This may include senior citizens, people with disabilities, young people, immigrants, people of various sexual orientations, and persons of diverse religions and ethnicities. This also includes people of diverse talents, skills, viewpoints, and experiences.

    The American Heart Association has built relationships with African-American organizations, Hispanic organizations, religious organizations, and community groups all across the country. Just as we promote our organization's products and services to as wide an audience as possible, we also promote our volunteer opportunities widely. Through these relationships we have shown our commitment to serving diverse communities and built relationships with individuals who have become volunteers.

    We even have outreach efforts to engage children as volunteers—after all, they represent the future of our volunteer ranks. Why not get them involved early? Jump Rope For Heart, for example, is a national educational fund-raising program that we cosponsor with the American Alliance for Health, Physical Education, Recreation and Dance (AAHPERD). This program engages elementary students in a physical activity (jumping rope) while raising funds from their friends and family to support heart and stroke research and programs. This educational program teaches the value of lifetime physical fitness and promotes the value of community service to students and their families. It shows students that they can contribute to their community's welfare. Even if you do not host events specifically for children, you can invite your volunteers to engage their children and grandchildren in their own volunteer efforts.

- **Emphasize that your staff is efficient and organized.** Volunteers of all types want to be part of a well-run organization where they feel that the time they are volunteering actually produces results. It's the same demand they have when they donate money: People want to know that any resources they donate are used efficiently and make a real difference for the causes they care about. You can demonstrate your efficiency and organization through the actions of your staff. Volunteers want to donate their time to work alongside staff members who are committed and organized and who can be counted on. The more you work on building staff talent, the more you will attract the best volunteers.

Lesson Learned

Volunteers want to be part of something about which they have a deep sense of pride. They will only donate their time and recruit friends and colleagues if they have confidence in the competence of their staff partners.

- **Consider ad hoc assignments.** It is generally far easier to recruit volunteers for ad hoc assignments with specific start and end dates and with a specific objective to accomplish. Busy people want to make a difference quickly and not engage in open-ended busywork. While there is always a need for volunteers who will commit to long-term projects or leadership roles, such as chairing a committee, you should also make room for people who can commit to only a short time period.

Recruiting for Key Volunteer Positions

Although all volunteers are important, some volunteer leadership positions require a recruiting strategy all their own. As with key positions in your paid staff ranks, volunteer leadership positions can have the most impact on your organization's success. They also require a more robust skill set and a larger time commitment. Here is the recruitment strategy I recommend for bringing the best high-level volunteers into your organization:

1. Create an ad hoc committee of existing volunteer leaders or board members and ask that they spearhead the effort to recruit for a key volunteer position—for instance, a chair for your annual fundraising walk. Call a face-to-face meeting of this committee and discuss the job description, the competencies required, and the kind of person you would like to have. For example, you might seek someone who is well known in the community, influential, and not shy about recruiting others; who has a proven track record with comparable community events; and who possesses great attention-to-detail and follow-through skills.
2. Then start brainstorming a list of individuals who meet the criteria you have laid out, without regard for whether these people have ever worked with your organization. Ask, "Who would we want to chair this walk if we could have anyone we wanted?" Think big! For the most part, when you ask people to help recruit volunteer leaders to important positions, there is a tendency to recruit down. This happens mostly because it's the course of least resistance. If I'm the president of a company, it's generally easier for me to recruit one of the company's VPs than one of my peers. Or if I'm recruiting someone from another company, it is easier to recruit an EVP than the CEO. It might be easier to do this, but the benefits of having a powerful, influential person chairing an event or taking on another important leadership role cannot be underestimated. Remind the search committee members to aim as high up the ladder as they can. If you don't request this up front, you can generally count on people to recruit down.

    Sometimes you are faced with a time-sensitive deadline, such that you need a chair or leader as soon as possible. When volunteers and staff feel too pressed to meet recruitment deadlines—particularly for important leadership positions—it is human nature to go for the quick fix and recruit someone who might not necessarily give the best performance but is ready and willing, instead of waiting to get the right person with the right influence. Even in time-sensitive situations, I still believe it is crucial to engage the very best person you can. The benefits of having the right volunteer on board outweigh the risks of waiting.
3. Once you have a list of five to seven names, rank your prospects in priority order. When you determine your top prospect, ask the

volunteer who nominated the individual whether he or she could open a door with this prospect. Assuming that the answer is yes, ask the volunteer to step outside the room and contact the prospect to ask for a meeting. Taking immediate action keeps the process moving forward.

Here is a basic script for the contact person: "Jean, as you may know, I'm a very active volunteer with the ABC organization, and we have a project coming up that I would like to talk to you about. I would like to stop by your office with a couple of my volunteer associates and tell you more about it. It shouldn't take more than about twenty minutes. Is there a day next week that would work for you?"

Ideally, you get an appointment, and the volunteer returns to the meeting with a positive report. Of course, you have to be flexible; the volunteer may not be able to get through or may receive a clear no. If the call goes through and an appointment is made, great. If the request is turned down, this also speeds up the process in that you can move on to the next candidate.

4. When you are able to set up a meeting, two or three of the volunteers from the original discussion and the staff responsible for the fund-raising walk make the visit. Your chances of a yes are good if the prospect has agreed to an in-person meeting. It is much more difficult to say no in person, and it is much more difficult to say no to a group than to a single individual. Use this to your advantage. As for an agenda, the volunteer who set up the meeting makes the introductions, then another volunteer talks for three to five minutes about the organization and its mission, and then the most appropriate volunteer talks about the specific initiative you would like this person to chair. The staff member reviews the job description and timelines for the project and discusses the staff support that will be provided. Finally, the volunteer making the appointment makes the ask.

5. In an ideal situation, you get an answer of "yes" on the spot. If the person says, "I need to think about it," the volunteer making the ask is in charge of follow-up. Ask how many days the prospect will need, and set up a date on which to call the prospect for a final answer. If you receive a "no" response, you don't have to reconvene a meeting of the original committee. Simply turn to the next name on the priority list and ask the volunteer who has the connection to make a call. The process begins again from there.

This process is time-consuming, but it is worth the end result if you get a really high-powered leader to chair your event. Does this process work every time? No, and nothing does, but will it significantly increase your success rate? Absolutely! There are also some residual benefits to this process. Having several volunteers involved in the process sets a good example, showing that the prospect is expected to roll up his or her sleeves and perform. It also demonstrates that the prospect will have lots of support if he or she accepts the opportunity. It is impossible for those volunteers making the visit to leave without saying, "If I can help in any way, let me know." That is also reassuring to the newly recruited chair.

GUIDING VOLUNTEERS

Once the best volunteers are on board at all levels, follow these guidelines to ensure that volunteer/staff interactions and projects run as smoothly as possible. Keep in mind that nonprofits must maximize the impact of volunteer work by focusing volunteer efforts on mission-related activities—activities that really move the needle and help them achieve their strategic goals.

- **Provide information about your organization to its volunteers.** Make sure that volunteers are informed of what needs to be accomplished to serve your mission, adhere to your strategic driving force, and move closer to your breakthrough goal. Use personal stories in training volunteers to make the mission and goals come alive.
- **Provide volunteers with job descriptions.** People function best if they are asked to complete a specific task with clearly established outcomes within a designated time frame. Problems occur when the role of your volunteers is not clearly delineated from the role of the staff. (It is also a problem if you make such a distinction but no one really agrees to it or abides by it.) The more thoughtful you are about assigning projects to volunteers, the more thoughtful they will be about completing them. Developing volunteer position descriptions is one of the best practices of volunteer management. Volunteer job descriptions can be short for ad hoc assignments— simply a bullet-pointed list of responsibilities and timelines—or, for longer-term volunteer assignments, they can read like staff

position descriptions. Whatever your document looks like, what is most important is clearly delineating the volunteer versus the staff responsibilities. You cannot anticipate every situation, but at least define some guiding principles for who is responsible for what.

- **Give volunteers enough to do.** Believe it or not, most organizations lose new volunteers at the board and committee levels because the volunteers are underworked not overworked. Too often we reach out to our go-to volunteers instead of approaching new volunteers, who may be unproven. But if a volunteer attends a meeting and feels ignored or leaves without a specific task, he or she might never return. Generally, people don't want to attend meetings just to attend meetings. They want to contribute. It is important to engage people who approach your organization quickly before they slip through your fingers.

    You can prevent this by ensuring that your staff and volunteer leaders are disciplined about assigning tasks. For instance, as the staff works with the board chair or committee chair to prepare an agenda for a board or committee meeting, there should be a discussion about the tasks that need to be assigned during the meeting. Pay attention to which volunteers are doing a lot of work and which volunteers could take on more responsibility. Pay particular attention to new volunteers to make sure they are engaged. This assessment and assignment work should be a regular part of the preliminary effort before each meeting.

- **Recognize volunteers for their contributions.** Everyone likes to be acknowledged, particularly those who are donating their time. Send frequent thank-you notes and e-mails, and include stories about volunteer accomplishments in your online and offline publications. Make sure that every volunteer sees how his or her work is making a true difference and fits into the big picture. The AHA often includes patient stories on its website and in volunteer e-newsletters and other communications to give volunteers a feeling of connection with the real people their work is supporting. Any nonprofit can personalize its mission through the sharing of well-chosen stories about the individuals it serves.

- **Solicit feedback.** Since volunteers do not have formal performance reviews during which they can share their motivations and goals, be sure to check in regularly and ask how they are doing.

You can do this through informal conversations or through online surveys.

> ### CAN YOU FIRE A VOLUNTEER?
>
> One of the most successful staff members I ever had was a young man named Richard Cole, who joined the American Heart Association right out of college. He had been a part-time youth minister and recruited many volunteers in that role. Part of his job at the AHA involved leading an effort of volunteers recruiting volunteers—similar to a pyramid structure. He would meet with the lead volunteer recruiters and provide each one with a specific job description. This included the number of volunteers each person was expected to recruit and a time frame for doing so.
>
> As the staff member in charge, he would follow up with each volunteer in advance of the recruiting deadline. I love this strategy—following up just before the deadline is a positive action. Following up after the deadline can be perceived as negative and makes the volunteer feel like he or she is being reprimanded. If the volunteer did not meet the deadline, Richard would adjust the timeline in an attempt to get the volunteer on track. If the volunteer did not meet the second deadline, Richard would say, "It is clear you do not really have the time to do this and we are being unfair to you. So I accept your resignation." Essentially, Richard was firing the volunteer, without making the person feel rejected. He had the courage to quickly move underperforming volunteers out of the organization so he could recruit more effective replacements. And I have never heard a complaint about his tactics. The volunteers were likely relieved by his decision and glad to be let off the hook.

DEVELOPING AND GUIDING THE BOARD OF DIRECTORS

Nonprofit boards are generally responsible for strategy, oversight, governance, budgeting, and overseeing the CEO or executive director. In smaller organizations, board members may also play a role in delivering the organization's programs and services and raising the funds necessary to sustain the organization. In larger organizations, the board generally works as a strategic partner to the staff leadership to set strategy and ensure that the organization meets its goals and commitments. In all cases, there is always plenty of interaction between board members and some of the paid staff. For this reason, it is best to always approach your work with the board in a spirit of unity. You are in this together and working toward the same goals.

Your organization should review the size and structure of your board periodically to make sure it is serving your organization's best interests. Here are some big-picture questions to ask about your board, which will help you recruit the best board members and work with them effectively.

How Many Members Should the Board Have?

According to Independent Sector's Panel on the Nonprofit Sector, a nonprofit board should have enough members to allow for full deliberation and diversity of thinking on governance and other organizational matters. Except for very small organizations, this generally means that the board should have at least five members. The board should not be so large that it is unwieldy or so small that it lacks a variety of perspectives. Today, the median size of a nonprofit board is fifteen members, and the trend is toward smaller and smaller boards. I think the ideal size is somewhere between twelve and twenty-four members. That may seem like a wide range, but the size of the board depends on several factors. A national board needing to provide representation to local components would be at the higher end, a local board that is implementing and raising funds might also be at the higher end, and a foundation or organization without local components would be at the lower end of the range. One size does not fit all—the size of your board should be tailored to the needs of your organization.

Look for board members with expertise in the mission-related aspects of your work. For example, the AHA board includes individuals with expertise in cardiovascular and stroke science and health-care delivery. Some private foundations might need to involve family members as well. Most organizations also need some board members who can open doors. Depending on the scope of your organization, your influential board member might be anyone from a well-known celebrity to a local VIP, such as a corporate executive, a prominent community activist, or a local news anchor.

When in doubt, my experience says that a smaller board is generally more engaged and provides more stringent oversight. The American Heart Association has downsized its board: Ten years ago, it had forty-three members; today, it has twenty-two members. This has allowed the AHA to work more effectively, thanks to crisper decision making and more engaged board members.

> **Recommended Resource**
>
> **BoardSource** (www.boardsource.org), formerly the National Center for Nonprofit Boards, is a comprehensive resource for all topics related to nonprofit board of directors management, including answers to frequently asked questions about nonprofit boards—helpful to start-ups and established pros.

What Type of Board Do You Need?

Some people think that a board is a board is a board, but that simply is not the case. There are different types of boards that operate in different ways and serve different purposes. It is important for you to assess what kind of board you have—and whether the type you have is best suited to your organization's needs. Depending on the type of organization and the historical moment of your journey (Is your organization just starting out? Well-established? In crisis? In need of innovation?), you are likely to have one of four major types of board. Note that no type of board is better or worse than any other. The important point is that you decide what the role of your board will be. If you don't, the tide will simply take you wherever it wants to and the role of your board will not be clear. Note also that most boards are probably a hybrid of more than one type, which is fine as long as you are aware of it.

Here are four major types of boards:

1. **Working/operating board:** This type of board acts as an executive management team. This is an option used by organizations that have

limited budgets for paid staff and is common for the board of a younger start-up.
2. **Policy board:** A policy board is perceived to be in control, allowing the senior staff to do things. This board is more powerful than its executive director or CEO when it comes to decision making. Virtually any type of organization can have this type of board, and many do.
3. **Traditional board:** In this case, the staff is stronger than the board, and the board essentially rubber-stamps decisions made by the staff. This board is purely for oversight and is also common to a wide variety of nonprofits.
4. **Governing board:** This is a collaborative partnership between the board and the staff but with different, clearly delineated accountabilities and responsibilities—a true partnership. Most decisions are made jointly, and the staff are considered a valued resource with a needed perspective rather than functionaries who take the minutes at the meetings. There is a delineation between board responsibility (setting strategy and direction and monitoring) and staff responsibility (execution and implementation). The American Heart Association has this type of board.

If an organization has a governing board, select board members and the staff leaders work together to draft a strategic plan. The plan is then taken to the entire board for consideration. Both volunteers and staff engage in the discussion, and finally the board—not staff—adopts a plan. Once the strategic plan is adopted, the staff is responsible for working with the committee chairs and committees to develop annual implementation plans. These plans are then presented to the board for their information, and the staff is held accountable for the execution of the plan. Key benchmarks are monitored by the board throughout the year.

Ultimately, the type of board your organization has may be determined by how your organization grows and evolves over time. To facilitate interactions and decisions, make sure that everyone on the board and the staff members who deal with the board are clear about the type.

How Diverse Is the Board?

The ideal board—regardless of which of the four types you adopt—includes members of diverse genders, ethnicities, talents, and backgrounds. Depending on your mission, this generally includes members with expertise in financial management, fund-raising, marketing, advocacy, law, and public relations. Diversity also means ensuring that your board has a diversity of ideas, experience, and knowledge. To find more diverse board members, you might need to look outside the usual sources from which board members have been recruited in the past or relax rules about allowing only board members who have served the organization for many years.

CONSIDER A COMPETENCY-BASED BOARD

As you are thinking about the makeup of your organization's board of directors, you might consider one additional model for structuring a board. This model is relatively recent in the history of the American Heart Association board, and it has been tremendously beneficial. It is a competency-based board. No matter which of the four types of boards your organization has and regardless of the board's size, using a competency-based approach is a way to refine the board and make it even more valuable to the organization. A competency-based board consists of directors who represent the key competencies your organization needs to achieve its strategic goals.

The American Heart Association has six key broad competencies that it must be good at if it is to achieve its strategic plan:

1. **Scientific knowledge:** Discovering and interpreting science.
2. **Advocacy:** Advocating for science and public health at the federal, state, and local levels.
3. **Communication:** Communicating cardiovascular and stroke health information to public and professional audiences.
4. **Health-care delivery:** Strengthening health-care delivery.
5. **Fund-raising:** Generating resources.
6. **Corporate operations:** Audit, finance, information technology, and so on.

So to have a competency-based board, the AHA needs board members who are expert in each of these areas: scientific knowledge, advocacy, communications, health-care delivery, fund-raising, and corporate operations.

Prior to 2002, we didn't think about the exact competencies we needed on the board. All we thought about was making sure that the board consisted of 50 percent medical professionals and 50 percent laypeople. It might happen that all of those people were talented, powerful, and committed, but in our case the AHA board had little to no expertise in advertising/marketing or advocacy. Using a competency-based approach, we ensure that the board has members with the expertise required to achieve the strategic plan. This provides a broader perspective and protects the organization from blind spots and missed opportunities.

Anyone nominated to the AHA board must have expertise related to one of the six competencies. The nominating committee uses this information to vet candidates. Let's say that in any given year there are six to eight open positions on a board of twenty-two members. We would look at the functional expertise of directors continuing to the next term. We would then determine which functions are underrepresented and give preference to candidates with expertise in those areas. For instance, several years ago, the AHA did not have board members with strong backgrounds in health-care delivery systems. Today, there are three members with strong backgrounds in health-care delivery. We are now able to engage in a better informed, more insightful, and more productive level of discussion because of their presence. This is true in other functional areas as well.

To guide your board toward a competency-based model, think about the key competencies you need to achieve your strategic goals. The early chapters in this book guided you through this process. This helps you assess the expertise you need that you do not currently have on your board. Once defined, include a discussion of competencies when you consider new people for the board of directors.

Without a competency-based board, the American Heart Association would not and could not have achieved the success it did in the area of paid advertising. The initiative needed an experienced and influential voice on the board. The organization needed people who knew the right questions to ask and the appropriate negotiation tactics to employ in the advertising world. Knowing that we were considering paid advertising as part of our communications competency, we added the CEO of an advertising agency. Not only did the AHA benefit from his advice, it also gained credibility in the advertising community by having his name associated with that of the organization. We had some staff competency in the area of marketing and advertising, but those staff people needed to have volunteer partners on the board. You cannot have one without the other. Well, perhaps you can, but you are much more effective with both.

Competency-based boards seem to be gaining some traction. I was on the board of Partnership for Prevention, a national membership organization that promotes disease prevention and supports health promotion policies. The chair of the board asked me to chair a task force to look at structure and governance, and we recommended a competency-based board. Partnership for Prevention adopted the model, and we realized that the organization had no board members with any expertise in marketing or communications. As a result, we recruited Peggy Conlon, CEO of the National Ad Council, and Rob Gould, who was at that time partner-in-charge of the public relations firm Porter Novelli. The process of defining needed competencies helps you focus. It becomes easy to narrow down the field of potential candidates and find the right board members.

Lesson Learned

Think of your board as a football team. You can't just take the most talented players. You need to select your team so you have players for a variety of positions. Imagine a football team with eleven quarterbacks on the field—you wouldn't score many touchdowns!

BEST PRACTICES FOR THE BOARD OF DIRECTORS

According to McKinsey & Company's research report *The Dynamic Board: Lessons from High-Performing Nonprofits*, "A strong board is a critical piece of the puzzle for increasing the effectiveness of a [nonprofit] organization; a nonprofit can only sustain high performance over the long term when it has a great board."[2] Here are the guidelines I recommend.

Follow Legal Protocol

First, a nonprofit board is a legal entity, and, as such, you must make sure that legal protocol is followed. Board members' legal responsibilities are clearly outlined under established principles of nonprofit corporate law. You certainly should consult with an attorney when it comes to writing any legal documents for the board. Here is a basic description of the three major responsibilities of a nonprofit board member:

- **Due care:** The board member must act with the same care and diligence as an ordinarily prudent person would exercise in his or her own personal business affairs.
- **Loyalty:** The board member must act in good faith, avoid conflicts of interest, and demonstrate loyalty to the organization and its best interests as a whole, not any constituent part or member.
- **Obedience:** The board member must perform his or her duties in accordance with applicable laws and the organization's charter, bylaws, and policies, and must ensure that the organization obeys the law and conducts its affairs pursuant to its governing documents.

Educate Board Members About Their Fiduciary Responsibilities

Orient new board members and periodically reorient all board members about how to read and interpret your organization's financial statements. Even board members with extensive financial management experience may not be familiar with the specifics of nonprofit finances or your organization's particular structure and issues.

Clarify Other Expectations

Depending on your organization, you may also require board members to make a personal donation or serve on at least one committee. Why would an organization require board members to donate? Most major gift donors and foundations want to know that all of your board members support your organization financially before they make a financial commitment. The amount of the gift is not as important as having 100 percent participation of your board members. Some boards have a "give or get" policy, which requires board members themselves to donate or solicit donations of a certain amount. Make sure you are very clear in the recruitment process about what is expected, especially from people who are new to serving on a nonprofit board. Have all of these discussions up front so everyone understands the expectations.

Have the Board Structure Mirror the Staff Structure

There are many variations of board structures, but the mirroring principle is important because it aligns the activities, goals, and priorities of volunteers and staff. One of the keys to the American Heart Association's success has been a national board of directors with committees that match the functional areas for which it has executive vice presidents. The volunteer committee leader (board member) and the functional EVP (a paid staff member) are knitted together from a structural standpoint. That makes it easier to keep that partnership going. We also insist that all board-level committee chairs have monthly teleconferences with the staff in between committee meetings. This ensures that the volunteers and staff members work in tandem.

Fully Educate Board Members About the Organization

Board members must become experts on your organization. This is to ensure their success as advisers, decision makers and external advocates. The American Heart Association holds a six-hour orientation session for new board members. During the orientation, new board members learn about their fiduciary responsibilities, and we try to make sure that they have a clear understanding of the AHA's strategic plan and how the organization operates. These presentations are given by staff and volunteer partners, who discuss activities and issues in that particular area for the past twelve months and what lies ahead in the next two to three years. We expect every new board member to attend these orientations.

Communicate with the Chair of the Board

Leaders must communicate frequently with the head of their board. In addition to my communication with officers as a group, I devote time to discussing issues with the chairperson (who is a business professional) and the president (who is a medical professional). On a biweekly basis, we have informal, one-hour conference calls to discuss a variety of topics. The main objective of these calls is to ensure that both of them know what is going on in the organization. I present items for discussion and then ask if they have any additional topics that they would like to discuss. It is very informal, and we take whatever time is needed to address specific issues.

Use Technology to Communicate

The AHA board is very comfortable communicating electronically. In addition to four face-to-face meetings each year, the board meets twice via Web conference or teleconference. These electronic meetings are generally about an hour in duration and are canceled if there is no business. We also send board members a bimonthly report via e-mail, which summarizes several key topics and provides them with e-mail links to the appropriate staff if they have questions or need more information. They also receive the weekly organization-wide e-mail newsletter, with news on science and association initiatives. Our job as a staff is to make sure that board members have the information they need to stay informed so that they can drive the strategic decisions.

Streamline In-Person Board Meetings

The AHA has tried to minimize the number of informational status reports given at formal board meetings. Reciting purely informational reports at a meeting just doesn't make sense in today's technology-driven world. Who says that when you bring people together you have to give status reports on various projects? Instead, my rule is this: When you need to tell people you have done something, do not wait for the meeting. Just send an e-mail! If we are communicating regularly outside of meetings, then when we come together in person or on a conference call, we can use our collective brainpower in more productive ways. It is hard to get people to change this mind-set, but at the AHA we find that transparency, immediacy, and diversity of communication channels—phone, one-on-one e-mails, and group e-mails—have helped, as described earlier.

To maximize its efficiency, the American Heart Association board has adopted a policy of *consent agendas* at in-person board meetings. As a part of the agenda packet sent out in advance of the meeting, we identify what we perceive to be routine business items—usually ten to twelve items per meeting. Appropriate documents for each of these items are included with the packet. These include things like board approval of Audit Committee members, signatories on a bank account, and approval of minutes. Unless a director requests otherwise, these items are voted on as a batch. If anyone asks that an item be pulled from the batch, it will be fully discussed and voted on separately. Consent on routine items is therefore achieved quickly and efficiently.

Next, we generally have two to three strategic items for discussion about which we need direction from the board. These consist of a twenty-minute presentation with an hour of discussion for each item. An example of a recent strategic discussion is Health Care Reform. We educated the board about the complexity of the issue and then had discussion about what role, if any, the AHA should have on this issue; at what level (principles versus detailed plan) we should be involved; whether we should join coalitions or form partnerships; and what kind of strategies we should employ. This discussion provided direction to the Advocacy Committee to then develop a plan and strategies. Obviously, this type of high-level discussion makes for a much better use of the expertise of the directors sitting at the table, as opposed to listening to ten status updates on routine matters.

Once a year a detailed budget report is presented for approval. Routine quarterly financial reports are sent electronically to the board and are not discussed at a board meeting unless there is something unusual or a request is made.

Address Potential Conflicts of Interest

To maintain the reputation of your organization, it is crucial to have a rock-solid ethics policy for board members. American Heart Association board members sign an ethics statement at the beginning of their tenure and submit a conflict-of-interest statement at any meeting when an issue arises that might be questionable. For example, if the AHA is considering forming a strategic alliance with an organization and an executive from that organization serves on the AHA board, the director would be recused not only from the vote but from any related discussion. As another example, we would never consider using a firm to conduct the annual audit if an employee of the audit firm served on the AHA board. The firm would not even be allowed to bid.

At the beginning of each board and committee meeting, the conflict-of-interest policy is referenced, and all members are reminded to declare before any topic of discussion where a conflict might be perceived. If that is indeed the case, the member is recused from the discussion and the decision making.

Encourage the Board to Assess Itself

The best boards are committed to self-improvement, which means that they periodically take a hard look at their own performance, identify opportunities for improvement, and change practices or leaders in order to close the gap."[3] Such boards accept self-improvement as a permanent responsibility and undertake disciplined reviews of their effectiveness. One way to accomplish this is to develop a form (online or in hard-copy format) to collect data annually from the directors. The form asks a series of questions related to how well the individual director thinks he or she performed and how the overall board performed as a group. The data can be collected anonymously and then compiled. Officers and staff can review the suggestions and then either take action on the suggestions or, where appropriate, ask the board to take action accordingly.

Build Your Bench

Just as you do with staff, make sure you have a process to identify future board and committee members, as well as future officers. Make sure you have an opportunity to observe these volunteers in action and that you get to know them and how they behave under different circumstances. Keep a short list of individuals you would like to see move up.

A UNIQUE WAY TO ENGAGE VOLUNTEERS: EXPERT PANELS

A few years back, the American Heart Association instituted a program of volunteer expert panels. Expert panels are not a formal part of the volunteer organizational structure and have no decision-making authority. Instead, expert panels typically consist of three or four people with a very specific expertise for which the organization has a need.

Let's say we are thinking about ways to improve our direct-mail campaign—which is about a $65 million effort annually—and we want input from outside eyes with niche expertise. We invite a few experts together for a chat. In this case, it might be a direct-marketing expert from L.L. Bean or the Neiman Marcus catalog. These people have no previous experience with the American Heart Association. We ask them to donate a few hours of their time, usually over the telephone, to provide their expert opinions. Typically, we accept some of their recommendations but not others. Panel members often have different points of view on the same topic, which gives us food for thought. There is no need to achieve a group consensus like there is on a board of directors or committee. This is simply about getting new ideas from different viewpoints.

I am always amazed at the number of experts who are willing to share their time and generously provide ideas and insight. As with technological issues, nonprofits—even large ones like the American Heart Association—often do not have the resources to be as cutting-edge as they would like. This is why insight from industry leaders can be so incredibly valuable. It helps nonprofits focus their resources on high-value solutions.

The purpose these expert panels serve is to supplement, not supplant, the AHA's internal oversight structure. It is simply a way to make sure we keep our eye on trends and best practices in the outside environment. Occasionally, we retain expert consultants as well—anything to make sure we are always thinking creatively. I once attended a conference lecture by a nineteen-year-old tech genius who just blew me away with his ideas and insights. So we called him up and asked if we could engage him for some consulting time. As you can imagine, he generated many nontraditional ideas for us to consider. This is but one avenue we use to stimulate creative thinking in staff and volunteers.

To develop an expert panel for your organization, think of people from whom you would like to receive advice—event planners, creative writers, experts on marketing to Generation Y—whatever would be valuable expertise for your organization to have. Then approach people who might be willing to volunteer their time and expertise for a good cause. To increase your chances of someone agreeing to speak with you, try to find an in with that person through a member of your board, a professional association you belong to, or a shared connection on a social networking website such as LinkedIn.com.

Many people are happy to volunteer a few hours. It is a relatively easy and commitment-free way to donate to a good cause. We also have received the feedback that it is fun for experts on a particular topic to approach the challenges of a nonprofit. If you have never tried this strategy, give it a shot. The worst anyone can do is say no.

CHAPTER 8 TAKEAWAYS

- **It is all about partnership.** The best framework for guiding volunteers is to think and talk about volunteer-staff partnerships. Partnership is about honesty, trust, communication, and the cultivation of complementary skills and diverse viewpoints as well as dual responsibility.

- **The better your staff, the better the volunteers you will attract.** Volunteers want to be part of a winning team. They want to donate their time to a mission and work with people who are competent, committed, organized, and, most of all, effective. Volunteers recruit other friends and colleagues only if they have confidence in their staff partners.

- **Recruit up.** When you are recruiting for an important volunteer role, begin with this question: "Who would we ask to volunteer to lead this project if we could have anyone we wanted?" Generate names, and try to get an in with each person and get a small group to make a recruitment call. As with recruiting staff, it is better to wait for an A candidate than to settle for a B or C candidate who is available immediately.

- **Regularly reassess your board of directors.** Think about the size, type, diversity, and responsibilities of your board. If necessary, shake things up a bit. Try a competency-based board that ensures you have experts in the functional work processes that will help you carry out your mission.

- **Implement best practices with your board.** These include preparing people to serve, working collaboratively, communicating frequently (particularly with the board chair), using technology to communicate, and setting clear goals. Always set clear expectations.

CHAPTER 9

INFLUENCING PUBLIC POLICY

Nonprofit Advocacy and Lobbying

Legend has it that President Ulysses S. Grant invented the term *lobbyists* at the Willard Hotel in Washington, D.C. He used the word to describe the political wheelers and dealers who used to approach him in the hotel's lobby to discuss their issues. "Those darn lobbyists," he called them.

As it turns out, the attribution is false. The *Oxford English Dictionary* dates the first usage of the term, meaning "persons who frequent the lobby of the house of legislature for the purpose of influencing its members in their official action" to 1808, before Grant was even born. However, the sentiment about "those darn lobbyists" (or stronger language!) is common today, thanks in part to recent scandals regarding lobbyists and their dubious relations with various politicians.

Currently, very few nonprofits lobby the government, perhaps in part because of the activity's negative connotations. Of the more than 249,000 charities that filed IRS Form 990 returns in 1999, only 1.6 percent reported spending any money on lobbying. Research by the Center for Lobbying in the Public Interest (CLPI), a nonprofit that helps charities advocate for their causes, suggests that the amount of reported lobbying may be understated. But even if it is twice that amount, it is too little. I strongly encourage more nonprofits to consider advocacy and lobbying at the local, state, or federal level. Every organization—

not to mention every American—has the opportunity to speak out on the issues they care about and advocate for better public policies.

If you are concerned that lobbying is too expensive or can be done only by large organizations, pay a visit to your local city council. You will surely find individuals and small groups of people speaking out about issues they believe in, ranging from leash laws to bike trails to green initiatives. Laws are adopted or changed frequently because a group of concerned citizens (probably without paid staff or even without forming a nonprofit) decided to take action.

As a nonprofit organization, you should at least consider lobbying and other types of advocacy. Public decisions are being made every day at the federal, state, and local levels that potentially affect the missions of nonprofit organizations in either a positive or a negative way. If you want to have a voice in the outcomes, you must become involved. In most instances, these decisions are being influenced by powerful interest groups. Many of these powerful interest groups are looking out primarily for their self-interest. In some instances there is an overlap with the public interest, but in many instances there isn't. Nonprofits can bring an objective, credible, and influential voice to public debate.

If you are successful in your advocacy efforts, a few wins in this area can accelerate progress toward achieving your goals. We can advance our missions one person at a time, or we can work with governments to enact laws that advance our missions on a far larger scale. In the words of Bob Smucker, founder of the Center for Lobbying in the Public Interest, "Much of the social change in America had its origin in the nonprofit sector. Nonprofit lobbying is the right thing to do. It is about empowering individuals to make their collective voices heard on a wide range of human concerns." As members of a democratic society,

Recommended Resource

The **Center for Lobbying in the Public Interest,** or CLPI (www.clpi.org), is a resource for nonprofits interested in advocacy and lobbying. According to its website, CLPI "promotes, supports and protects 501(c)(3) nonprofit advocacy and lobbying in order to strengthen participation in our democratic society and advance charitable missions."

we have the privilege—and the responsibility—to influence the laws that govern the American people.

DEFINITIONS OF LOBBYING AND ADVOCACY

Although many people use the terms interchangeably, let's pause here to make a distinction between *lobbying* and *advocacy*. It is important to understand the distinction, because nonprofit lobbying expenditures are regulated and capped by the federal government and must be reported on your 990 tax return, even if your lobbying activities are strictly local. It is important that you know the difference so that you can accurately complete your tax return and reporting requirements.

Lobbying is a specific type of advocacy work. It refers to advocacy efforts that attempt to influence legislation at the federal, state, or local level or to influence the public in a referendum, initiative, or constitutional amendment. Lobbying activities include all the time, efforts, and expenditures related to your attempt to influence legislation, such as directly contacting or communicating with members or staff of a legislative body or urging the public to do so.

Advocacy is the broader term that refers to any effort a nonprofit makes to affect some aspect of society. This might include appealing to companies about their policies (such as promoting the offering of heart-healthy products in their cafeterias or encouraging them to become a "Fit Friendly Company"), educating members of the general public about their behavior, or lobbying the government to change its laws. Everything that you do in advocating is not necessarily lobbying. Here are some examples of advocacy work that are *not* defined as lobbying:

- Offering a nonpartisan (full and fair representation of facts) analysis, research, or study that presents to the public an independent and objective view of a particular issue, disclosing all sides of the issue, and not promoting an opinion
- Providing technical advice or assistance to a legislative committee or subcommittee in response to a written request
- Disseminating to the public objective information about legislation, such as summaries of debates that are objective and impartial

- Engaging in self-defense lobbying regarding such issues as legislations affecting tax-exempt status or deductibility of contributions for nonprofit organizations
- Advocating to influence regulations of government agencies

Note that nonprofits that are tax exempt under Internal Revenue Code 501(c)(3) may never engage in advocacy work that involves endorsing or hosting fund-raisers in favor of a political candidate. Nonprofit advocacy work is about promoting causes not candidates.

IT IS LEGAL FOR NONPROFITS TO LOBBY

Many in the nonprofit sector mistakenly believe that lobbying the government is prohibited for tax-exempt organizations. The U.S. Constitution establishes the right of individuals and organizations to interact with government. In 1976, Congress made it quite clear that nonprofits have the right to lobby by writing into the income tax laws authorization for each such organization to spend a certain percentage of its income on lobbying. In 1990, the IRS issued rules that gave all but the largest nonprofits a great deal of latitude in public advocacy—including all of the activities mentioned in the preceding list.

The law does specify certain limitations. An organization that conducts lobbying activities may opt to come under *election H*, which provides for a $1 million cap on lobbying activities. This is more than adequate for most smaller organizations. Most larger organizations use the *substantial part* election, which allows the organization to document that its lobbying is not a substantial part of its activities.

On January 1, 2008, new lobbying ethics and disclosure laws went into effect. These complex new rules, coupled with IRS requirements for nonprofits, are creating new opportunities and challenges for organizations that engage in lobbying at the local, state, and federal levels. Noncompliance with the new rules carries significant penalties, including fines and prison time, for the officers who sign the statements that are submitted to the clerks of the House of Representatives and the Senate. The new rules also call for regular, random auditing of lobbying disclosure filings.

It is part of our jobs as nonprofit professionals to stay on top of all laws and regulations related to advocacy and lobbying. This is a very complex issue and entire books are written on the subject, so you should get legal advice before pursuing any lobbying activities.

> **Recommended Resources**
>
> To stay abreast of developments related to laws affecting lobbying by nonprofits, look to **independentsector.org** and **irs.gov**.

NONPROFIT ADVOCACY AND LOBBYING ACROSS THE COUNTRY

Many organizations across the country are looking at formidable challenges and thinking differently about how to achieve their missions. They are pulling back from business as usual and taking a fresh perspective on how to effect more systemic change, get at the root cause of problems, and give a greater voice to their constituents. Like all of us, they want to do more for the people they serve. Lobbying and advocacy work make this possible.

Consider the Capuchin Soup Kitchen, founded eighty years ago to provide emergency food and shelter to Detroit residents. A few years back, the executive director was determined not to become the "McDonald's of soup kitchens" and began to transform the organization to be more than a place for homeless people to get a quick and easy meal. They wanted to advocate on behalf of the homeless and help people reenter society or find psychiatric or drug abuse treatment if they need it. The Capuchin Soup Kitchen now works with families to identify the things that are keeping them in poverty and helps them develop strategies to overcome the barriers. They also provide a voice for those they serve by speaking out on issues affecting homeless people.

Our Kitchen Table, a group of parents and health-care providers concerned about the level of lead paint poisoning among minority children in the Grand Rapids area, applied for a federal grant and received $100,000 over three years to explore the environmental impact of lead poisoning on African-American and Latino families in their community. They formed a cross-race coalition to conduct research and provide a voice for the issue, educating the public about the dangers of lead paint poisoning.

Both of these groups were assisted by an organization known as the Building Movement Project (www.buildingmovement.org), a nonprofit that supports other nonprofit organizations as they work toward social change in integrating advocacy and movement building into their work.

Another example of a local lobbying effort is the United Community Ministries (UCM) in Fairfax, Virginia, a nonprofit social service agency with a mission to assist families and individuals to improve their quality of life and build self-esteem. To share just some of their successes, Sharon Kelso, their longtime executive director, noticed that people coming to the food pantry also had medical and dental needs, so she recruited some doctors and dentists and converted a couple of rooms into a clinic, which was open on Saturday mornings. Demand required them to also open on Tuesday and Thursday evenings, and eventually this service was taken over by the county. To serve an even larger audience, UCM began lobbying the county on issues related to quality of life for families. They chose to lobby against the county's proposed closing of a local child care center. Their lobbying efforts worked, and today the child care center is open and thriving in its community.

HOW TO BUILD A LOBBYING EFFORT

Lobbying—attempting to influence legislation—has incredible potential as a tool to achieve your mission and breakthrough goals, so I will walk through the process of building a nonprofit lobbying effort. Following are steps the AHA has taken to build its lobbying efforts and that your organization can take to lobby effectively on behalf of your mission, whether you choose to do so at the local, state, or federal level. You do not have to take these steps in order; each one is important in building a strong and effective lobbying effort.

1. Decide That Advocacy/Lobbying Fits with Your Strategic Goals

First and foremost, lobbying or advocacy work must make sense with your mission and strategic goals. I am so strongly in favor of advocacy and lobbying because of their potential to reach people and make change on a larger scale than any program initiative can achieve on its own. However, you must weigh the benefits of advocacy work against the time, resources, and effort it requires. Organizations mentioned in this chapter, such as the Center for Lobbying in the Public Interest and the Building Movement Project, can help you get a sense of the potential costs and benefits for your organization.

2. Build Staff and/or Volunteer Competence

To build a strong advocacy effort, some people on your team—paid staff or volunteers—need to build their skills and experience in this area. Ultimately, seasoned staff should lead your advocacy efforts, but do not let that prevent you from beginning the journey. Advocacy skills can be taught to pretty much anyone on your team who is willing to learn. The AHA decided to lobby at the federal level, so we needed more people with experience in congressional offices on Capitol Hill. If you are looking to lobby at the local or county level, you may need to hire staff or recruit volunteers with some experience in local government or send existing employees or volunteers to training courses or workshops that teach lobbying and public advocacy skills.

When we identified advocacy as a priority at the American Heart Association, we conducted an assessment of our staff competence in this area. Since, to that point, we had not focused on advocacy as a high priority, we knew we needed to have more staff with a proven track record. As part of our reorganization into fewer affiliates, we added new staff positions throughout the country that were focused entirely on lobbying/advocacy.

Once we built staff competence, we also sought out volunteers at all levels—federal, state, and local—with experience in government relations. The AHA has made progress in passing clean indoor air ordinances in many smaller communities throughout the country without having paid local staff. Insider expertise at any level of government helps you understand how the legislative process really works and often gives you a head start on building relationships with decision makers.

3. Select Your Policy Issues

Determine which issues will be the focus of your lobbying and other advocacy efforts. You have two main criteria to consider:

- What issue(s) will have the biggest impact for your mission and breakthrough goals?
- What issue(s) are most likely to succeed legislatively?

The American Heart Association has identified nine issues that constitute its public policy agenda. Smaller organizations might choose to focus on only a few or even begin with just one. How can you know which to choose? Be data-driven in your decision making. Take the pulse of the public through free online polling, surveying through phone interviews, hosting discussion groups, or finding publicly available data, such as the research provided by the nonprofit, nonpartisan organization Public Agenda. Continually seek out statistics, analysis, and statements from leading experts that can support your advocacy arguments.

Take the pulse of politicians through personal relationships (ideally, those cultivated through your staff and volunteers) and by attending legislative hearings and generally following the news. Try to determine whether the issue you want to pursue is "ripe": Is it getting a lot of attention in the news? Is it on the agenda for legislative meetings? Is it being covered on the websites and in the newsletters of the politicians you want to reach? If it is not the right time to advance your issue, even the best lobbying effort will fail.

Remember as well that the political environment can change quickly. The economy could slide, a war could break out, or a major legislative issue unrelated to your mission might become urgent. You have to be fluid enough to be willing to change your priorities, perhaps shifting your focus to other areas. When determining your policy priorities, always do your homework, ask questions, and get a realistic assessment of your chances of success.

Recommended Resource

Public Agenda (www.publicagenda.org) is a nonprofit, nonpartisan organization that produces unbiased research about what the public thinks about issues including education, foreign policy, immigration, religion, and civility in American life.

Ten years ago the Transportation and Land Use Coalition was formed in the Bay Area in California to advocate on behalf of healthy, vibrant, walkable communities that provide all residents with transportation choices and affordable housing. They determined that lobbying the government for funding would be the most effective use of their resources and energy. The coalition advocated on behalf of issues such as protecting and increasing transportation funding, monitoring emissions that affect the climate, providing safe routes to school, and building new homes in walkable neighborhoods near transit and jobs. One of the coalition's success stories involves their lobbying to get $375 million in government funding shifted away from highway expansion to mass transit.

4. Build a Grassroots Network

The American Heart Association employs staff members in every state who are responsible for lobbying and other advocacy efforts. It has local staff in the larger metro areas as well. Ultimately, however, the success of these advocacy efforts depends on grassroots volunteers. When it comes to lobbying, numbers matter.

Grassroots lobbying involves appealing to the general public—including your organization's donors and volunteers—to contact public officials about issues important to your mission. This might take the form of a letter-writing campaign by parents seeking a safer public playground for their children or an e-mail campaign by supporters of a domestic violence shelter to receive funding from the local government. Having a strong, active, and vocal volunteer community supporting your advocacy and lobbying efforts can make a tremendous difference at every level of government.

In 2003, the American Heart Association unified and branded its database of 35,000 advocacy volunteers as the You're the Cure™ grassroots network. Organizing volunteers into this branded network has proved to be a significant success. Volunteers feel more connected to each other and the cause, and lawmakers can easily identify volunteers related to our various efforts. The brand gives a context to the volunteers' work, providing a constant reminder about the goal of their efforts—helping to find cures for heart disease. This branding also helps members of the network recognize advocacy messages in their inbox. Finally, the You're the Cure brand also creates more of a sense of being part of a movement, which builds loyalty.

> **Lesson Learned**
>
> Organizing your grassroots advocates into a branded network helps to bring a sense of community to your volunteers and also creates a group identity that is recognized by lawmakers.

Since 2003, the You're the Cure network has grown to more than 175,000 volunteer advocates nationwide. These advocates receive action alerts by e-mail from the American Heart Association and respond by sending e-mails, flooding legislative offices with phone calls, writing letters to the editors of newspapers, making visits to their legislators' offices, attending lobby days, and encouraging friends to become active, too.

The You're the Cure network conducts in-person lobbying and advocacy as well. On AHA's Annual Lobby Day, 600 to 700 volunteers, heart disease survivors, and staff travel to Washington, D.C., for a day of meetings on Capitol Hill. The American Heart Association leaders determine two or three issues to address that day (such as supporting legislation to increase funding of medical research by the National Institutes of Health), and then we train people how to promote those issues to elected officials and their staff members. We train volunteers in presentation skills, talking points, and answers to various questions that might arise. We do our best to help everyone feel confident and not intimidated to be meeting with elected officials. On the day, we meet with members and/or the staff of every congressional district in the country to educate them on certain issues related to the AHA's mission. You will read more about our public policy agenda—and how to select yours—later. Lobby Days are also conducted in most states throughout the country.

In addition to a strong grassroots effort, you also need a "grass-tops" network. This is a smaller group of highly influential volunteers who have relationships with government officials. The goal is to have officials receiving phone calls and personal visits from people they know in addition to the mass e-mails and/or phone calls from the broader network.

> ### Lesson Learned
> In addition to a grassroots lobbying network, cultivate a "grass-tops" network—people who have personal relationships with high-level officials and can exert influence on a different level.

All of the American Heart Association's lobbying achievements would not be possible without the personal investment and efforts of You're the Cure advocates. Even when we are lobbying/advocating against powerful interest groups with virtually unlimited funds, a strong grassroots network proves difficult to beat.

5. Build Strong Relationships with Legislators and Their Staff Members

Relationships are the key to effective lobbying. Committee members change with every election, and power shifts frequently. You must maintain your existing relationships and also constantly build new relationships to sustain your effectiveness. One of the biggest lessons I have learned is how much political activity, deal making, and agenda setting happens behind the scenes in government at all levels. Pay attention to the political winds through your own observation and also through your insider network. Really spend time with people—in the cutthroat world of politics at every level of government, trust and loyalty are extremely valuable commodities.

6. Form Coalitions

When it comes to lobbying, seldom will you be able to go it alone. Look for partner organizations that can help increase the volume of your voice and bring more resources to the table. Discuss partnerships with other organizations that share common interests—you can likely find advocacy partners among the organizations you are already working with on your programs. Ideally, you should partner with organizations that have some influence or expertise in advocacy work—those with a track record of dealing with legislation. You also should partner with organizations that are easy to work with and will assume their share of the responsibility.

Partnering with other organizations in your lobbying can help you add resources, credibility, and sheer numbers to your efforts. If you can produce a document that ten other organizations have signed as well, you will get more attention from legislators. My one caution is to make sure you have a streamlined decision-making process in larger coalitions in order to respond quickly to the rapidly changing legislative environment.

Strategic partnerships are an important part of the advocacy success of the American Heart Association. In 2007, along with the CEOs of AARP, the Alzheimer's Association, the American Cancer Society Cancer Action Network (ACS CAN), and the American Diabetes Association, we helped to lead rallies in support of health-care reform. We led the rallies at simultaneous events in Iowa, New Hampshire, Nevada, and South Carolina—four states with early primaries for the 2008 presidential election.

Together, we rallied to call attention to America's health-care crisis and launched a campaign called Are You Covered? This coalition is nonpartisan and does not endorse any specific candidate's plan. Rather, it insists that all candidates propose health-care plans that integrate our coalition's fundamental goals: quality health care for all, health care that's affordable, health care without the red tape, and health care when and where people need it. Although each of the partner organizations in this effort may sponsor separate activities, our goal is the same: to increase public awareness about the importance of health-care reform and to encourage candidates to address the issues.

Why is the American Heart Association part of this lobbying coalition? It goes back to our mission and our breakthrough goal of reducing cardiovascular diseases and stroke by 25 percent by 2010. Health-care reform is an important issue for the 81 million Americans who suffer from cardiovascular diseases and are struggling with access to quality, affordable health care. The World Health Organization estimates that 80 percent of heart disease, stroke, and type 2 diabetes could be prevented if the major risk factors of tobacco use, poor nutrition, physical inactivity, and obesity were addressed earlier. Yet health-care providers are not reimbursed or paid to prevent or delay the diseases altogether. They get paid for sick care, not for health. All of these factors add up to the necessity that the American Heart Association advocate for health-care reform on behalf of the American public.

7. Stay Committed

The AHA generally works on several issues at a time, and lobbying/advocacy for each policy initiative may take five years or more at the federal level. Lobbying is definitely a marathon, not a sprint. It takes patience, tenacity, flexibility, and lots and lots of heart. Is it worth all of the hard work? Absolutely. Working to change or implement a law can impact the lives of millions of people all at once.

ADVOCACY AND LOBBYING AT THE AMERICAN HEART ASSOCIATION

At the American Heart Association, we believe public advocacy is one of the best and most effective ways we can spend funds that donors entrust to us. In a recent survey, 98 percent of our grassroots network and researchers and 96 percent of our volunteer physicians said it is important for the American Heart Association to play such a role. The majority of our volunteers and supporters understand the difference between a corporation lobbying for its self-interest and a nonprofit lobbying on behalf of the public interest. Politicians debate heart and stroke issues frequently, and we must be part of that dialogue. Our mission requires changing the behavior of individuals, and it also includes changing public policies. That is why we engage in advocacy efforts.

To make sure our advocacy efforts have the maximum impact, the AHA adopted its Federal Public Policy Agenda for 2006 to 2010, the year we hope to reach our breakthrough goal of reducing cardiovascular diseases and stroke by 25 percent. Although there are many worthy initiatives for which we could lobby, we have selected nine areas that will have the most impact toward achieving our breakthrough goal. These nine areas are communicated to the You're the Cure network and appear on our website:

1. Heart disease and stroke research
2. Heart disease and stroke prevention

3. Tobacco control
4. Obesity prevention
5. Quality and availability of care
6. Chain of survival (strengthening each step in the chain of events for someone having a health event—from a good 9-1-1 system, through quick response from EMS, proper care en route to the hospital, proper care and triage in the emergency room, and, ultimately, to proper care and treatment in the hospital)
7. Stroke treatment and systems of care
8. Health disparities
9. Nonprofit issues

Our advocacy efforts related to these issues include lobbying at the federal, state, and local levels. This is accomplished by attempting to influence legislation, doing regulatory work with government agencies, leveraging the voices of our You're the Cure advocates and coalition partners, and influencing the media. The American Heart Association also remains a credible, nonpartisan source of information on which public officials can rely for vital information about heart disease and stroke.

Lesson Learned

In addition to active lobbying, nonprofit organizations can serve as advocates on behalf of their issues. You and your staff can provide information, education, statistics, and insight to elected officials.

FIGHTING BIG TOBACCO

Let's look at one of these advocacy areas in depth: tobacco control. Influencing public policy is essential, but it is by no means easy. This is especially true when you are lobbying against the interests of a wealthy and powerful opponent, as we have in our advocacy efforts on behalf of antismoking legislation. Our opponents in this fight are the Big Tobacco companies, the largest cigarette manufacturers such as Philip Morris, British American Tobacco, and R.J. Reynolds. These cigarette manufacturers are powerful, and, based on my twenty-five-plus years of opposing them, I would go so far as to say they are cunning, using every weapon at their disposal.

We cannot be afraid to fight fire with fire. Faced with a foe known for unleashing every bit of firepower in its arsenal, the American Heart Association has been aggressive in its lobbying efforts against Big Tobacco. Why? Tobacco kills 440,000 Americans each year, and about one-third of those deaths are cardiovascular related. The biggest killer of Americans is not heart disease, stroke, or cancer; it is tobacco. And tobacco is the single greatest cause of preventable death in this country.

Tobacco companies spend tens of millions of dollars on lobbying each year to keep Americans using their products. As we know, due to the nicotine, use of cigarettes, chewing tobacco, and other harmful products results in addiction. So it is not too much to say that tobacco companies spend billions of dollars for advertising and marketing to keep Americans addicted. To that end, their activities include direct lobbying of government officials as well as sophisticated public relations campaigns. As a result of this lobbying, tobacco products, unlike other consumer products sold in the United States, have escaped significant government regulation. Virtually anything can be added to tobacco products, including arsenic (the same chemical used in rat poison), hydrogen cyanide, formaldehyde, benzene, and ammonia. What's worse is that there are more regulations for orange juice and pet foods than for tobacco.

The antitobacco lobby (of which the AHA is an active part) has lobbied aggressively to change this lack of regulation. Unfortunately, in the late 1990s, the antitobacco lobby was unable to pass legislation that would grant the Food and Drug Administration (FDA) authority to regulate tobacco products. Determined not to give up, we changed tactics and took the battle to the state and local level, in part because the large tobacco companies find it more difficult to fight on multiple fronts.

A note of caution about working at the state level: You must be aware of the concept of preemption. Preemption is a clause in state or federal legislation that outlaws the passing of stronger regulations at the local level. Preemption, in my opinion, is a tactic often used by Big Tobacco to get a very weak bill drafted at a state level to prevent stronger, more meaningful legislation from being passed locally. Be aware of how your opponents might use preemption as well.

Lesson Learned

Be prepared to shift your battles. If the door closes at the federal level, shift to the state and/or local level.

In addition to our strong volunteer network at the American Heart Association, we also have dedicated partners in our antismoking efforts, including the American Cancer Society, the American Lung Association, and the Campaign for Tobacco-Free Kids. We work together on various issues and campaigns. Here are some specifics about our joint advocacy and lobbying efforts against smoking and Big Tobacco, primarily at the state and local levels. In each case, you can see how our lobbying priorities are determined by the number of people legislation could help.

- **Secondhand smoke:** The American Heart Association has never advocated banning tobacco products altogether (Prohibition demonstrated that strategy does not work), but we do have a goal for all public places to be smoke free. The number of people who die each year from secondhand smoke—40,000 to 60,000—is comparable to the number of people who die annually from breast cancer. Rather than telling people not to smoke in public places, it is much more effective to lobby for city and state ordinances. Along with our partners, including the American Cancer Society, the American Lung Association, and the Campaign for Tobacco-Free Kids, we have been quite successful in our efforts. Today, more than 65.1 percent of the country's population is covered by clean indoor air laws compared to just 42.7 percent two years ago.

- **Consumption taxes on cigarettes:** We are also working to increase the state consumption (excise) tax on cigarettes. Increasing cigarette taxes reduces smoking and saves lives. It also raises revenue and reduces health-care costs, which is beneficial for governments. Studies, as well as experience in state after state, show that higher cigarette taxes are one of the most effective ways to reduce smoking among both youth and adults. Every 10 percent increase in the price of cigarettes reduces youth smoking by about 7 percent and overall cigarette consumption by about 4 percent. So far, our efforts in this area have been successful. Since 2002, the state average cigarette tax has increased from $0.42 per pack to $1.18 per pack. This does not include city and county taxes, which have also increased considerably.

In addition to these state- and local-level efforts, we have recently turned our antitobacco lobbying against tobacco at the federal level (as the political winds have shifted back in that direction). Our most recent efforts support the Family Smoking Prevention and Tobacco Control Act, federal legislation that would grant the FDA full authority to regulate the manufacture, distribution, sale, labeling, advertising, and promotion of tobacco products. This law would especially eliminate the advertising, marketing, or availability of tobacco products for children.

I have no doubt that tobacco companies will continue to aggressively market cigarettes in an effort to create new customers for their products. The American Heart Association and its partners are committed to fighting them every step of the way.

* * *

As you can see from these examples of large and small organizations, nonprofit doesn't mean noncombative. If we want to achieve breakthrough goals and change the world for the better, particularly when opposing the interests of wealthy and powerful parties, it is necessary to use every tool available. This includes aggressive lobbying and advocacy on behalf of the causes we believe in.

CHAPTER 9 TAKEAWAYS

- **Advocacy involves many activities, including lobbying.** Advocacy includes any activity to influence public opinion about an issue. Lobbying is a type of advocacy that involves attempting to influence legislation at the federal, state, or local level. This distinction is important because lobbying is regulated by the government and must be reported on a nonprofit's 990 tax return.
- **It is legal for nonprofits to lobby.** The law is clear that nonprofit organizations may lobby public officials directly or conduct grassroots advocacy efforts to influence the outcome of other legislation, so long as such efforts constitute an "insubstantial part" of their overall activities.
- **Advocacy and lobbying should be considered by nonprofits large and small.** We have a responsibility to speak out on issues that affect our constituents and advocate for better public policies. If advocacy activities, and lobbying in particular, fit with your mission and strategic goals, they are an excellent way to reach large numbers of people and promote causes you believe in.
- **A strong volunteer network is a key component of effective advocacy work.** Your grassroots advocates can send e-mails, flood legislative offices with phone calls, write letters to the editors of newspapers, make visits to their legislators' offices, and encourage friends to become active. If you are not able to have a dedicated staff person responsible for advocacy, volunteers can step in.
- **Declare a focused public policy agenda.** In the beginning, you may have only one issue, but the impact might be significant, so begin the journey. You can build staff and volunteer competence and coalition partners over time.

CHAPTER 10

HEART-TO-HEART ALLIANCES

Becoming a Partner of Choice

In early September 2004, former president Bill Clinton underwent successful open heart surgery. His physicians said that President Clinton, whose overall physical condition had improved as a result of better eating and exercise habits, noticed that he was experiencing some chest constriction and shortness of breath. Then, he had "an episode of discomfort," lasting fifteen to twenty minutes, that led to hospitalization and an angiography that showed extensive blockage in each of the vessels supplying blood to his heart muscle.

At the age of 58, President Clinton had been headed for a serious heart attack. He had a very common form of coronary artery disease that affects about 20 million people in North America alone. He then underwent a very common bypass surgery performed about 300,000 times a year, or roughly 1,000 times a day.

The former president's quick response to his symptoms and the ensuing successful treatment was a credit to him and his team of physicians, but it also presented an unexpected opportunity for the American Heart Association to enlist a highly visible figure in its fight against cardiovascular disease. Of course, we did not rush to his bedside with flowers and a proposal, but I did begin exploring ways that we could work together as soon as he recovered fully.

The result of those efforts is one of the most successful programs the AHA has executed in recent years: the Alliance for a Healthier Generation, which is a partnership between the American Heart Association and President Clinton's philanthropic foundation. It is a comprehensive, pragmatic initiative that works to prevent childhood obesity by helping children make healthier choices and develop healthier lifestyles.

Childhood obesity is a national epidemic. Fighting it alone would consume more resources than the AHA has available. However, by joining with the William J. Clinton Foundation and forming the Alliance for a Healthier Generation, we are able to enjoy synergies that increase our impact exponentially.

In fact, the American Heart Association has a wide range of relationships, which includes over ninety partner organizations at the national level. Each time we engage with a new partner, we strive to become what you might call a *partner of choice*. In other words, we want our potential partners to think of us as desirable to work with. Make sure that when you engage in partnership activities, you strive to make your organization a partner of choice as well.

Being a partner of choice means that when an organization thinks about working with another organization, you are top of mind as one that is credible, fulfills its commitments, and is a desirable partner to work with. You want to be known as an organization that brings value to relationships. The Clinton Foundation could have worked with just about any heart-related organization, but the American Heart Association was their partner of choice. When Steve Joseph was working through the class-action lawsuit against McDonald's for not removing trans fats in preparing their products as they had publicly promised, he could have chosen a number of nutrition-based organizations to accept some of the settlement to conduct educational programs, but the AHA was his partner of choice. Both of these decisions resulted in a much greater impact by the American Heart Association than would have occurred otherwise. If you want to build your organization's success, then do not miss out on such exciting and beneficial opportunities.

ASSESSING POSSIBLE PARTNERS

The key to developing successful partnerships is that they are mutually beneficial and support the mission and strategic goals of both organizations. They also must have a high impact at a reasonable cost to be worth your investment of time and money. At the American Heart Association, this means partnering in ways that (1) support and promote its mission of building healthier lives free of cardiovascular diseases and stroke, and (2) move the AHA closer to its breakthrough 2010 goal. Here are some things to consider in looking at partnerships:

- Does the organization have a good reputation and is it credible?
- Will the public see it as an organization that makes sense for you to be working with?
- Does a joint initiative fit within your strategic priorities, and will it extend your reach and accelerate movement to achieve your goals?
- What are the projected direct and indirect costs, and does this project compete well against other opportunities?
- Will both parties bring synergy to the relationship, allowing you to do together what neither organization could do alone?
- Is the process for making joint decisions acceptable and workable?
- Does this relationship constrain you from working with other groups?

The American Heart Association's strategic alliances include:

- Professional associations
- Federal, state, and local government agencies (although the AHA does not accept government grants because we believe this may be perceived as a conflict of interest if some of the funds generated by our advocacy initiatives flowed back to the American Heart Association).
- National nonprofit organizations
- Health-care insurers (such as HMOs)
- Media outlets
- For-profit corporations in a variety of industries

As you think about partnership opportunities for your organization, consider all of these types of organizations and others. There is no need to limit your thinking when it comes to potential allies, as long as you always keep your mission and breakthrough goal top of mind.

FORMING AND EXECUTING STRATEGIC PARTNERSHIPS

When it comes to forming and managing strategic partnerships, there are a number of critical things you can do to exponentially increase the chance of the partnership being successful. Here are nine specific suggestions:

1. **Develop a *strategic alliance value proposition* to guide your partnership strategy.** This may sound complicated, but it is actually a simple statement that defines, first, what you bring to the table in a partnership and, second, what your organization wants to receive from partner organizations. The American Heart Association's strategic alliance value proposition for every potential partnership is this:

   > **AHA provides access to credible scientific knowledge and brand identification that strengthens the ability of alliance organizations to achieve their desired outcomes. Strategic alliances expand AHA's ability to reach more people and improve the quality of patient outcomes.**

   The strategic value proposition shows your desire to form a mutually beneficial partnership with the maximum amount of synergy. Think of it as a mission statement that you can turn to for clarity and share with partners. The clearer you are at the beginning of a relationship, the less likely you are to have misunderstandings and problems later.

2. **Consider your organization's culture.** A cultural fit with a partner is just as important as a strategic fit. Include the organization's core values in any discussion of a potential alliance partner. Two organizations can be aligned in their missions but clash in the area of culture. Pay attention to whether everyone can get along.

3. **Honestly assess what your organization can offer.** There is a crucial difference between what you would like to do in a partnership and what you can really achieve. It is always better to underpromise and overdeliver, particularly when you are working with an organization larger than your own.

4. **Address potential conflicts of interest or ethical concerns up front.** The American Heart Association is very careful to protect its good name with a firewall that includes stringent corporate relations policies, guidelines, conflict-of-interest disclosures, and a comprehensive approval process for working with for-profit businesses. Our Ethics Policy and Conflict of Interest Policy are available at AmericanHeart.org, and they operate or appear prominently in any discussions with potential partners.

> **Lesson Learned**
>
> Create ethics policies that regulate any partnership activity prior to beginning a partnership relationship. Make sure they are transparent to each partner and consistently enforced as the relationship develops.

5. **Approach relationships with an attitude of abundance versus scarcity.** When you think there is only so much to go around, you start focusing on the wrong things. To be sure, it is not always easy to have an abundance mentality. We are all working to make our organizations the best they can be, so it can be difficult to share information, ideas, resources, and, ultimately, credit for successes. But this is the way that strong partnerships endure and continue to grow.

    Nonprofits and their leaders tend to share more with each other than might be possible for most for-profit leaders. Perhaps this is because profit is not our motivating factor, and we do not work under the pressure of Wall Street analysts. As an example, I am particularly close with John Seffrin, CEO of the American Cancer Society, who has been a tremendous mentor to me. We are highly competitive when it comes to seeking donor dollars for our organizations, but we still want each other to succeed in our respective missions. As I mentioned earlier, when the former Leukemia Society was looking to change its name to incorporate the word *Lymphoma*, we shared our experience in creating the American Stroke Association. We also lent our expertise to the American Lung Association and the Arthritis Foundation when they were undergoing a reorganization similar to ours. It would be unlikely that you would see this kind of organizational sharing in the for-profit world, but we are all stronger in the nonprofit world when we work together and help each other.

> **Lesson Learned**
>
> Instead of fighting over pieces of the pie, we create a bigger pie for all of us when we work together and support one another.

6. **Say no when necessary.** Having an abundance mentality does *not* mean saying yes to every opportunity. It is very tempting to wander from one's mission or align with a lower-priority issue to take advantage of an exciting partnership opportunity. Always keep your mission, core values, strategic driving force, and breakthrough goal foremost to make sure a partnership really is a good idea.
7. **Maintain continuity of people.** This applies to both paid staff and volunteers. People are the most important element of a partnership, so pay attention to relationships and trust. Think of partner organizations as important VIP clients. When working with partner organizations, you shouldn't have a new point person every year or a different volunteer leader each year. As an example, if you are going to involve your organization's volunteer chair of the board in a partner relationship, involve the chair-elect as well, so that there is continuity with the partner when the chair steps down.
8. **Do not keep score.** It is important to confirm partnership relationships and deliverables in writing through a formal contract or a memorandum of understanding (MOU). An MOU stops a little short of being a contract, but it outlines the purpose of the relationship, the responsibilities of each party, and the terms for terminating the relationship if necessary. Then, once you have a document outlining who is going to do what, put your entire attention on the work in front of you. Keep your focus on your mission and the ability of this partnership to move you closer to your goals. Do not worry about who gets the credit or whether the work is exactly evenly divided. At various points, various people carry different shares of the load.
9. **Partner with heart.** Personal alliances drive professional alliances. The more you network professionally and spend time with people

who believe in your mission, the more opportunities you will find for mutually beneficial partnerships. It's a kind of partnership karma.

PARTNERING WITH A FORMER U.S. PRESIDENT

Let's get back to the American Heart Association's partnership with the Clinton Foundation. When we built a relationship with President Clinton, we certainly realized that we were taking a risk. As a politician, he is viewed by many through the lens of partisan politics. That meant that people had both positive and negative opinions. We knew that we might face some criticism in the media for the alliance, but ultimately we decided it was a partnership that aligned so completely with our mission, strategic goals, values, and breakthrough goal that other considerations paled in comparison.

In this instance, our alliance came about because we focused on the *who* of partnering before we focused on the *what* or *how*. Sometimes this is the right strategy—when you see a partner with a similar mission—as we saw with Bill Clinton, whose heart attack experience moved the agenda of his foundation. You do not always need to know exactly how you will work with a particular partner before approaching that person or organization to discuss an alliance.

This has proven to be a wise decision and a groundbreaking partnership. Our first meeting took place in New York, where we met with President Clinton's chief of staff in a conference room at his offices. The meeting was going well, and we were talking about our ideas. The next thing we knew, the door opened and President Clinton walked in. He was friendly and engaging, walking around the table to shake everyone's hand. Eventually he looked down at the table and saw the proposal we had brought outlining our idea for a partnership. "Is this it? Is this what you want me to do?" he asked with genuine excitement. I said, "Yeah, as a matter of fact it is."

The proposal briefly outlined three high-impact ideas from which President Clinton could choose. We wanted to leave open the opportunity for him to cocreate the program with us, rather than saying that we had one idea written in stone. We were 100 percent sure we wanted to work with him, but we wanted him to work on the topic about which he felt most passionate. Sometimes you seek partners to work on specific programs. In other cases, such as the AHA's partnership with the Clinton Foundation, you share several high-impact ideas and develop a program together.

After a few months of discussions, President Clinton agreed to form a partnership. He opted to work on a program related to childhood obesity and declared that the program—named the Alliance for a Healthier Generation—would be his foundation's number one domestic priority. Since that moment, the Clinton Foundation's volunteers and staff members have been true partners in this effort. In particular, Ira Magaziner, current chairman of the Clinton Foundation policy board, and Bruce Lindsey, who heads the foundation, deserves particular acknowledgment for work in forming our partnership arrangement.

Together, the Clinton Foundation and the AHA set a breakthrough goal for the Alliance for a Healthier Generation program. In other words, what would we attempt to do if we knew we could not fail? We set a goal to stop the increasing prevalence of childhood obesity in the United States by 2010 and reduce the prevalence of childhood obesity by 10 percent by 2015. Today, we are making great strides toward this objective.

President Clinton has been an excellent partner and is far more than a figurehead. He is engaged in teleconferences, appears at fund-raisers, speaks at news conferences, and opens doors. President Clinton and Ira Magaziner helped us to win an initial $8 million grant from the Robert Wood Johnson Foundation for the work we are doing in schools and a partnership with Nickelodeon to help spread the Alliance for a Healthier Generation message to kids. The Robert Wood Johnson Foundation followed up with an additional grant for $20 million.

It could well have taken us five to ten years of working state to state to get the beverage agreement that our alliance with President Clinton landed a year after we teamed up. We worked with representatives of Cadbury Schweppes, Coca-Cola, PepsiCo, and the American Beverage Association to establish new guidelines to limit portion sizes and reduce the number of calories available to children during the school day. Under these guidelines, only lower-calorie and nutritious beverages are sold to schools. This agreement affects close to 35 million students across the country. In 2007, we announced that the program's first-year report card showed a drop of 40 percent in sales of sweetened soda in schools.

A year after the beverage announcement, we negotiated a comparable agreement with five of the nation's leading food manufacturers. Campbell Soup Company, Dannon, Kraft Foods, Mars, and PepsiCo joined us in establishing the first-ever voluntary guidelines for snacks and side items sold in schools, to provide healthier food choices for children. The five food industry leaders agreed to invest in product reformulation and new product development, while encouraging broader support of the AHA's nutritionally sound guidelines. The guidelines cover foods and snacks, desserts, side items, and treats sold throughout schools—including school vending machines, school stores, snack carts, and fund-raisers. Thanks to these changes, we expect to see good news about healthy eating behaviors, and ultimately about improved children's health, in the future.

Needless to say, the former president has also guided us through the political implications of our work. Among his first recommendations was to ensure the alliance was bipartisan by involving a Republican as a cospokesperson. This led to the involvement of Mike Huckabee, who at the time served as governor of Arkansas and chairman of the National Governors Association. Diagnosed with type II diabetes in 2003, Governor Huckabee lost 110 pounds over the following few years and changed his health habits. This made him an excellent spokesperson on nutrition and exercise issues.

In 2007, after Mike Huckabee's gubernatorial term ended, California governor Arnold Schwarzenegger was named a colead of the Alliance for a Healthier Generation. Schwarzenegger issued the Governor's Challenge for a Healthier Generation to encourage other governors across the country to enroll the highest percentage of schools of any state across the nation in the Alliance's Healthy Schools Program. The Governor's Challenge provides a mechanism for governors to do two important things: (1) pledge their commitment to building healthier school environments and (2) draw attention to a free and comprehensive resource available to all schools—public, private, and parochial—that helps schools to implement programs and policies promoting healthy eating and physical activity among students and staff. As a result of these wins, the AHA's alliance with President Clinton is creating a comprehensive, pragmatic initiative to help prevent childhood obesity by helping children make healthier choices, develop healthier lifestyles, and, ultimately, live healthier lives.

Until the Alliance for a Healthier Generation existed, nobody was addressing childhood obesity from a comprehensive standpoint. Why?

Because nobody was sure exactly what to do. There was no blueprint to follow, no books to read. Never before had a former president and a nonprofit organization come together to take on such a big issue. But we did it together. President Clinton opened doors in private industry, media, and foundations. The American Heart Association provided the science credibility and a grassroots network. This combination has created opportunities far beyond anything either of us initially envisioned, and we are deeply grateful for his leadership, vision, and dedication to what is now a mutual mission. The Alliance for a Healthier Generation is an ideal example of synergy—how, together, we can achieve things that would be impossible for either organization to achieve alone.

PARTNERING WITH A TECHNOLOGY LEADER

On October 4, 2007, the American Heart Association launched a new Web-based program in partnership with the Microsoft Corporation to help people manage their high blood pressure. While the Clinton partnership brought us exposure and connections, the Microsoft partnership has brought us increased technological capacity.

The Blood Pressure Management Center (www.bpmc.heart.org) is an online tool that allows people to manage their blood pressure through storage of personal health information on the Internet—with complete privacy protection. In addition to tracking one's blood pressure online, patients can track their physical activity and weight to help them manage their overall health. Our goal is for this to be the first in a series of Web-based disease management solutions made available to consumers by the AHA and Microsoft.

Although the application was codesigned with Microsoft as part of its HealthVault program, it is housed on the American Heart Association's Web server. We aligned with Microsoft on the strategy of encouraging consumers to equip themselves with their own health information to help them make more informed health-care decisions. The partnership helps the American Heart Association implement its vision for personal health records to empower Americans to:

- Own and maintain a personal health record—which includes the blood pressure tool as one of its components—that is portable and interoperable and contains a historical record of the individual's health. Think about the people who had to evacuate New Orleans because of Hurricane Katrina. How many of them went to a new health-care provider in a different city and could not remember their exact medications and dosages? With this online tool, all of that information is retrievable online.

- Leverage the personal health record features as a step toward taking personal responsibility for their own health and health-care decisions. High blood pressure wreaks a lot of havoc with people's health. When you can monitor your own blood pressure, exercise, and diet, you are more likely to control your risk of a heart attack or stroke. The tool is about prevention. To date, over 200,000 people have referred to the tool and about 25,000 people are using it regularly.

Our objective in this partnership with Microsoft and the blood pressure application is that it help move us close to our 2010 breakthrough goal. If we had tried to create this product ourselves, it would have cost a small fortune not only to build but also to maintain and support over time. However, because we are a partner of choice, we were able to create this tool in collaboration with Microsoft and its HealthVault program. Our next project together will be a comparable tool to manage elevated cholesterol.

How did this partnership arise? Microsoft approached us as a nonexclusive partner, meaning that a relationship with Microsoft did not preclude us from pursuing other relationships involving the distribution of disease management programs or the development of public health records. Eleven weeks later, we had a fully working module. We were the first nonprofit to distribute this kind of software. In addition to working on the software itself, we had to get everything through the appropriate legal reviews—and we did so in record time. This first-mover advantage gave us the opportunity to be center stage at the soft launch.

Note that the nonexclusive nature of our partnership turned out to be quite important. You should always address exclusivity when considering partnerships. In this case, the American Heart Association went on to sign an agreement with Google to help that company launch a personal health record as well.

Windows of opportunity open and close very quickly, particularly when working with technology companies. In this case, Microsoft had a specific timeline based on the planned launch of their HealthVault program—their product through which a person can access his or her own personal health record online. If you want to work with high-tech partners, your organization must be quick and flexible, as well as committed to discipline and excellent at execution.

> **Lesson Learned**
>
> One of the many benefits of being clear about your mission and strategic driving force, focused on achieving your breakthrough goal, aware of external trends, and working with High-Potential staff and volunteers is that you are prepared to act quickly when great partnership opportunities arise.

PARTNERING TO SUPPORT A CAUSE

The American Heart Association has many corporate partnerships, and its relationship with Jiffy Lube is a good example of extending the organization's reach to raise new dollars and provide a "good citizen" benefit to a corporate partner. In February 2008, the AHA and Jiffy Lube launched a fund-raiser and education program to support Go Red For Women. In conjunction with the Car CheckUp online tool on their website, Jiffy Lube drove consumers to the Go Red Heart CheckUp on the AHA website, helping us reach our goal of having 1 million women take the Heart CheckUp. For a two-month period, Jiffy Lube customers were given an opportunity to donate $3 to the Go Red For Women movement at more than 1,750 participating service centers across the United States. In return, each customer received a Maintenance Partners for Life savings book that offered more than $100 in preventive-maintenance savings, healthy recipes and tips, and a sweepstakes ticket for a chance to win prizes.

The program, which effectively tied car maintenance to health maintenance, resulted in over $1 million raised for AHA in addition to the educational outreach. Jiffy Lube benefited significantly as well: Participating service centers saw a 7.6 percent increase in new-customer visits while nonparticipating locations saw a 2.7 percent decrease. This is a good example of a win-win for both organizations.

PARTNERING WITHIN THE NONPROFIT COMMUNITY

Partnering with fellow nonprofits is another important option. In 2004, we joined forces with the American Cancer Society and the American Diabetes Association for a three-year education campaign. The campaign, Everyday Choices for a Healthier Life, conveys to consumers that simple health decisions they make every day when it comes to food, exercise, not smoking, and regular checkups have major long-term health consequences. Each organization pitched in a third of the $3 million total cost over three years to launch a public service campaign with the Ad Council.

The partnership is so powerful because 60 percent of us will die from cancer, diabetes, or heart disease, and you can dramatically decrease your chance of getting any of these diseases if you eat better, exercise regularly, don't smoke, and have regular checkups. Working together, we were able to have a much stronger impact on public awareness. It is effective when the American Heart Association says to eat right to avoid disease. It is exponentially more effective when the American Cancer Society and the American Diabetes Association promote the exact same message with us. We can reach more people by joining together with the same message, and we can also maximize the impact of the research each organization has produced. Our partnership allows us to promote the fact that there is a consensus among all three organizations about the kind of tests that should be administered by health-care providers during physical exams based on age and risk factors. That had never existed before. Partnerships can maximize the number of people you reach, the value of your research, and your promotional opportunities.

Three large nonprofit organizations had never collaborated in this way. We had worked together on specific issues but never on any campaign of this reach. Credit goes to the National Health Council (NHC) for bringing the three CEOs together. All three of us served on the NHC's board and as a result had built relationships of trust and a genuine desire to help one another. When we agreed to this initiative, we charged our various teams with getting together and making it work. I am sure that at times the teams experienced some frustrations, but our trust and commitment at the CEO level were deep enough that the foundation was there to build a successful program.

> **Lesson Learned**
>
> Trust is a critical element in making organizational alliances work.

ADDITIONAL PARTNERSHIP OPPORTUNITIES

Because of the size of the American Heart Association, it has the unique opportunity to partner with very large organizations. Part of the reason we are a partner of choice, in addition to our science credibility, is that we are flexible, creative, and open-minded about how to work with various organizations. Here is an overview of the wide variety of ways that nonprofits can partner—on projects, marketing, fund-raising, and more.

- **Create joint content.** Articles, op-ed pieces, books, manuals, blogs, podcasts, and other content are significant credibility builders for nonprofits. These are also great partnership opportunities—to share the writing, editing, production, or distribution of such materials. As an example, the American Heart Association partners with the American College of Physicians (ACP) on a variety of joint publishing initiatives including a joint special report patient education piece titled "Understanding Emergency Care." In addition to partnering on content creation, the ACP also provides a distribution channel for existing AHA content. As a result of our collaboration, the ACP regularly distributes the new AHA guidelines, statements, and advisories to its 119,000 members.

- **Publicize programs.** Media outlets are always looking for credible sources of information, advice, and stories. Nonprofits are natural partners and credible content providers. The American Heart Association formed a mutually beneficial relationship with *Parade* magazine, among the most-read magazines in the United States. *Parade* designated 2005 as the Year of the Heart and highlighted cardiovascular diseases in five issues, with circulation of about 37 million readers per issue.

Many publicity opportunities exist with professional publications as well. For instance, the American Heart Association partners with the American College of Obstetricians and Gynecologists (ACOG) in a mutually beneficial way. The college serves on the AHA Women's Guidelines writing group and helps us publicize important health information to women. The Secondary Stroke Guidelines were highlighted in the May 2006 edition of *ACOG Today*, an ACOG member newsletter with a circulation of over 50,000.

- **Create joint guidelines or best practices.** Depending on your area of specialization, your organization can provide research or guidance to the general public. This might include a list of recommendations for better dental health, suggestions for how to grow a small business, or best practices to conserve energy. Since 1980, the American College of Cardiology (ACC) and the American Heart Association have jointly engaged in the production of guidelines in the area of cardiovascular disease. This effort is directed by the ACC/AHA Task Force on Practice Guidelines. Its charge is to develop and revise practice guidelines for important cardiovascular diseases and procedures. These practice guidelines are intended to assist physicians in clinical decision making by describing a range of generally acceptable approaches for the diagnosis, management, or prevention of specific diseases or conditions. (Of course, the ultimate judgment regarding care of a particular patient is made by the physician and patient.)

- **Advocate for strategy and legislation.** Many government agencies at the local, state, and national levels are interested in forming strategic partnerships with nonprofit organizations. In such cases, nonprofits can provide education, information, statistics, personal stories, and much more.

The American Heart Association has partnered with the Centers for Disease Control and Prevention (CDC) to identify specific opportunities for joint efforts and activities to develop a comprehensive national health strategy to prevent heart disease and stroke. We are in close communication with the CDC and provide input, advice, feedback, lobbying support, and other help to make sure cardiovascular diseases are foremost among CDC's efforts.

The American Heart Association's State Health Alliance (SHA) teams are tasked with leveraging the resources of external partners at a state level to further the goals of the American Heart Association. State-level partners have more direct access to—and influence on—specific populations, groups of health-care providers, and others who influence the health-care system. Our State Health Alliance teams identify key target partners, bring cross-functional teams together to determine appropriate strategies, and manage relationships. State-based relationships include state health departments, professional medical associations, offices of emergency medical services (EMS), and departments of education. Joint activities include cosponsoring events, speaking at conferences, adopting recommendations, sharing advertisement opportunities, jointly seeking grant money, finding spokespeople, and disseminating information in local communities.

- **Provide expert advice.** You also can work toward your mission by developing more informal relationships with other organizations. This may include serving on one another's advisory boards or ad hoc panels, sharing information by phone or in meetings, and attending each other's events. During the 2005–2006 fiscal year, the AHA and the Alliance for a Healthier Generation identified the American Academy of Pediatrics (AAP) as a key alliance organization for the childhood obesity cause. An exploratory call was held with AAP to discuss the potential for a relationship and actions related to the childhood obesity epidemic. This led to a member of the AAP serving as an advisory board member for the Alliance for a Healthier Generation campaign and two other members serving on the American Heart Association Childhood Obesity Panel.

- **Offer professional education and development opportunities.** Partnership opportunities exist in the arena of professional education as well. Nonprofits can partner with other for-profit or nonprofit organizations in a training capacity. This might include providing speeches and offering educational seminars, online learning modules, or professional consulting. An example is the American Heart Association's Get With The Guidelines program, which educates and empowers health-care teams to save lives and reduce costs. The program includes in-hospital quality improvement training, instruction about best practices, patient education materials, and decision-support tools that generate real-time reports. Hospitals implementing the program see measurable improvements in patient outcomes that often translate to an improved bottom line and, most important, lives saved. More than 1,000 U.S. hospitals (20 percent of the market) are using this quality improvement program to provide heart and stroke patients with a proven standard of care to reduce their risk of a future attack. In 2004, Get With The Guidelines became the very first in-hospital program to receive the Innovation in Prevention Award from the Health and Human Services secretary, who at the time was Tommy Thompson.

- **Participate in fund-raising.** Nonprofits can work with corporate partners to access funding opportunities as well. For example, the American Heart Association developed the concept for the Pharmaceutical Roundtable (PRT), a strategic coalition of the AHA and ten leading pharmaceutical companies that provide financial support for cardiovascular research and programs and discuss key trends in cardiovascular health care. It allows the American Heart Association and members of the pharmaceutical industry to identify and pursue common objectives to improve cardiovascular health in the United States through research, patient education, and public and professional programs. Since its inception in 1988, this premier corporate funding group has committed more than $55 million to cardiovascular and stroke research alone.

PERSONAL ALLIANCES: THE IMPORTANCE OF SECTOR AND PROFESSIONAL NETWORKING

Most partnerships arise through personal commitment and connections. It is crucial for leaders to become active in sector and professional associations in order to maximize exposure to partnership opportunities. Particularly if you lead a small organization or you are new to the nonprofit world, it is vital that you begin building personal relationships that will lead to organizational relationships.

Through my various association memberships, committee positions, board memberships, and professional relationships, I have gained invaluable experience, information, ideas, and connections. Here is the trick to making the most of your affiliations: The more involved you personally become (i.e., the more of your time and energy you give), the more you and your organization will benefit.

That said, time and energy can be finite resources, particularly against the backdrop of our personal lives. Where should you invest your time and energy? First, you must focus on areas related to your organization's mission and breakthrough goal. Here are a few categories of organizations you might consider. Think of these organizations as supporting partners of your organization:

- **Nonprofit associations.** There are several excellent national organizations that allow you to expand your network of nonprofit colleagues and build relationships that can lead to alliances for your organization. As a member, you can also take advantage of valuable conferences, publications, and websites. Chief among these are Independent Sector (www.independentsector.org), the American Society of Association Executives (www.asaecenter.org), and the National Human Services Assembly (www.nassembly.org). For younger leaders, there are organizations such as the Young Nonprofit Professionals Network (www.ynpn.org) and FLiP, Future Leaders in Philanthropy (www.flip.onphilanthropy.com).
- **Associations related to your organization's mission.** These will vary according to your mission and focus areas. In my case, this includes many health-related organizations, such as the National Health Council, Partnership for Prevention, Campaign for Tobacco-Free Kids, Research!America, and Campaign for Public Health. If you are uncertain of the organizations in your focus area, ask around your professional networks or use Google to search for relevant groups that meet in person or have discussions online.
- **Local community organizations.** Particularly if your work focuses on the local community, it is essential for you or your organization to join local professional organizations, such as the chamber of commerce, Rotary Club, or religious institutions.
- **Online networks.** Today, it is important to connect with other leaders online as well as in person. ASAE, for example, has an active discussion board, and many nonprofit leaders connect on such social networking sites as LinkedIn.com and Facebook.com.

> **Lesson Learned**
>
> Professional partnerships are built on strong personal relationships. In the words of Mark McCormack, author of *What They Don't Teach You at Harvard Business School* (Bantam, 1985), "All things being equal, people will do business with a friend; all things being unequal, people will still do business with a friend."

As an organization or an individual, you cannot do everything alone. We all must find partners to share the load and help us achieve our missions. As long as you stay true to your mission and work with like-minded partners, alliances can carry you across the finish line to achieving your biggest, boldest goals.

CHAPTER 10 TAKEAWAYS

- **Partnerships must be mutually beneficial.** The key to developing successful partnerships is to ensure that they support the mission and strategic goals of all participating organizations and are likely to have a high impact to justify the investment of time and resources.

- **Develop a specific and realistic strategic alliance value proposition.** This is a simple statement that defines: (1) what you bring to the table in a partnership and (2) what your organization expects to receive from partner organizations. Beware of overpromising and/or underdelivering, particularly when you are working with an organization larger than your own.

- **Become a partner of choice.** To attract the best partners, you have to have a solid reputation and be quick, but you also have to be good. This comes from being clear about your mission and strategic driving force, focused on achieving your breakthrough goal, and aware of external trends, as well as working with A-level staff and volunteers. When your organization works with these elements in a focused and disciplined way, you can take advantage of great opportunities.

- **Consider a wide variety of partnerships.** There are many opportunities to partner, in areas such as content creation, publicity, strategy and legislation, professional development, and fund-raising.

- **Personal alliances drive professional alliances.** Maximize the likelihood of meeting potential partners by networking professionally. This includes networking within the nonprofit community, within your professional discipline (such as CEOs or financial managers, technology managers, or public relations managers), in your particular topic or mission area, and in your local community.

CONCLUSION

> *What we have done for ourselves dies with us. What we have done for others remains, and is immortal.*
>
> —ANONYMOUS

If I have achieved my goal, the previous ten chapters have inspired you to try some new strategies and approach your role and your organization from a fresh perspective. The tips, lessons, and dos and don'ts have all been selected to have the most impact. You are now well on your way to increasing your organization's operational effectiveness by 5 percent (or better!) over your current projections.

To review our work together in this book, we have explored the ways that defining an organization's mission, strategic driving force, and breakthrough goal will propel it to new heights. We have discussed branding, technology, and diversity initiatives that will expand your organization in new directions. We have defined all of the ways in which staff and volunteers are the lifeblood that keep us energized and moving forward every day. We have walked down the halls of Congress to witness how advocacy and lobbying can bring a mission to the masses. And finally, we have reviewed the importance of partnering with other organizations to achieve our shared goals together.

As I think back over these topics and the way I have applied them to our work at the American Heart Association, I am deeply proud. I am proud that the American Heart Association's practices, strategies, and achievements are on par with some of the best-managed for-profit corporations in the world. I am proud that we are well on our way to our breakthrough goal of reducing coronary heart disease, stroke, and risk by 25 percent by 2010. And I am proud that we are saving lives every day.

Most of all, I am proud of my relationships with the mentors, staff, volunteers, survivors, partners, and friends with whom I have connected over the past forty years. No leader can succeed alone and, frankly, no leadership job would be much fun without dedicated, smart, and passionate people surrounding you. My final Lesson Learned is a reminder to appreciate all of the personal moments of connection that bond us not only to our missions but also to one another.

Finally, I will return to a comment I made in the Introduction—that this book is for people at all levels and that simply by picking up a book on the topic you have declared yourself to be a leader. The corollary to that rule is that each of us continues to be a leader even when we no longer hold an official title. During the final stages of writing this book, a transition committee was in the process of making its final decision about the person who would follow me as CEO of the American Heart Association after my retirement in 2008. I knew that one day soon they would announce their decision.

I also knew, deep down, that I would wake up the morning following the announcement and I would be the same person I was the day before, just as I was the same person the day after they named me CEO. A title is only a title. But leadership is a calling. Nonprofit leadership, in particular, is a commitment to continually bettering ourselves, our communities, and the world around us. It is a lifelong journey, and its greatest benefit is the knowledge that our good work will have a positive effect for generations. As my favorite quotation states, "What we have done for ourselves dies with us. What we have done for others remains, and is immortal." I have enjoyed sharing this stage of my journey with you, and I wish you all the best on yours.

NOTES

CHAPTER 1

1. National Center for Charitable Statistics (http://nccsdataweb.urban.org/PubApps/profile1.php?state=US).
2. "Average and Median Amounts of Household Giving & Volunteering in 2002," The Center on Philanthropy at Indiana University, March 2006.
3. Association of Fundraising Professionals DonorPulse survey, conducted by Harris Interactive. The survey was conducted by telephone in the United States, April 7–10, 2006, among a nationwide cross section of 1,008 adults. The survey has a 95 percent certainty with a statistical precision of plus or minus three percentage points.

CHAPTER 2

1. Mike Freedman, "Driving Force: Central Hook for Setting and Implementing Strategy," *The Art and Discipline of Strategic Leadership*, McGraw-Hill, 2002, pp. 55–57.

CHAPTER 4

1. Harvard case study citation.

CHAPTER 6

1. F. L. Schmidt, J. E. Hunter, and K. Pearlman, "Assessing the Economic Impact of Personnel Programs on Workforce Productivity," *Personnel Psychology* 35 (1982), pp.333–347.

CHAPTER 7

1. Erin White, "Authentic Ways of Leading," *The Wall Street Journal*, December 3, 2007, p. B3.

CHAPTER 8

1. Corporation for National and Community Service, "Issue Brief: Volunteer Retention."
2. McKinsey & Company, "The Dynamic Board: Lessons from High-Performing Nonprofits," 2003, p. 5.
3. Ibid., p. 21.

INDEX

AARP, 43, 191
abundance mentality, 202–203
ACC/AHA Task Force on Practice Guidelines, 212
accountability:
  in achieving goals, 70, 73
  in fund-raising, 104
  of management, 146, 150
  recommendations for, 25–28, 29
ACOG Today newsletter, 212
Acute Stroke Treatment Program, 115
Ad Council, 83, 115, 210
advertising:
  benefits of, 83–84
  corporate sponsorships and, 24
  drawbacks of, 84
  in image creation, 82–83
  in marketing campaign, 92
  for staff, 128
  tobacco-related, 194, 196
advisory boards, 114, 213
advocacy. See also lobbying
  definition of, 182–183
  function of, 180–182, 197
  nonprofit mission and, 183–184, 185
  partnerships for, 212–213
  procedure for, 185–192
  strategic role of, 48
affinity groups, 113, 119
AHA Federal Public Policy Agenda, 192–193
Alliance for a Healthier Generation, 11, 58, 198–199, 205–207, 213
alliances. See partnerships
Alzheimer's Association, 191
American Academy of Family Physicians, 116
American Academy of Neurology, 116
American Academy of Pediatrics (AAP), 213
American Alliance for Health, Physical Education, Recreation and Dance (AAHPERD), 159
American Beverage Association, 205
American Cancer Society, 10, 28, 53, 62, 80, 82, 195, 202, 210
American Cancer Society Cancer Action Network (ACS CAN), 191
American College of Cardiology (ACC), 212

American College of Obstetricians and Gynecologists (ACOG), 212
American College of Physicians (ACP), 211
American Diabetes Association, 53, 80, 191, 210
American Express Charitable Gift Survey, 107
American Heart Association (AHA), 70
  achievements of, 11–13
  advertising/marketing by, 75, 76, 81–82, 84, 90–91, 101
  affinity groups of, 113
  board of directors of, 166, 167, 168, 169–171, 173–175
  core values of, 40, 58
  corporate culture at, 102, 132, 145
  customer focus of, 97–99
  decision making by, 38, 58–59, 132
  distribution channels of, 46, 48, 50
  diversity initiative of, 110–114, 159
  ethical stance of, 31, 32–33, 202
  expert panels at, 176–177
  full disclosure by, 34
  fund-raising by, 103, 104
  goal setting by, 61, 62–66, 72, 191, 192, 200, 208
  honors/awards received by, 10, 13, 214
  key competencies of, 48–49
  lobbying/advocacy by, 186–196
  market research by, 84–88
  mission of, 32, 52, 58, 191, 192
  organizational structure of, 11, 50–53, 114
  partnerships of, 13, 24, 28, 70–71, 93–96, 112, 115, 198–201, 204–214
  products/services of, 46–48, 50, 58
  salary ranges at, 122
  staff performance at, 125–126, 135, 136
  staff recruiting/retention at, 49, 123, 124–125, 127–130, 141
  strategic driving force of, 41–42, 43, 45–50
  successes of, 10, 219
  tagline of, 80
  technology used by, 105, 109–110
  volunteers at, 157, 159, 164
  website of, 12, 13, 18, 34, 107, 202

American Heart Association programs:
  Alliance for a Healthier Generation, 11, 58, 198–199, 205–207, 213
  Are You Covered?, 191
  Childhood Obesity Panel, 213
  Choose to Move, 90, 110
  Everyday Choices for a Healthier Life, 210–211
  Food Certification, 12, 85–88
  Get With The Guidelines, 13, 58, 213–214
  Go Red For Women, 11, 58, 74, 76, 88–94, 112, 114, 209
  Go Red Heart CheckUp, 92
  HeartGuide, 86–87, 103
  Heart Profilers, 58
  Heart Walks, 12, 62–63, 105
  Jump Rope For Heart, 159
  Let's Just Play Go Healthy Challenge, 18–19
  Passion Project, 81–82
  Physician's Toolkit, 91
  Power of Love, 90
  Power To End Stroke, 111–112, 114
  Primary Stroke Center Certification, 13
  Professional Membership, 12
  State Health Alliance teams, 213
  Women's Guidelines writing group, 212
  You're the Cure network, 188–189, 190, 192, 193
American Hospital Supply, 43
American Legacy Foundation, 95
American Lung Association, 53, 95, 195, 202
American Society of Association Executives (ASAE), 15, 215
American Stroke Association (ASA), 11, 115–117, 202
Amigos Haciendo Amigos, 113
Amnesty International Human Rights Now! campaign, 89
Amway, 44
Annual Lobby Day, 189
antitobacco movement, 85, 193–196
Are You Covered? campaign, 191
Armstrong, Lance, 105
Arthritis Foundation, 44, 53, 80, 202
arts/culture/humanities organizations, 4
AT&T, 44
audits:
  conflicts of interest in, 176
  lobbying and, 183
automated external defibrillators (AEDs), 66
Avon:
  Breast Cancer Crusade, 88–89
  product distribution by, 44
  Walk for Breast Cancer, 20, 23

awards:
  for diversity initiatives, 114
  Innovation in Prevention, 13, 214
  WGA Seal of Approval, 10
baby boomers, 59, 121
behavioral event interviews, 129–130, 142
benchmarking:
  board-monitored, 168
  for employee performance, 134
  for organizational performance, 32–33
best practices:
  for boards of directors, 171–176
  creating, 212
  in diversity, 110–114
  function of, 102, 119
  purging activities and, 117–118
  sharing of, 117
  using technology in, 107–110
Big Brothers Big Sisters, 80
blogging, 110, 119, 141
Blood Pressure Management Center, 207
board of directors:
  communication with, 173–174
  competency-based, 169–171
  diversity on, 168–169
  donations from, 172–173
  ethics policy for, 175–176
  performance of, 176
  reassessing, 179
  responsibilities of, 165–166, 168, 172
  size of, 166–167
  structure of, 173
  types of, 167–168
BoardSource, 15, 167
Book Buddies, 113
Bornemann, Jeannie, 1–3
brand:
  AHA as, 11
  analysis of, 78–79, 117
  ASA as, 116
  definition of, 76–77
  function of, 99
  in grassroots lobbying, 188–189
  in nonprofit marketing, 75, 77–80, 84
  online, 101, 108
  protecting, 96
Brest, Paul, 25
Bridgespan Group, 121
British American Tobacco, 193
Buckingham, Marcus, 147
Bugher Foundation, 115
Building Movement Project, 185, 186
Built to Last (Collins), 33
business model:
  assessing, 54–57, 59, 60
  in decision making, 38, 59

Index

definition of, 54
marketing and, 101

Cadbury Schweppes, 205
call to action, 83, 84
Campaign for Public Health, 215
Campaign for Tobacco-Free Kids, 195, 215
Campbell-Ewald ad agency, 82
Campbell Soup Company, 206
cancer, deaths from, 210
Capuchin Soup Kitchen, 184
cardiopulmonary resuscitation (CPR), 12
cardiovascular disease. *See* heart disease
cause-related marketing, 7, 20, 23, 88–89
Center for Lobbying in the Public Interest (CLPI), 180, 181, 186
Center for Nonprofit Management, 39
Center on Philanthropy (Indiana University), 22, 107
Centers for Disease Control and Prevention (CDC), 13, 115, 212–213
Centers for Medicare and Medicaid, 13
CEO Diversity Advisory Cabinet, 114
Chafee, John, 87
chain of survival, 193
chambers of commerce, 21, 215
Childhood Obesity Panel, 213
children:
 as AHA volunteers, 159
 hunger program for, 89
 obesity in, 11, 58, 199, 205–207, 213
 smoking and, 85, 205
cholesterol levels, 72, 208
Choose to Move program, 90, 110
CIDS interview, 130–131
Cities Go Red campaign, 93
civic leagues, 21
Clinton, Bill, 198, 204–207
Clinton Foundation. *See* William J. Clinton Foundation
Coca-Cola, 43, 205
Coffman, Curt, 147
Cole, Richard, 165
collateral marketing materials, 91
college courses, 122
Collins, Jim, 5, 33
communication:
 through advertising, 83
 with board of directors, 173–174
 as competency, 48, 169
 of goals, 69, 71, 73, 149
 internal, 33–34
 by leaders, 16
 between management and staff, 144–145, 151–152
 between management and volunteers, 156
 within partnerships, 158

as soft resource, 17
technology for, 174
compensation:
 comparative, 122
 hiring and, 126, 127
 oversight of, 27
 performance-based, 123
competencies:
 in achieving goals, 70
 board of directors based on, 169–171
 developing, 47–49
 foundational, 137, 138
 key, 138
 in lobbying/advocacy, 186
 strategic driving force and, 43–47
CompuMentor, 109
ConAgra Foods Feeding Children Better program, 89
Cone Inc., 74, 89–90
conflicts of interest:
 for board of directors, 172, 175–176
 disclosure of, 34
 government grants and, 200
 partnerships and, 202
 perception of, 94, 96
 policies on, 96
Conlon, Peggy, 171
consent agendas, 175
consumption taxes, 195–196
content providers, 211–212
continuous learning, 147
core values:
 as constants, 59, 60
 corporate relationships and, 95
 in decision making, 38
 determining, 39–41
 marketing and, 101
 staff recruiting and, 131–132
corporate culture:
 best practices and, 102
 informality in, 145
 partnerships and, 201
 staff recruiting and, 124, 132
 values and, 40
Corporation for National and Community Service, 156
corporations:
 donations from, 30
 in fund-raising partnerships, 214
 nonprofit relationships with, 24–25, 30–31, 94–96, 209–210
 sponsorships by, 30, 90, 92, 93
Count Me in for Women's Economic Independence, 62
customer database, 97, 105
customer loyalty, 43, 98–99
customer pathways, 99

Index

customer satisfaction, 96–97, 98, 100, 101
customer service:
  employee engagement and, 98
  as key competency, 43
  in nonprofit marketing, 75
  quality of, 34
  testing, 99, 100

Dannon, 206
Darigan, Kristian, 90
decision making:
  in advocacy coalitions, 191
  board of directors and, 167, 168, 173, 174
  business model in, 54
  conflicts of interest and, 94
  core values in, 39–41
  customer data and, 97
  framework for, 37–38, 57–59
  goal setting and, 67
  in partnerships, 200
  on public policy, 181
  by staff, 152
  strategic driving force in, 41–42
Delta Sigma Theta sorority, 112
demographics:
  corporate sponsorships and, 95
  of volunteers, 159
diabetes, 191, 206, 210
direct-mail fund-raising, 56
direct marketing, 95
disclosure:
  as ethical requirement, 34
  about lobbying, 183
distribution:
  for AHA content, 211
  as strategic driving force, 43, 46, 49
diversity:
  best practices in, 110–114, 119
  on board of directors, 168–169
  of competencies, 57
  marketing efforts and, 99
  in recruiting volunteers, 159
DiversityInc, 111
Diversity Week, 114
donations:
  from board members, 172–173
  from cause marketing, 88
  corporate, 30
  disclosure of, 34
  of experts' time, 177–178
  via Internet, 22, 105, 107–108
  showing results from, 159
The Dynamic Board: Lessons from High-Performing Nonprofits (report), 171

e-blasts, 108, 128
educational/research organizations, 4

80/20 rule (Pareto principle), 68
election H, 183
e-mail:
  for board communications, 174
  in lobbying efforts, 188, 189, 190, 197
  viral marketing via, 90, 101
  from volunteers, 158
employee engagement, 98
e-newsletters, 108, 141
  for board communications, 174
  as employee development tool, 141
  volunteers recognized by, 164
  as website driver, 108
environmental/animal organizations, 4
ethics:
  of board of directors, 175–176
  core values and, 39, 40, 60
  corporate relationships and, 95–96
  guidelines for, 25–26
  in leadership, 149, 153–154
  for lobbying, 183
  of nonprofits, 9–10, 29, 30–32
  partnerships and, 202
  in staff performance evaluations, 132
Everyday Choices for a Healthier Life campaign, 210–211
expert panels, 90, 176–178, 213

Facebook, 34, 74, 90, 101, 108, 158, 215
Family Smoking Prevention and Tobacco Control Act, 196
First, Break All the Rules (Buckingham and Coffman), 147
501(c)(3) organizations, 21, 28, 51, 83, 181, 183
focus groups, 86, 87, 88
Food and Drug Administration (FDA), 87, 88, 194, 196
Food Certification Program, 12, 85–88
for-profit organizations:
  accountability in, 150
  in alliances with nonprofits, 24, 94–96, 200
  cause-related marketing by, 20, 88–89
  management techniques of, 143
  marketing techniques of, 77
foundational positions, 137–140
fund-raising:
  business model and, 54–55
  corporate partners in, 214
  direct-mail, 56
  goals for, 103–104
  revenue from, 104–105
  strategic role of, 49
  technology in, 105
  volunteers in, 105–106, 119
Future Leaders in Philanthropy (FLiP), 215

Gates, Bill, 22
Gaudieri, Millicent, 121
General Motors, 43
Generation Y, 59, 106, 110
George, Bill, 144
Get With The Guidelines program, 13, 58, 213–214
Girl Scouts of the USA, 53
goals:
    creating, 63–66
    executing, 67–71
    focus on, 151
    funding, 103
    importance of, 61
    lobbying/advocacy for, 181, 185, 187
    partnerships and, 200
    promoting, 71–72
    purpose of, 62–63, 73
    staff performance and, 136–138, 142
    staff recruiting and, 128
    volunteer efforts and, 163
Going and Growing Through Grief, 113
Good to Great (Collins), 33
Google, 44, 208, 215
Google Analytics, 107
Go Red For Women campaign, 11, 58, 74, 76, 88–94, 112, 114, 209
Go Red Heart CheckUp, 92, 209
Gould, Rob, 171
governing board, 168
Governor's Challenge for a Healthier Generation, 206
grants, 23, 55, 200, 213
grassroots efforts:
    lobbying, 188–190
    volunteers, 157
guideline creation, 212

Hafner, Dudley, 42, 50
Harvard Business Review, 15
head-hunting agencies, 128
health-care reform, 191–192
health records, online, 207–209
health services organizations, 4
HealthVault program (Microsoft), 207–209
Healthy Schools Program, 206
heart attack, 13, 208
heart disease:
    deaths from, 72, 82, 210
    diversity and, 110–112
    guidelines on, 212
    information on, 193
    prevention of, 191, 192, 212, 214
    smoking and, 94–95
    treatment of, 198
    in women, 11, 58, 76, 90
HeartGuide program, 86–87, 103

Heart Profilers, 58
Heart Walks, 12, 62–63, 97, 104, 105
high blood pressure, 72, 207–208
High-Impact Interview Questions: 701 Behavior-Based Questions to Find the Right Person for Every Job (Hoevemeyer), 130
High-Potential employees, 125–128, 132, 133, 135, 136, 138, 140, 142, 158
Hoevemeyer, Victoria A., 130
Home Depot, 39
Huckabee, Mike, 11, 58, 206
human resources, 128, 129
human services organizations, 4
Hunn, Marilyn, 52–53
Huselid, Mark, 136, 137

Independent Sector, 15, 25, 26, 29, 39, 96, 166, 184, 215
Indian Health Service, 112
innovation:
    as key competency, 44
    market research and, 86
    nonprofit function of, 102
    purging/prioritizing and, 117–118, 119
    stimulating, 64
Innovation in Prevention Award, 13, 214
In Search of Excellence (Waterman and Peters), 61, 145
Internal Revenue Service (IRS), 21, 156, 183, 184
international/foreign affairs organizations, 4
International Stroke Conference, 116
Internet:
    fund-raising via, 105, 107
    marketing via, 101
    memorials on, 108
    nonprofit growth and, 22
    nonprofit strategies and, 7
    nonprofit watchdogs on, 27
    personal health records on, 207–209
IRS Form 990, 180, 182
It's Personal campaign, 82

Jiffy Lube, 209–210
job descriptions, 163–164, 165
job interviews, 128–132, 142
Johnson & Johnson, 43
Joint Commission of Healthcare Organizations, 13
Joint Commission on Accreditation of Healthcare Organizations, 116
Joseph, Steve, 199
Josserand, Dave, 80
Jump Rope For Heart program, 159
JustGive.org, 22

Index

KaBOOM, 30
Kellogg Foundation, 30
Kelso, Sharon, 185
Kepner-Tregoe (KT), 42, 43
key positions:
  for paid staff, 125, 135–140, 142
  for volunteers, 160–163
King, Yolanda, 111–112
Kintera software, 99, 105
Kiva.org, 28–29, 44
Kraft Foods, 206

Lance Armstrong Foundation, 104–105
Landry, Robyn, 80
leadership. *See also* management
  assignments from, 164
  consistency in, 146
  as learned skill, 13–14
  in nonprofits, 14–16
  ongoing nature of, 220
  for volunteers, 160–163
legislation:
  antismoking, 196
  on disclosure requirements, 183
  on food labeling, 86–87
  influencing (*see* lobbying)
  nonprofit oversight and, 25–27
  partnerships and, 217
  preemption in, 194
  Sarbanes-Oxley, 7, 32
Let's Just Play Go Healthy Challenge, 18–19
letter-writing campaigns, 188, 189, 197
Leukemia & Lymphoma Society, 117, 202
Lindsey, Bruce, 205
LinkedIn, 158, 178, 215
Listservs, 141
LiveStrong wristbands, 104–105
lobbying. *See also* advocacy
  definition of, 182
  function of, 180–183, 197
  legal limits on, 183–184
  nonprofit mission and, 184–185
  procedure for, 185–192
  public interest vs. self-interest in, 192
Low-Potential employees, 126, 127, 132–135, 142

Macy's, 24, 92
Magaziner, Ira, 205
Make Mine a Million $ Business, 62
management:
  best practices of, 149–155
  by board of directors, 167–168
  characteristics of, 146–148
  coaching by, 134, 150
  by example, 144
  of paid staff vs. volunteers, 157

recruiting for, 121
succession planning by, 122
by wandering around (MBWA), 145–146
March of Dimes, 80
marketing:
  brand and, 77–80
  function of, 75–76, 99, 101
  online, 100
  techniques for, 91–93
  by tobacco companies, 194, 196
  via volunteers, 158
market research, 43, 85–88
markets, 43, 97
Mars Inc., 206
McCormack, Mark, 216
McDonald's, 199
Meals On Wheels, 79
media relations, 91–92, 100
Medium-Potential employees, 126, 127, 132, 133, 135, 142, 158
meetings:
  of board of directors, 174–175
  of committees, 173
  communication in, 151–152
  decision making and, 38
  electronic, 174
  for recruiting, 162
  to train volunteers, 106
  volunteer involvement in, 164
memorandum of understanding (MOU), 203
memorial Web pages, 108
Merck, 92
microfinance, 28
Microsoft Corporation, 23, 24, 207–208
mindshare:
  acquiring, 76, 78
  competition for, 23, 24, 36, 89
  definition, 75
  expanding, 110
minority-owned businesses, 33
minority populations, 112, 159
mission:
  board members and, 166
  communicating, 33–34
  defining, 32
  executing, 19–20, 122, 151
  goal setting and, 67
  importance of, 18–19, 23–24, 35, 36, 59
  in lobbying, 184, 185, 187, 192
  marketing and, 101
  partnerships and, 94, 95, 216
  passion for, 23, 33, 81, 144
  personalizing, 164
  professional associations related to, 215
  staff recruiting and, 123, 124, 131–132
  strategic driving force and, 42

tagline and, 80
volunteer efforts and, 163
mission statements, 18, 32, 36
Moms@Work, 113
MTV, 23
museums, 4, 20, 121
MySpace, 74, 108

National Center for Cultural Competence, 111
National Committee for Quality Assurance, 13
National Council of Nonprofit Associations, 26
National Food Processors Association, 87
National Football League (NFL), 13
National Health Council (NHC), 15, 96, 210, 215
National Heart, Lung and Blood Institute, 93, 115
National Human Services Assembly, 15, 215
National Institute for Neurological Disorders and Stroke, 115, 116
National Institutes of Health, 189
National Minority Health Month Foundation, 112
National Minority Supplier Development Council, 113
National Wear Red Day, 76, 92–93
Native Americans, 112
Ness, David, 42
networking. *See also* social networking
  in advocacy efforts, 197
  via affinity groups, 113
  grassroots, 188–190
  with other organizations, 112
  partnerships and, 203–204
  via professional associations, 214–216, 217
Nickelodeon, 19, 205
Nike, 104
Nonprofit Leadership Trifecta, 67
nonprofit organizations:
  accountability in, 9–10, 25–28, 29, 36, 150
  advertising by, 82–84
  associations of, 215
  best practices for (*see* best practices)
  boards of directors of, 165–176
  branding by, 76–80
  business models for, 54–57
  categories of, 4
  compensation at, 27, 122–123, 126, 127
  competitors of, 20, 21–22, 24
  as content providers, 211–212
  culture of, 201
  decision making by (*see* decision making)
  diversity initiatives at, 110–114
  ethics of, 30–32, 60, 153
  for-profit practices adopted by, 28–30, 88
  fund-raising by (*see* fund-raising)
  future position of, 59

goal setting by, 62–73
hard vs. soft resources for, 17
leaders of, 14–16
lobbying by (*see* advocacy; lobbying)
management of (*see* management)
marketing by (*see* marketing)
measuring success in, 20–21, 23, 25, 63
mission of (*see* mission)
partnerships of (*see* partnerships)
purpose of, 6
recruiting by, 33, 49, 70, 105, 108, 122–124
resource allocation by, 54, 55–56, 68, 73
sharing among, 202–203
strategies for, 7, 32–34 (*see also* strategic driving force)
training for (*see* training)
workers at (*see* staff; volunteers)
"The Nonprofit Sector's Leadership Deficit" (report), 121
Nye, Joseph, 15

obesity:
  cardiovascular disease prevention and, 191, 193
  in children, 11, 58, 199, 205–207, 213
Ogilvy, David, 77
Omidyar, Pierre, 22
Omidyar Network, 22
Our Kitchen Table, 184
oversight. *See also* watchdog agencies
  by board of directors, 168
  effects of, 28
  expert panels and, 177
  financial, 26
  by government, 27
  need for, 25

Panel on the Nonprofit Sector, 4, 25, 29, 166
Parade magazine, 211–212
Pareto principle (80/20 rule), 68
partner of choice, 199, 211, 217
Partnership for a Drug-Free America, 83
Partnership for Prevention, 171
partnerships:
  to achieve goals, 70–71
  for administrative functions, 28
  assessing, 199–200
  board/management, 166
  board/staff, 168
  conflicts of interest and, 175
  with corporations, 24–25, 30–31, 94–96, 209–210
  in diversity initiatives, 112, 119
  executing, 201–204
  for lobbying/advocacy, 190–192, 197
  nonexclusivity in, 208
  opportunities for, 211–214, 217

partnerships: (*Continued*)
    with other nonprofits, 93, 210–211
    through professional networking, 214–216
    volunteer/staff, 157–158, 179
Passion Project, 81–82
PepsiCo, 205, 206
performance:
    of board of directors, 176
    of staff, 105, 125, 127–128, 132–135, 150–151, 160
    of volunteers, 164–165
Peters, Tom, 61, 75, 145
Pfizer, 24, 92
Pharmaceutical Roundtable (PRT), 214
philanthropy:
    generational trends in, 106
    increase in, 22
Philip Morris, 193
Physician's Toolkit, 91
podcasts, 109–110, 119
policy board, 168
political candidates, 183
Power of Love program, 90
Power To End Stroke initiative, 111–112, 114
preemption, 194
Primary Stroke Center Certification Program, 13, 116
Principles for Good Governance and Ethical Practice: A Guide for Charities and Foundations, 25, 29
private foundations, 21, 166
process improvement, 44
product development, 43
products/services:
    mission-related, 104
    as strategic driving force, 43, 46, 49
Professional Membership Program (AHA), 12
professional networking, 214, 217
Public Agenda, 187
public policy:
    influencing (*see* advocacy; lobbying)
    setting agenda for, 189, 190, 192–193, 197
public service announcements, 83, 92, 116, 210
public/social benefit organizations, 4, 21

recruiting:
    for board of directors, 166–171
    by employees, 128
    for paid staff, 33, 49, 70, 105, 122–128
    by volunteers, 158, 159, 165
    for volunteers, 105, 108, 158–163, 165
Reebok Human Rights Award, 89
reference checks, 132, 142
religious organizations, 4, 21, 156

reports:
    financial, 175
    on project status, 174–175
    superfluous, 118
reputation:
    conflicts of interest and, 94
    online, 108
    partnerships and, 200
    preserving, 31
Research!America, 215
resource allocation, 54, 55–57, 68, 73
return on investment (ROI), 22, 95
revenue streams. *See also* fund-raising
    diversifying, 104–105
    increasing, 103
    marketing and, 101
    sustaining, 55–57
Rhapsody in Red event, 93–94
R.J. Reynolds, 193
Robert Wood Johnson Foundation, 205
Rogers, Kathy, 89
Rotary Club, 215
Rule of Three, 105, 119

salary. *See* compensation
sales, 43, 44
Sarbanes-Oxley Act, 7, 32
Schwarzenegger, Arnold, 206
Scientific Sessions (AHA), 12
Secondary Stroke Guidelines, 212
secondhand smoke, 195
Seffrin, John, 202
Slutsky, Lorie, 25
Smart, Bradford D., 125, 126, 127, 130
smoking:
    cardiovascular diseases and, 94–95, 194
    lobbying against, 193–196
    market research and, 85
    reductions in, 72, 193, 195
Smucker, Bob, 181
social networking (online):
    in best practices, 108, 119
    as employee development tool, 141
    for expert panels, 178
    Go Red For Women and, 74
    in marketing, 101
    partnership opportunities via, 215
    for volunteers, 158
soft power, 15
solicitation letters, 105
sponsorships (corporate), 30, 90, 92, 93
staff (paid):
    accountability of, 70, 146
    advocacy by, 186
    compensation for, 122–123, 126
    continuity of, 203
    development plans for, 139–142

foundational positions for, 137–140
hiring, 120
interviewing, 128–132, 142
key positions for, 125, 135–140, 142
managing, 134
partnerships with board, 168
partnerships with volunteers, 157–158, 179
performance of, 105, 125, 127–128, 132–135, 150–151, 160
positive feedback for, 147, 152–153, 155
recruiting, 33, 49, 70, 105, 122–128
reference checks for, 132, 142
retaining, 123, 125, 133, 134, 135, 142
shortage of, 121
State Health Alliance (SHA), 213
strategic alliance value proposition, 201, 217
strategic driving force:
  competencies for, 47–49, 169
  corporate relationships and, 94
  in decision making, 38, 41–42
  determining, 43–54, 60
  goal setting and, 67
  marketing and, 101
  reevaluating, 59
  staff management and, 124
  volunteer efforts and, 163
Strengthening Transparency, Governance, and Accountability of Charitable Organizations (report), 25
stroke:
  AHA programs on, 114–117
  cultural background and, 111
  death rate from, 72
  information on, 193
  prevention of, 191, 192, 208, 212, 214
Stroke Connection magazine, 116
Stroke Family Warmline, 116
substantial part election, 183, 197
succession planning, 139–141
supplier diversity, 33, 113, 119
SurveyMonkey.com, 98
surveys:
  of customers, 88, 97
  of paid staff, 98
  on public policy issues, 187
  of volunteers, 165
Susan G. Komen for the Cure Breast Cancer Foundation, 30, 80
SWOT analysis, 64
synergy, in partnerships, 199, 200, 201, 207

tagline, 79–80, 101
talent reviews, 139–140
tandem interviews, 131
taxes:
  consumption, 195–196
  exemption from, 9, 51, 183 (*see also*
  nonprofit organizations; 501(c)(3) organizations)
Teach For America program, 122
technology:
  in achieving goals, 70
  best practices using, 107–110, 118, 119
  for communication, 174
  in fund-raising, 105
  partnership role of, 207–209
  as strategic driving force, 44
Think MTV, 23
Thompson, Tommy, 214
tobacco companies, 193–196
Topgrading: How Leading Companies Win by Hiring, Coaching, and Keeping the Best People (Smart), 127
Topgrading process, 125–127, 130, 135
training:
  employee development and, 140, 141
  for hiring managers, 129
  for key positions, 139
  for lobbying/advocacy, 186, 189
  partnerships for, 213–214
  staff performance and, 133
  staff retention and, 123, 142
  for volunteer fund-raisers, 106
Transportation and Land Use Coalition, 188
True North: Discover Your Authentic Leadership, 144
trust:
  in advocacy relationships, 190
  in customer relationships, 98
  between managers and staff, 147–148, 149, 155
  in nonprofit alliances, 210, 211
  between paid staff and volunteers, 158
  between public and nonprofits, 31–32, 36
  as soft resource, 17
tuition reimbursement, 140

UNICEF Millennium Development Goals, 62
United Cerebral Palsy, 80
United Community Ministries (UCM), 185
United Way, 55
Univision Network, 112
U.S. Department of Agriculture (USDA), 87, 88
U.S. Department of Health and Human Services:
  food labeling and, 87
  Innovation in Prevention award, 214
  Office of Minority Health, 112
user-generated content, 108, 119

values. *See* core values
viral marketing, 90, 91, 101, 109

Index

volunteers:
  ad hoc assignments for, 160, 163
  continuity of, 203
  diversity among, 110
  expert panels as, 176–178
  growth in, 21, 121
  guiding, 163–165
  importance of, 156
  in lobbying efforts, 186, 188–190, 197
  recruiting, 105, 108, 158–163, 165, 179
  responsibilities of, 105–106, 119, 164
  terminating, 165
  in U.S., 19
volunteer/staff partnerships, 157–158

watchdog agencies, 21, 27
Waterman, Bob, 61, 145
webcasts, 109, 119
website:
  advertising on, 92
  communicating goals via, 71
  as customer pathway, 99, 100
  fund-raising via, 22, 105, 107–108
  professional networking via, 215
WeddingChannel.com, 23
What They Don't Teach You at Harvard Business School (McCormack), 216
Wheeler, Cass:
  as AHA CEO, 17, 50, 75, 145, 219–220
  background of, 8–9, 10
  Yolanda King and, 111–112

Wieden + Kennedy ad agency, 104–105
William J. Clinton Foundation, 11, 13, 19, 58, 71, 199, 204–207
Winfrey, Oprah, 22
Wise Giving Alliance (WGA), 9–10, 27
women:
  health information for, 212
  heart disease in, 11, 58, 76, 90
  marketing to, 91–92
  physical activity program for, 110
women-owned businesses, 33, 62
Women's Business Enterprise National Council, 113
Women's Guidelines writing group, 212
word-of-mouth marketing, 91, 101
workforce development plans, 139–142
World Health Organization, 191
World Wide Web. *See* Internet

Yahoo!, 44
Yancy, Clyde, 109
Young Nonprofit Professionals Network, 215
You're the Cure network, 188–189, 190, 192, 193
YouTube, 109
YWCA, 80

Zoomerang.com, 98